# PROCEEDINGS

OF THE

# NATIONAL

# COMMERCIAL CONVENTION,

## HELD IN BOSTON,

FEBRUARY, 1868.

PUBLISHED BY ORDER OF THE CONVENTION.

BOSTON:
1868.
J. H. EASTBURN'S PRESS.

# TABLE OF CONTENTS.

# INTRODUCTORY NOTE.

---

THE Commercial Convention held in Detroit, in 1865, was the first occasion on which the merchants of the nation assembled together, to consult in reference to those great industrial and financial questions in which they have a common interest. That Convention was called in the hope and belief, that the members composing it, forgetting for the moment the particular branch of enterprise with the prosperity of which they were as individuals more especially identified, and laying aside also temporarily, local considerations and preferences, would endeavor to ascertain what would best advance the interests of the country at large, as it was then situated, and give definite expression to the opinions which they might reach, for the information of their fellow-citizens, and especially of the representatives of the people charged with the duty of framing the national legislation. The experiment was in a good degree successful. The attendance of delegates was large; the discussions were sustained with ability; germane and valuable statistics were supplied; and broad and comprehensive views were unfolded of the resources, the capabilities and the necessities of the nation. It was encouraging to hear commercial questions debated so thoroughly, upon their merits, by men who had a practical knowledge of what they were talking about, and entirely apart from all political and party considerations.

The Detroit Convention, if it produced no other result, impressed business men with a new conviction of the important influence which, in the sphere appropriate to its exercise, they might legitimately exert upon public sentiment, by unity of purpose and of action. The activity and efficiency of the various Boards of Trade and Chambers of Commerce, undoubtedly received from it a new impulse; but it had become apparent that something more than the agency of these associations, in their individual and independent capacity, was necessary to the complete attainment of the desired result. It was determined therefore, not only to hold a second general Convention, but also, to use the occasion for the organization of a National Chamber of Commerce, by means of which relations of an intimate and a permanent character might be established between the bodies which would be assembled in it.

The duty of calling this Convention was devolved upon the Boston Board of Trade. A Committee, who for some time had the subject under advisement, reported favorably in reference to it, on the second of December, 1867, and the Board voted to adopt their recommendations, on the sixteenth of the same month. A Committee of Arrangements was chosen, with the Hon. F. W. LINCOLN, Jr., for Chairman; and the text of the call to be issued, was agreed upon, as follows:

"You are hereby cordially and respectfully invited and requested to appoint delegates, on the basis of one delegate to every fifty members, to a Commercial Convention representing all the Boards of Trade and Chambers of Commerce in the United

States, organized at the present date, to be holden in this city on Wednesday, the fifth of February, 1868, at eleven o'clock, in the forenoon, and succeeding days, for the consideration of the following subjects:

"The improvement of our inland and interior means of transportation.

"The adoption of an uniform system for he measurement of grain.

"The adjustment of the currency question in a manner which will reconcile conflicting sectional views, while at the same time promoting the welfare of the whole country.

"The restoration of the foreign commerce of the country from its present greatly depressed condition.

"The organization of a National Board of Trade, or Chamber of Commerce.

"And such other subjects, not of a local or political character, as may properly come before the Convention."

The Convention met at the time appointed. The invitation had been cordially responded to, even by those associations who could not accept it, and the attendance was quite as full as could have been anticipated, considering the season of the year. Fourteen States were represented; and thirty-six associations, situated in thirty-two cities. The number of delegates present was two hundred and forty-five. This volume contains a full record of the proceedings, reported by Mr. J. M. W. YERRINTON, a skilful Stenographer, and is published under authority of the Convention. Upon the manner in which these proceedings were carried forward, and upon the general result reached, the members have good reason to congratulate themselves. Of course, it would have been impossible, within the limits of a four day's session, to exhaustively discuss abstract questions of political economy, or to critically examine underlying principles; nor was anything of the kind attempted. It was sought rather to give, in simple outline, a practical and suggestive statement of the present and pressing necessities of the country in connection with the currency, taxation, internal improvements and foreign commerce. It was believed that such an expression of opinion, coming from a representative body constituted as this was, would be welcomed by business men, as furnishing a commercial platform on which they could stand and work together; and that it would prove useful to Congress, as indicating the views of those who are most closely identified with and deeply concerned in the industry and enterprise of the nation.

The various resolutions adopted, have been printed together in the form of a Memorial, and sent to Washington, in behalf of the Convention. They have received additional weight, since their passage, by the approval given to them by most if not all the associations to whom they have been reported by the delegates; and they have received very general commendation from the press.

The following estimate of the Convention and its work, is extracted from the report of the delegates of the Philadelphia Board of Trade:

"We may here be permitted to say a word of the *personnel* of the Convention as it impressed us during the sessions.

"It consisted of men of acute minds who had come profoundly impressed with the magnitude of the subjects they were to consider, and the probable influence their discussions would have in shaping public opinion and legislation.

"They had brought with them deep conviction of what they deemed desirable for their several sections, and they defended these convictions with wisdom, intelligence and eloquence; and it is quite probable that the thoroughness of discussion and the enlarged comparison of views and conflicting opinions on many points, led to the adoption of reports and resolutions, which, as nearly as was possible, brought their deliberations to an harmonious and safe ground on which each sacrificed a part for the good of the great whole.

"In such a result the bodies that sent them will have great satisfaction; and the voice which they have spoken, will, we think, be accepted to so large an extent by the people, that it will have a salutary influence in tending to settle some of the vexing and dangerous tendencies of the times in a safe and honorable way."

The tone of the discussions was thoroughly national. The essential harmony of all the great branches of industry, each with the rest, was fully recognized; and the feeling manifested mutually, on the part of the representatives of the various sections of the country, was hearty and fraternal. Those present from some of the Southern cities, were especially welcomed; and it was only regretted that they were so few in number. Letters had been received from Richmond, Wilmington, (N.C.,) Charleston and New Orleans, expressing entire sympathy with the objects proposed, although they were unable to send delegates. A quotation from one of these letters will illustrate the spirit of them all. The President of the New Orleans Chamber of Commerce, wrote:

"I am instructed by the Chamber to return thanks to the Board of Trade for its polite invitation to us to send delegates to represent our Chamber in the Convention, and to state that whilst fully appreciating the importance of the subjects to be considered, the condition of our commercial community at present is such, and the leaving home at the time mentioned would be so inconvenient to our merchants, that the Chamber will most reluctantly be compelled to forego the advantages of being represented in the Convention."

Had these gentlemen witnessed the manifestation of kindness and good-will with which, on the third day, a resolution was passed in reference to "the destitution and suffering existing in the Southern States;" they would have been much impressed. It was an earnest of the Union which is to be. Such meetings are calculated to do more perhaps than anything else to hasten the day, of which one of our New England poets has sung, when

"—North and South, together brought,
Shall own the same electric thought,
In peace a common flag salute,
And, side by side in labor's free
And unresentful rivalry,
Harvest the fields wherein they fought."

The Convention took important action in deciding upon the formation of a National Chamber of Commerce. This Chamber promises to be to the associated bodies, very much what these are to their individual constituents; and upon the country generally, its influence may be made most valuable. It will tend to correct hurtful misapprehensions, to conciliate opposing sentiments, to modify sectional preferences, to harmonize and adjust conflicting interests, and to create a public sentiment which will demand well-considered, well-balanced and truly national legislation on all industrial questions. Its sessions will have advantages over Conventions such as those of Detroit and Boston, in that they will be held at regular intervals, and will probably be more protracted, the rules of procedure will be settled, and the business to be taken up will be definitely notified in advance. A meeting will be called shortly, probably in Philadelphia, to organize the Chamber and to determine its plan of action.

The Boston Board of Trade avails itself of the present opportunity to express its great gratification at the manner in which its efforts in behalf of the recent Convention have been appreciated by the associations embraced in the call, from many of whom it has received, since the adjournment, courteous and generous acknowledgments. The Board begs also to express its thanks to the people of Boston, who so warmly seconded and supported its plans; as well as to His Honor the Mayor and the municipal authorities, and to His Excellency the Governor and the honorable members of the State Legislature, who extended welcome and hospitality to its guests. They, no less than the members of the Board, have an interest in the kind words respecting our City and our Commonwealth, which the occasion has called forth, in such free and hearty utterance, from their fellow-citizens of the East, West and South.

H. A. H.

BOARD OF TRADE,
BOSTON, March 31, 1868.

# NATIONAL COMMERCIAL CONVENTION.

## FIRST DAY.

WEDNESDAY, FEBRUARY 5, 1868.

THE Convention met in the large hall of the Board of Trade Building, Chauncey Street, Boston, on Wednesday, the fifth of February, 1868, at eleven o'clock in the forenoon, and was called to order by Mr. CHARLES G. NAZRO, President of the Boston Board of Trade, who invited the Rev. EDWARD N. KIRK, D.D., of Boston, to open the proceedings with prayer.

At the conclusion of the prayer, Mr. NAZRO delivered the following

## ADDRESS OF WELCOME.

GENTLEMEN OF THE CONVENTION:—

In the name of the Boston Board of Trade, and in that of the merchants and business men of this city, I bid you a sincere and cordial welcome. And I beg you, gentlemen, not to take these as mere words of formal courtesy, but as the honest and heartfelt sentiments of the people of New England, as they greet their brethren and fellow-citizens from all parts of the land; here to take friendly counsel together; here to strengthen the ties that bind us each to each, and all in one; citizens of one common country; owing allegiance to, and protected by, one common flag; and determined, come weal or woe, to stand or fall together. (Loud applause.)

We have met, gentlemen, for mutual consultation; to compare views in relation to the various plans which are devised to bring us back to a state of prosperity; to see wherein we can all work together to restore the business which has been so sadly deranged by the late terrible rebellion; it gives me pleasure to meet here friends from so many different places who so largely represent the industrial and business interests of the country, and I trust that our deliberations will not be in vain.

We have, of course, no authority; we can only express opinions; but it is well at some periods for the representative men of the nation to meet together and interchange views; and the opinions of such a body, if they be well considered and the result of calm deliberation, cannot fail to have an important influence, and to receive the respect to which they are entitled.

Permit me to say here, gentlemen, that Boston is not alone responsible for the assembling of this Convention. Friends in other places were desirous that we should make the call, and we most cheerfully and readily did so. But notwithstanding we are so glad to call our friends together, and earnestly as we wish to enter into all the discussions, Boston has no objects to attain other than those which are common to all, and our meeting here has no local significance. Everything that benefits one section, must of necessity, in a general point of view, benefit the whole. We should, therefore, as far as possible, put away all sectional feelings and endeavor so to shape our counsels that all may equally share in the good we hope to obtain.

It is unnecessary in a country like ours to have any feelings of jealousy between different parts. There is room enough for all; there is work enough for all; and if instead of looking with uneasiness when we see another portion of our community moving forward, we seek to coöperate with and aid them, we shall at the same time benefit ourselves. Noble emulation and friendly intercourse between the different members of our great family will in the end not only produce material gain to each part, but will serve to knit closer the bands by which we are held together as a body politic; and the glorious motto "*E Pluribus Unum*" shall be true not only in a governmental, but in a social and commercial acceptation; and we shall show to the world that a Christian republic can not only live as a strong and powerful nation, but that it can teach those great principles of noble emulation, which, while it causes each part to strive for a high position in all that raises a people in moral dignity, yet inculcates only that competition which scorns to obtain a good which shall unjustly work an evil to its neighbor.

Our forefathers sought only religious freedom. No dream of founding an empire entered their minds. Could they have had a glimpse of the future, could they have known that in less than two hundred and fifty years a republic would spring up whose territory should reach from the St. Croix to the Rio Grande; from the

Atlantic, across that vast chain of mountains to the Pacific; a country so powerful, and so vast in its operations, that when by an internal dissension its wheels of business were partially stopped the whole commercial world should feel a shock and all its affairs be deranged; quite likely they would have sought to lay a different foundation; and yet, could they have thus become cognizant of the future, no better or more enduring one could have been devised; first recognizing God and building on His word, and secondly establishing colleges and seminaries of learning, and implanting in the minds of their descendants those principles of stern integrity and unblemished honor, which alone can form the basis of true prosperity. (Applause.)

New England has played no small part in the history of this country, and we think she has had some hand in shaping its destiny; but we look with pride and astonishment at the rapid strides which have been made in other parts of the land.

When we look at the great Northwest, with its untold wealth, its rich soil, its immense crops, its mineral treasures, its men of enterprise and indomitable perseverance, we rejoice that it is a part of our common country, and that these are our fellow-citizens, members of our own family. And so with the great Southwest, abounding in wealth, and although checked by recent events, it will, we trust, soon emerge into the bright sunshine of prosperity. (Applause.)

Again, as we turn our eyes from the contemplation of these pictures and cast them upon the sunny South, we wear "a countenance more in sorrow than in anger." We remember that they inherited from the mother country a curse which has been interwoven in all their history. The ways of Providence are inscrutable, but always right; and when man's wisdom fails, then an unseen hand guides our steps and shapes our destiny. The whirlwind and the storm bring forth the clear and healthful atmosphere, and God rides upon that whirlwind and directs that storm; and when they have done their appointed work, He says to the raging sea, peace, be still, and He is obeyed. May we not hope that wise counsels, chastened by past experience and guided by that kind Providence, may prevail in that fertile part of our land; that the acts of the General Government may be guided by wisdom, firmness and discretion; that a feeling of forbearance and brotherly kindness may prevail all over the land; and that the loyal people in the South shall receive a warm-hearted welcome as they resume, which I trust in God they soon will, their places in the councils of the nation, and thus the terrible tornado that has swept over them result in their ultimate good, and the wrath of man be made to praise the Almighty Ruler of the universe? (Applause.)

And let me speak with pride and satisfaction of the Middle States. The ancient and noble Commonwealth of Pennsylvania, which has done so much in time past for the prosperity of the whole country, and which is now in the zenith of her maturity; New York, the great Empire State, whose far-sighted statesmen early inaugurated the system of internal improvements and thereby laid the foundation of her present great prosperity; can any American, located wherever he may be, have other than feelings of pride and admiration as he contemplates these parts of our domain?

The great City of New York, the commercial metropolis of this country, and by-and-by to be the commercial and financial metropolis of the world,—her prospective greatness looms up before our minds in gigantic proportions. We admire her enterprise, and we feel justly proud of her; albeit she is at times a little facetious, and patronizingly pats her little sister on the head and calls her the "little village of Boston;"—(laughter)—*that* we can forgive, for to us it appears like a man whistling in the dark to keep his courage up. But while we love her and cherish these feelings of pride toward her, we want all to understand that we mean to keep both eyes open, and do all we can to maintain the ancient reputation of our own beloved city. (Loud applause.) And we also wish it to be understood that we intend at some future time to become a big affair. We are annexing all the adjacent cities, and we are not sure but that as we go on increasing the circle, the City of New York may become an environ of Boston, and that we shall finally annex her. (Great merriment.)

When we look beyond the mountains and see that great country which so short a time since had only a few semi-barbarous people, owing allegiance to a foreign nation, but now forming one of the most important States of the Union, it seems as though from its very distension our Government must be broken into fragments, were it not that we see on the other hand the great network of railroads and telegraphs binding and cementing together the various parts, and by annihilating, as it were, both time and space, rendering that possible which has hitherto seemed impossible, and thus, however apparently dissevered the various parts, making one harmonious whole. And this leads me to speak of those great thoroughfares, those continental highways which are to connect us with those distant parts of our land, and so materially shorten the distance to the great countries of the East. Should we not strive to have all these roads completed at the earliest possible moment, that we may have free communication with our Pacific possessions?

Gentlemen, it is not for me at this time to set before you at any length the various topics which will engage your attention. They embrace subjects connected with the prosperity of the whole country. Some of the most important are:

The means of transporting the products of the land from the point of production to the point of consumption or exportation. This is a question which affects us all vitally; the West and the South as producers, and the Middle and New England States as the consumers or the medium through which these products find their way to foreign markets. Much attention has been given to this subject, and great improvements have already been made, and if there were no other matter to be brought before the Convention, this alone would seem to be worthy of its assembling.

Vitally connected with this, is the great shipping interest, now so prostrated, and which it is for the interest of all should regain its wonted vigor. By what means this end can be attained, deserves, and doubtless will receive the very serious attention of the Convention. Interwoven with this, are the great questions of steam navigation, the tariff on imports, and many other incidental subjects, such as the reciprocal trade with Canada and other foreign places on this continent.

The third great question is that of the finances of the country, which have assumed such gigantic proportions and the management of which in such a manner as to do justice to all, is a very difficult problem to solve. There is evidently a disposition in some quarters not to carry out, what fairly construed would be the plighted faith of the Government; and should the Convention, after careful deliberation, form and express an opinion upon the subject, it would doubtless have much weight.

Another great problem is that which relates to taxation. The amount to be raised is so large, and it bears so heavily upon some interests, and it is so important that it should operate equally and fairly upon all, that doubtless those with whom it lies to regulate the matter would be glad to have the views of such an intelligent body of the business men from all parts of the land as are here assembled.

The measurement of grain is another subject which will probably receive your attention, whether we shall continue the present plan, or adopt some uniform system.

The organization of a National Board of Trade or Chamber of Commerce commands the attention of all. This subject has been seriously considered by many of the local Boards, and cannot fail to attract the notice of this Convention; and it can receive more full and careful examination by so large a representation of various Boards, than it could do by correspondence.

These, and such other topics as your wisdom and experience shall suggest, will doubtless occupy the attention of the Convention, and if there be agreement of opinion and unity of action in all essential particulars, I have full confidence that all the members of the Convention will feel that they have accomplished much good by their presence here.

In thus briefly sketching the features of our country and its institutions, and touching upon some of the topics which will engage your attention, is it not a pertinent question to ask of such a Convention as this, composed of men of so much intelligence, can we afford to trifle with these great advantages which Providence has placed in our hands, and for the right use of which we shall be held responsible? Ought we to allow any sectional feeling, or rivalry, or jealousy, to weaken us? Should not the West and the East, the Centre and the South, all unite to seek the benefit and best good of all? Should there not be one united voice going up to Congress from the great body of the whole people, asking it to enact and construe all laws in a manner that can have no doubtful subterfuges, but will proclaim to the world: "This is a nation which acts in good faith, and on those high principles of honor and rectitude which will bear the test of time and the scrutiny of the world, and the people will sustain us in so doing." (Applause.) Let such a voice go from this Convention, and it will find a response all over the land; for, no matter what set of politicians may rule the hour, no matter what particular line of policy may be adopted, the people are honest and intelligent, and on all great questions decide substantially for the right. The people can be trusted. Get them together — let them meet face to face — let them understand each other, and the result cannot be doubtful. It is this, more than almost anything else, that causes me to rejoice in this convocation. It is this faith in the intelligent, educated American people, that gives me confidence that God has high purposes for our land. Where on the face of the globe can you find a nation or a people, who, from a state of entire peace, with no belligerent thoughts, each pursuing his quiet avocation, could, when the tocsin sounded, spring at once to arms; become one vast army; improvise the most powerful navy in the world; fight a hundred battles; destroy half a million lives; spend three thousand millions of dollars; standing firm as adamant, ready to meet the world should it come against us even at our weakest moment; and yet, after the exigency is passed, lay down their arms, return to their homes, resume their occupations, and set themselves to work honestly to pay off the great debt? (Applause.)

This, fellow-citizens of the United States, is the American people. These are the fruits of the teachings of the Pilgrims; these are the results of the baptism of blood on Plymouth Rock; these are the effects of an open Bible; these are the fruits of diffused education among the masses. May God in His infinite mercy ever keep us true to himself, true to ourselves, and true to our posterity; may we hand down to our children, and they to theirs, the rich inheritance we have received from our fathers; and when in the lapse of time our thirty-seven stars shall have increased to a hundred, and our forty millions of people to five hundred millions, may the same glorious motto be raised on high, written in letters of living light, and "*E Pluribus Unum*" be as true of us then as it is at the present moment, and we continue a nation that honors God, and therefore one whom God delights to honor; and the period never arrive when the stars and the stripes shall blush in the presence of the Banner of the Cross, but side by side, folded and entwined together, may they shelter and protect our people to the latest period of time; and may the frequent interchanges of opinion and friendly greetings among the citizens of different parts of our land thus keep us an united, homogeneous and happy people.

I again extend to you, gentlemen, a most cordial greeting; and I trust that your sojourn among us may be of such a nature that, although we may have met as strangers, we shall part as friends, and that each and all of us shall look back to this occasion as an era when all the great interests of the country received a new impulse, the ties of fraternal love and kindly feeling were strengthened, and our love for our common country was made deeper and stronger by our friendly intercourse with each other. (Prolonged Applause.)

The first business in order will be the temporary organization of the Convention, by the choice of a President and Secretary *pro tem.* With your permission, I will nominate for the office of temporary President the Hon. FREDERICK FRALEY, of Philadelphia, and for temporary Secretary, Mr. HAMILTON A. HILL, of Boston.

These nominations were unanimously ratified, and the Hon. OTIS NORCROSS and Mr. ERASTUS B. BIGELOW, of Boston, were appointed a Committee to wait upon Mr. FRALEY and conduct him to the chair.

This Committee having discharged this duty, the President *pro tem.* addressed the Convention as follows:

## ADDRESS OF MR. FRALEY.

I am profoundly sensible, gentlemen, of the honor which you have conferred upon Pennsylvania, and of the still greater honor that you have conferred upon me, by electing me to this temporary presidency. After the searching and touching prayer to which we have just listened, after the eloquent address we have just heard, what is there that remains for me to say? The whole ground of your assembling has been covered, all the objects that you are to consider have been presented, and if I were to comply with my own feelings, I would bow my acknowledgments merely for the honor you have conferred, and take my seat. But when I reflect upon what has brought us together, the great interests that we are about to consider, the necessity that there will be for a careful comparison of views and weighing of opinions, I may be permitted, perhaps, to say a word or two upon some of those topics which are to be considered here.

First, of our great lines of internal communication — the railways and the canals of the Union; those iron and water links binding us now together as a Union, destined to bind us still more closely together and to magnify us among the people of the earth as the greatest and the most powerful nation upon which the sun shines, and upon which God bestows His blessings. The more closely we consider those lines of internal communication, the more shall we be disposed to put forward all the strength of our influence, and all the might of our authority to make them complete and to diffuse them over the whole land.

Again, on the great subject of the currency, which we are to consider, what conflicting opinions prevail among us upon that vital and important topic, lying as it does at the foundation, almost, of the social structure of society, entering into every man's business, entering into every household in one shape or another, and commanding the attention and the scrutiny of those who have devoted their minds to the study of such problems, and who look to us to present those views in order that they may be carefully compared, and that out of our deliberations upon this subject there may go up to Washington a voice that will be respected — that will put this question upon foundations that shall not be shaken, which will, in the edifice which shall be reared on these foundations, restore us to the condition we enjoyed before the rebellion broke out, and which will so place the currency of this country in the future before the world that it shall be considered not only the best and most reliable currency, but the one which will be most beneficial to the wide and extended population that will use it.

In regard to the question of taxation, we have a broad field before us. We have in connection with that subject to consider the great manufacturing, industrial, and agricultural interests of the country; to balance the claims of each; to consider how they bear upon each other, and to bring about such a harmony of these interests as that each shall receive its due reward, and that the agriculture, the commerce, and the manufactures of this country shall go forward, hand in hand, prospering and to prosper.

In regard to the organization of a National Board of Trade, this assemblage shows, I think, the advantages that will be derived from such an institution, bringing together, as it will, from all parts of our country intelligent minds operating in different lines of business, following different modes of thought, representing different sectional interests and all shades of opinion. Through such an organization the influence of the business men of the country will be potently felt throughout the land for the good of the whole people.

Coming as I do from Pennsylvania, having had considerable experience in matters of business, having been tolerably familiar with the history of this country during the present century, and having seen the vast strides that our country has made in arts, in manufactures, in science, in intellectual cultivation, when I contemplate what has come out of the seed that has thus been sown, and look forward to the future, I realize to the fullest extent these blessings which have been so ably sketched by the President of the Boston Board of Trade who opened these proceedings, in the admirable speech he has just delivered. When I look at the influence that the construction of the great canals of New York had upon opening the great West and making New York the great outlet of the internal commerce of the country; when I look at the rapidity with which Pennsylvania followed in those steps and organized her lines of internal improvement; when I consider that the examples thus set by New York and Pennsylvania have been followed so largely by the Western States; and when I realize, gentlemen, the benefits that have flowed from this enlarged system of internal improvement, I have thought that every dollar, nay every million of dollars that may be expended in constructing such great highways of trade, is like the seed sown in the prolific soil of the West, that brings forth an hundred fold. (Applause.) And when I recollect, gentlemen, the condition the manufactures of this country were in at the breaking out of the war of 1812, how unfitted we were at that time to enter upon the struggle with the powerful empire of Great Britain, and recall the effect that war had upon developing the industry of this country and shadowing forth its resources; when I consider the foundations that were then laid for our manufacturing industry, which were built upon at the close of that war by the protective tariff, which set in motion the energies of New England in the first instance, and afterwards set in motion the energies of all the other States; when I consider the influence that that system had in preparing us for the still greater struggle that we have just passed through, and see to what an extent the manufacturing industry of this country enabled us to breast the great rebellion and to overcome it; and find that we had the ability not only to make blankets for our soldiers, but clothing for them also; to create all the artillery of war; to construct the most magnificent steam navy that ever floated upon the waters of the ocean; when I look, I say, upon the field that has thus been cultivated from 1812 to 1868, I confess that I glory in my country, and that I anticipate for her quite as noble a future as has been so eloquently portrayed to us in the address to which we have just listened. (Applause.)

Now, gentlemen, it is for you to consider these great questions; to consider them in that spirit of forbearance, and harmony, and deference to preconceived opinions, that these great questions demand; to bring out of what may seem in some of them antagonistic elements, the simplicity, and perfectness, and unity of truth; for truth upon all these questions, permit me to say, is an unit, and what is the interest of the agriculture of this country is equally the interest of the manufactures of this country; what is the interest of the manufactures of this country is the interest of the commerce of the country. These are blended so intimately together that one cannot suffer without compelling the others to suffer, and we might as well expect the body to move in soundness of health and perfectness of organization deprived of its limbs, leaving it merely a heart, as to suppose that our country can move on without the complete harmony of all these great interests. (Applause.)

Permit me to say, that we of Pennsylvania have endeavored by diversifying the employments of our people to shadow forth an example of this unity of interests of which I speak. Our commercial centre, subordinate, it is true, to the commercial power of the great City of New York, cultivates foreign and domestic commerce; the transportation of the products of the interior to the seaboard and the exportation of such of those products as we have to spare and cannot consume at home, to foreign countries; giving employment to a much smaller number of ships, it is true, than sail from the port of New York, but balancing their excess against other interests of the Commonwealth, so that those who participate in trade and commerce shall reap their proportion of the golden rewards which commerce brings. So of our manufactures. We give them all the protection and encouragement that we can. We invite the largest possible investments of capital in those branches of business. We hold out, by liberal legislation, to those residing outside of the territory of the Commonwealth, the opportunity to come in by a free law for the incorporation of manufacturing, mining, and trading companies, giving them abundant opportunities to plant themselves on our soil, and to avail themselves of our resources; and we have seen, in the growth of our great Commonwealth, and the rapid advances she is making in wealth and population, that we realize the true idea in this harmony of interests of which I speak. Our fields glow with abundant harvests; our farmers reap a rich reward for their labors, mainly by the proximity of manufacturing establishments to their farms. They are not obliged to transport their products, even over our liberally conducted system of railroads, for extraordinary distances, in order to reach a market and to get a return for their labor. And what we of Pennsylvania have found so beneficial to us we wish to put forward as an example for our sister States, so that they may participate in and enjoy the advantages which we do; and which to a great extent I acknowledge we have copied from the thriftiness and example of New England. (Applause.)

Now, gentlemen, I again present to you my thanks for the honor you have conferred upon me; and when I look upon this Convention and see the faces that are turned toward me beaming with intelligence, and remember the varied interests they represent, and the various sections from which they come, I am sure, gentlemen, that the deliberations of such a body upon all those topics which are presented for our consideration in the circular of the Boston Board of Trade, with such others as the wisdom of this Convention may suggest, will be honestly, honorably, and fairly treated; so that when we separate, coming here together as strangers, as has been said by the President of the Boston Board of Trade, we shall continue to the end of our respective lives, fast and firm friends (applause,) bound together by the ties of a national brotherhood, by the sympathy of a common interest, and by the hope (as has been asked for us by the servant of God in his prayer) of a reünion in that higher and enduring country, where we shall receive the reward of labors well done here upon earth. (Loud applause.)

Mr. WALBRIDGE, of New York: I move the appointment of a Committee, consisting of one member from each Board of Trade and Chamber of Commerce represented in the Convention, to nominate permanent officers, to prepare rules of order for the government of the Convention, and to report a ratio of voting.

Mr. MCCHESNEY, of Chicago: I move a division of the question, and the appointment of an independent Committee to prepare rules of order.

Mr. WALBRIDGE accepted the amendment; and the first part of the motion was carried.

Mr. WETHERELL, of Philadelphia: It seems to me hardly necessary to appoint a separate Committee for the purpose of preparing rules and determining the ratio of voting, for I presume that the rules and the ratio of voting will be the same as were adopted at the Detroit Convention, and which are fully understood. Time is a matter of importance to us, and as the appointment of another Committee will take time, I hope the motion will not prevail.

The PRESIDENT: Do you make a motion to amend in that way?

Mr. WETHERELL: I do, Sir.

Mr. BRYSON, of St. Louis: I cannot see the propriety of referring this subject to the Committee just agreed upon. If the object is to save time, certainly two Committees will do a certain amount of work in less time than one Committee can do it. We can do no business until the Committee on Permanent Organization have reported, and while they are preparing their report, this other Committee can decide upon the rules of order and the basis of voting which they will recommend for our adoption.

The question was put, and the amendment was lost.

The motion for the appointment of a separate Committee on Rules of Order and Basis of Voting was then adopted.

Mr. MUNN, of Chicago: I move that in the Committee on the nomination of officers, members be empowered to cast the votes to which their respective delegations are entitled.

The PRESIDENT: That would seem to conflict with the vote already passed, the Convention not having fixed any scale of representation.

Mr. MUNN: The motion was made merely as a guide for the action of the Committee, not as a permanent rule in the action of the Convention. It is but right that the various bodies assembling here to-day should be fairly represented, even in the incipient stages of the proceedings, and it is for this reason that I made the motion. However, if the Chair decides that it conflicts with any previous vote, or that it is out of order, I will not press it.

Mr. WETHERELL: I would suggest that the Committee on Rules make their report before the Committee on Organization; and then the Convention will be bound by it. That is the reason why I wanted the whole matter to go to one Committee.

A Delegate from Cleveland: What number does the gentleman from Chicago propose the members of the Committee should vote for — for the number of delegates present, or for the number of members in the bodies they respectively represent?

Mr. MUNN: My motion contemplated their casting as many votes as they are entitled to in this body.

The PRESIDENT: The Chair decides, that as the ratio of voting has not yet been settled by the Convention, that proposition is out of order.

On motion of Mr. WALBRIDGE, a recess of ten minutes was taken to enable the several delegations to nominate the members of the Committees ordered.

Upon the reassembling of the Convention, the two Committees were announced as follows:

## COMMITTEE ON PERMANENT ORGANIZATION.

| | | |
|---|---|---|
| Hiram Walbridge, | Chamber of Commerce, | New York. |
| Frank Chamberlain, | Board of Trade, | Albany. |
| N. G. Hichborn, | Maine Shipbuilders' Asso'n, | Augusta. |
| William D. Sewall, | Board of Trade, | Bath. |
| Charles G. Nazro, | Board of Trade, | Boston. |
| Avery Plumer, | Corn Exchange, | Boston. |
| P. S. Marsh, | Board of Trade, | Buffalo. |
| T. W. Barhydt, | Board of Trade, | Burlington. |
| Murray Nelson, | Board of Trade, | Chicago. |

| | | |
|---|---|---|
| S. Lester Taylor, | Chamber of Commerce, | Cincinnati. |
| J. H. Clark, | Board of Trade, | Cleveland. |
| E. B. Ward, | Board of Trade, | Detroit. |
| H. Lowry, | Produce Exchange, | Dubuque. |
| A. P. Cook, | Board of Trade, | Jackson. |
| W. W. Alcott, | Board of Trade, | Kalamazoo. |
| J. J. Porter, | Board of Trade, | Louisville. |
| John Bradford, | Chamber of Commerce, | Milwaukie. |
| E. S. Brown, | Produce Exchange, | New York. |
| James Y. Leigh, | Board of Trade, | Norfolk. |
| D. W. C. Brown, | Board of Trade, | Ogdensburgh. |
| J. W. Pitkin, | Board of Trade, | Oswego. |
| Samuel V. Merrick, | Board of Trade, | Philadelphia. |
| C. J. Hoffman, | Commercial Exchange, | Philadelphia. |
| James I. Bennett, | Board of Trade, | Pittsburgh. |
| Woodbury S. Dana, | Board of Trade, | Portland. |
| C. A. Ropes, | Board of Trade, | Salem. |
| W. J. Dill, | Board of Trade, | Sandusky. |
| Moses Ellis, | Board of Trade, | San Francisco. |
| George Coray, | Board of Trade, | Scranton. |
| Nahum H. Andrews, | Board of Trade, | Springfield, O. |
| J. H. Britton, | Board of Trade, | St. Louis. |
| A. W. Fagin, | Union Merchants' Exchange, | St. Louis. |
| Joseph A. Wheelock, | Board of Trade, | St. Paul. |
| M. D. Carrington, | Board of Trade, | Toledo. |
| Thomas A. Tillinghass, | Board of Trade, | Troy. |
| Edward Betts, | Board of Trade, | Wilmington. |

## COMMITTEE ON RULES.

| | | |
|---|---|---|
| John C. Dore, | Board of Trade, | Chicago. |
| William S. Preston, | Board of Trade, | Albany. |
| B. C. Bailey, | Board of Trade, | Bath. |
| Joseph S. Ropes, | Board of Trade, | Boston. |
| Samuel G. Bowdlear, | Corn Exchange, | Boston. |
| E. S. Prosser, | Board of Trade, | Buffalo. |
| T. W. Barhydt, | Board of Trade, | Burlington. |
| Robert Hosea, | Chamber of Commerce, | Cincinnati. |
| R. T. Lyon, | Board of Trade, | Cleveland. |
| Moses W. Field, | Board of Trade, | Detroit. |
| H. Lowry, | Produce Exchange, | Dubuque. |
| A. P. Cook, | Board of Trade, | Jackson. |

| | | |
|---|---|---|
| W. W. Alcott, | Board of Trade, | Kalamazoo. |
| John Tait, | Board of Trade, | Louisville. |
| W. P. McLareu, | Chamber of Commerce, | Milwaukie. |
| L. J. N. Stark, | Chamber of Commerce, | New York. |
| Edward Hincken, | Produce Exchange, | New York. |
| James Y. Leigh, | Board of Trade, | Norfolk. |
| W. L. Proctor, | Board of Trade, | Ogdensburgh. |
| F. B. Lathrop, | Board of Trade, | Oswego. |
| J. P. Wetherill, | Board of Trade, | Philadelphia. |
| George L. Buzby, | Commercial Exchange, | Philadelphia. |
| George H. Thurston, | Board of Trade, | Pittsburgh. |
| Samuel J. Anderson, | Board of Trade, | Portland. |
| Washington Ryan, | Maine Shipbuilders' Asso'n, | Portland. |
| John C. Osgood, | Board of Trade, | Salem. |
| Rush R. Sloane, | Board of Trade, | Sandusky. |
| Alfred DeWitt, | Chamber of Commerce, | San Francisco. |
| George Coray, | Board of Trade, | Scranton. |
| Nahum H. Andrews, | Board of Trade, | Springfield, O. |
| M. A. Bryson, | Board of Trade, | St. Louis. |
| George Pegram, | Union Merchants' Exchange, | St. Louis. |
| Russell Blakely, | Board of Trade, | St. Paul. |
| C. A. King, | Board of Trade, | Toledo. |
| James Forsyth, | Board of Trade, | Troy. |
| George G. Lobdell, | Board of Trade, | Wilmington. |

Mr. HOFFMAN, of Philadelphia: I move that the members of the Committee on Organization have power to cast the votes of the number by which their respective bodies are represented here. Otherwise the smaller bodies might make the organization, while the larger bodies would have only one vote.

The PRESIDENT: I think that, in the absence of any fixed rule in regard to voting, that motion is not in order.

Mr. HOFFMAN: It seems to me that such a rule ought to be adopted. We do not want to have the report of the Committee on Organization come in here, and then have any unpleasant feeling in regard to it. I do not know that there will be any, but here is one city represented by twenty delegates, another by thirty, while there are other organizations represented by one or two, whose votes may elect the officers of this Convention. That is my point, and I think the motion is in order.

Mr. CHAMBERLIN, of Cleveland: This proposition has more in it than appears upon the surface. In the first place, it implies the want of a disposition, on the part of this Committee, to act fairly; and, in the next place, it assumes to carry with it a method of voting that is uncertain, and only regulated by the number who happen to be here present represented on that Committee. Now, I do not apprehend that there is any disposition to act unfairly by anybody. This is merely a preliminary step. A Committee has been appointed to present to the Convention a plan of organization. It will be for this Convention to ratify the action of this Committee or not, just as it pleases. I should be very sorry to see, at the outset, any apprehension manifested that there would be any unfair advantage taken of anybody. On the part of the small delegations, it implies that the large ones are going to overslaugh them; on the part of the large delegations, it implies that we are afraid the small ones will take too much into their hands. I hope this proposition will be withdrawn, and the whole matter submitted to the Committee, and let them act in their good discretion, for the benefit of us all. (Applause.)

Mr. HOFFMAN: I have no feeling upon the subject at all, but I ask the question whether the motion is in order. The Committee on Rules will not report until the Committee on Organization have made their report. Now, to obviate the very difficulties to which the gentleman has referred, I have made this motion. I do not know that there will be any unpleasant feeling occasioned by the report of the Committee; but suppose the Committee shall report a list of officers with which the larger delegations are not satisfied, they will vote the report down. Now, which is the most unpleasant, to have the matter fairly and quietly considered in the Committee, or to have the report brought before this body, and the Convention refuse to ratify it?

Mr. THURSTON, of Pittsburgh: I will ask if a resolution of instructions to this Committee would be in order?

The PRESIDENT: That would be in order.

Mr. THURSTON: I would move, then, that this Committee be instructed to vote for the officers in the manner adopted by the Detroit Convention, that is, according to the representation of the several States in Congress.

Mr. CHAMBERLIN: I move to amend by substituting, "according to the membership of the respective Boards of Trade, or other organizations here represented," instead of according to the representation of the several States.

This amendment was carried.

Mr. STRANAHAN, of New York: I merely wish to move, inasmuch as there seems to be no feeling whatever on this subject, (for all declare this to be the fact,) that the whole subject matter of instructing the Committee lie upon the table.

The motion to lay on the table passed.

Mr. WALBRIDGE: I move that the Committees have leave to retire to perform the duties devolved upon them by the Convention.

Mr. NAZRO, of Boston: Before that motion is put I have a word to say. It seems to me that there should be some action taken in regard to the credentials of members, before these Committees proceed to act upon the subjects committed to them. If there should be any organizations represented here who do not belong here, it will be too late to remedy the difficulty after these Committees have reported. I do not know that there are any such organizations here — I presume there are none — but it seems to me that, as a preliminary matter, we should have a Committee on Credentials. I move the appointment of such a Committee, to consist of nine members.

Mr. TOBEY, of Boston: I move the postponement of Mr. WALBRIDGE's motion, in order that a Committee on Credentials may be appointed. I am constrained to make this motion, from the fact that there is at least one organization, if not more, who feel that they are embraced within the call, on which question there may be a difference of opinion. I do not know who can determine that question so well as a Committee on Credentials, and it is for that reason, I am sure, that the gentleman from Boston has made his motion.

Mr. TOBEY's motion to postpone Mr. WALBRIDGE's motion was carried.

Mr. CHAMBERLIN: If this Committee is to prevent the action of any other Committee until it has made its report, thereby delaying the business of the Convention, I object to it. I should rather prefer that each Committee, which is the judge of its own members, just as each branch of Congress is the judge of its own members, should expel any one whom they find not entitled to be there.

Mr. HOFFMAN: I move to amend the motion by substituting as follows: that a Committee of three, to be composed of members of the Board of Trade of Boston, be appointed as a Committee on Credentials.

Mr. NAZRO: I hope that motion will not prevail. The Boston Board of Trade would be sorry to reject any body claiming a right to be represented here. We have called the Convention together in good faith, and we have designed to have, so far as possible, a fair representation of all business bodies entitled to meet in such a Convention as this from all parts of the land. For one (and I presume I express the opinion of all my colleagues,) I should be very sorry to reject any organization, of a respectable character, claiming to come here as business men; but if the Convention will choose a Committee from various sections, they can act impartially, and there will be no ill-feeling occasioned by their action. The Boston Board of Trade has desired to act with entire impartiality, in perfect good faith, and, so far as possible, to make its call as wide as the limits of the land. I hope, therefore, that the motion will not prevail.

Mr. SLOANE, of Sandusky, Ohio: I simply rise to say, that if the proposition of the gentleman from Boston is to be considered at all by this Convention, there is great propriety in the motion submitted by my friend on my right (Mr. HOFFMAN.) This Convention has assembled by an invitation of the Boston Board of Trade, extended to all the Boards of Trade regularly organized throughout the country, and it seems to me it would be much more proper that the Committee on Credentials should consist of three members of the Boston Board of Trade, than that it should be composed of nine members, appointed by the Chair, when we have twenty or twenty-five organizations represented here. I ask this Convention, before they pass any resolution providing for the appointment, by the Chair, of a Committee of nine on Credentials, to consider that it is a very important question bearing upon the status of the Convention, and one which may materially affect its deliberations and results. Either give us a Committee of three, composed of members of the Boston Board of Trade, or give us a Committee on Credentials upon which every delegation here present may have a representation.

Mr. ROPES, of Boston: I would inquire if there is any practical difficulty in the way of the Committee on Organization acting also as a Committee on Credentials? The Chairmen of the several delegations have the credentials of their delegates, or may have them, and it seems to me the matter may be very well referred to the Committee on Organization, and be settled by them in the readiest way possible.

Mr. WETHERILL, of Philadelphia: I would suggest that this whole matter had better be postponed, and that the different delegations be called upon to present to the Chair their credentials. That is the ordinary way of organizing conventions, and why should it not be pursued in this instance? It would save trouble to the Committee, and the whole matter could be settled in fifteen or twenty minutes. I doubt not that all present are fully prepared to say that they have a right to sit in this Convention.

I move that the whole matter be indefinitely postponed, and that the several delegations be called and their credentials presented.

This was agreed to, and the motion giving the Committees leave to retire was put and carried.

The credentials of delegates were then handed in. The list, as finally perfected, was as follows:

## LIST OF MEMBERS.

**Board of Trade, Albany, N.Y.**

| | | |
|---|---|---|
| Frank Chamberlain, | William S. Preston, | A. K. Sheppard, |
| James McMartin, | | William H. Taylor. |

**Board of Trade, Bath, Me.**

| | | |
|---|---|---|
| B. C. Bailey, | | William D. Sewall. |

**Board of Trade, Boston.**

| | | |
|---|---|---|
| Edward Atkinson, | Charles G. Nazro, | Solomon R. Spaulding, |
| Erastus B. Bigelow, | Otis Norcross, | Edward S. Tobey, |
| Francis Dane, | George C. Richardson, | George L. Ward, |
| William Endicott, Jr., | Joseph S. Ropes, | Samuel H. Walley, |
| Charles W. Freeland, | | Charles O. Whitmore. |

**Corn Exchange, Boston.**

| | | |
|---|---|---|
| Samuel G. Bowdlear, | Otis Munroe, | T. Albert Taylor, |
| Edmund W. Clap, | Harrison E. Maynard, | Calvin M. Winch. |
| | Avery Plumer, | |

**Board of Trade, Buffalo, N.Y.**

| | | |
|---|---|---|
| E. P. Dorr, | P. S. Marsh, | Jason Parker, |
| Israel T. Hatch, | E. S. Prosser, | Elmore H. Walker. |

**Board of Trade, Burlington, Iowa.**

T. W. Barhydt.

**Board of Trade, Chicago.**

| | | |
|---|---|---|
| T. N. Bond, | W. H. Low, | W. Nason, |
| E. W. Blatchford, | L. F. Leopold, | Thomas Parker, |
| B. F. Culver, | T. P. Lawrence, | I. W. Preston, |

| | | |
|---|---|---|
| John F. Beaty, | Ira Y. Munn, | W. E. Richardson, |
| John C. Dore, | S. H. McCrea, | A. A. Stone, |
| D. H. Denton, | R. McChesney, | V. A. Turpin, |
| P. W. Dater, | Hugh McLennan, | C. L. Wilson. |
| | Murray Nelson, | |

**Chamber of Commerce, Cincinnati.**

| | | |
|---|---|---|
| R. M. Bishop, | A. L. Frazar, | Henry Lewis, |
| L. T. Barr, | John A. Gano, | T. W. Moffatt, |
| S. F. Covington, | A. T. Goshorn, | Henry Pearce, |
| F. G. Cleneay, | Robert Hosea, | W. R. Phipps, |
| Thompson Dean, | William Harvey, | William Resor, |
| James Espy, | John W. Kirk, | S. Lester Taylor, |
| Thomas H. Foulds, | Samuel B. Keys, | Adolph Wood. |

**Board of Trade, Cleveland, Ohio.**

| | | |
|---|---|---|
| Philo Chamberlin, | A. Hughes, | R. T. Lyon, |
| J. H. Clark, | | J. C. Sage. |

**Board of Trade, Detroit, Mich.**

| | | |
|---|---|---|
| George F. Bagley, | Moses W. Field, | Thomas McGraw, |
| H. J. Buckley, | James F. Joy, | Edmund Trowbridge, |
| George B. Dickinson, | | E. B. Ward. |

**Produce Exchange, Dubuque, Iowa.**

H. Lowry.

**Board of Trade, Jackson, Mich.**

A. P. Cook.

**Board of Trade, Kalamazoo, Mich.**

W. W. Alcott.

**Board of Trade, Louisville, Ky.**

| | | |
|---|---|---|
| Julius Dorn, | George A. Owen, | J. J. Porter, |
| John B. Green, | | John Tait. |

**Maine Shipbuilders' Association.**

| | | |
|---|---|---|
| N. G. Hichborn, | Edwin Reed, | Washington Ryan. |

**Chamber of Commerce, Milwaukie, Wis.**

| | | |
|---|---|---|
| P. D. Armour, | Edward D. Holton, | W. P. McLaren, |
| John Bradford, | C. Holland, | James S. Peck. |
| | M. B. Medbery, | |

**Chamber of Commerce, New York.**

| | | |
|---|---|---|
| S. D. Babcock, | D. Colden Murray, | John A Stevens, Jr., |
| Martin Bates, Jr., | L. J. N. Stark, | William M. Vermilye, |
| J. J. Comstock, | J. S. T. Stranahan, | Hiram Walbridge, |
| William H. Guion, | | John M. White. |

**Produce Exchange, New York.**

E. S. Brown,
William Blanchard,
John H. Boynton,
Edward Hincken,
W. H. Harris,
Harvey E. Hicks,
J. Hobart Herrick,
L. Haseltine,
A. H. Philips,
Isaac H. Reed,
Thomas Rigney,
Francis P. Sage,
W. W. Wickes,
Paul Worth,
H. Youngs, Jr.

**Board of Trade, Norfolk, Va.**

James Y. Leigh.

**Board of Trade, Ogdensburgh, N.Y.**

D. W. C. Brown,
George A. Eddy,
O. C. Lee,
W. L. Proctor.

**Board of Trade, Oswego, N.Y.**

D. G. Fort,
A. H. Failing,
F. B. Lathrop,
J. W. Pitkin,
George B. Sloan.

**Board of Trade, Philadelphia.**

George N. Allen,
Samuel T. Canby,
Frederic Fraley,
Samuel V. Merrick,
D. C. McCammon,
Thomas Potter,
E. A. Souder,
George N. Tatham,
John P. Wetherill,
Henry Winsor,
Edward R. Wood.

**Commercial Exchange, Philadelphia.**

Thomas Allman,
George L. Buzby,
C. H. Cummings,
Robert Ervein,
C. J. Hoffman,
H. S. Hannis,
Philip B. Mingle,
Seneca E. Malone,
John H. Michener,
S. L. Ward.

**Board of Trade, Pittsburgh, Pa.**

James I. Bennett,
Felix R. Brunot,
George W. Cass,
C. B. Herron,
George W. Hailman,
D. McCandless,
George H. Thurston.

**Board of Trade, Portland, Me.**

Samuel J. Anderson,
Woodbury S. Dana,
T. C. Hersey,
Charles H. Haskell,
M. N. Rich,
A. K. Shurtleff,
George W. Woodman.

**Board of Trade, Salem, Mass.**

Charles Harrington,
John C. Osgood,
W. P. Phillips,
C. A. Ropes,
J. O. Safford.

**Board of Trade, Sandusky, Ohio.**

S. W. Butler,
W. J. Dill,
F. E. Foster,
J. O. Moss,
Rush R. Sloane.

**Chamber of Commerce, San Francisco.**

William T. Coleman,
Alfred DeWitt,
Moses Ellis.

**Board of Trade, Scranton, Pa.**

George Coray.

**Board of Trade, Springfield, Ohio.**

Nahum H. Andrews.

**Board of Trade, St. Louis.**

M. A. Bryson, J. H. Britton, R. W. Crittenden, Martin Collins, James P. Fiske, E. W. Fox, John R. Lionberger, W. H. Pulsifer, E. C. Pike, N. W. Warne.

**Union Merchants' Exchange, St. Louis.**

J. H. Alexander, J. E. Carpenter, Nathan Cole, J. P. Colcord, D. D. Duncan, J. C. Ewald, A. W. Fagin, W. T. Hazard, Wm. Heinrichshofer, William Hunicke, George H. Morgan, Thomas Morrison, George Pegram, M. L. Pottle, W. W. Sanford, William Wallace, H. R. Whitmore, H. C. Yaeger.

**Board of Trade, St. Paul, Minn.**

Russell Blakely, James W. Taylor, Joseph A. Wheelock.

**Board of Trade, Toledo, Ohio.**

Frederick Bissell, M. D. Carrington, John B. Carson, R. Cummings, George W. Davis, E. W. Harris, C. A. King, William T. Walker.

**Board of Trade, Troy, N.Y.**

Thomas Coleman, Charles Eddy, James Forsyth, Thomas A. Tillinghast, Perry E. Toles.

**Board of Trade, Wilmington, Del.**

John H. Adams, Edward Betts, Francis Barry, Samuel Bancroft, Jr., G. G. Lobdell, E. T. Warner, Jr.

A communication from Mr. HORACE H. DAY, of Niagara Falls, New York, was read by the Secretary, asking for himself admission to the Convention on the ground of his long and intimate connection with the transportation interests of the country.

Mr. BRADFORD, of Milwaukie: I move that Mr. DAY be admitted.

Mr. CHAMBERLIN, of Cleveland: I should be very glad to have the gentleman admitted as a member of this Convention, but if you once open that door, you cannot close it. The call is for a "Commercial Convention." The moment you go beyond that, you will have this room so full you cannot breathe.

A Delegate: It is quite competent for the Convention to close the door at any time.

Mr. HATCH, of Buffalo: I merely rise to say, that Mr. DAY is very largely concerned in the construction of a work of national importance, and is therefore deeply interested in the action of this Convention. For one, sir, I should hope that the Convention would admit Mr. DAY as a member.

Mr. WOOD, of Philadelphia: I recollect that some such question came up at Detroit, and I think the gentleman was invited to attend the meetings of that Convention, but without the privilege of voting. I should think this would be the proper way to put the question now.

Mr. BRADFORD: I made my motion upon this ground. I feel that we are here as a Convention of business men, to take counsel together. I have not sympathized with those gentlemen who were earnest upon the question of credentials. I would not shut out any gentleman, from any part of the country, who is a prominent business man, who comes here with any fair credentials, or any fair claim to represent any one of the important interests we have before us. Mr. DAY is well known all over the country as a gentleman who has taken a very deep interest in one of the most important questions which will come before this body; and upon this ground I made my motion that he should be admitted. There is force in the suggestion of the gentleman who said that we reserve to ourselves the right to shut the door whenever we please.

Mr. CHAMBERLIN: I know both Mr. DAY's project and himself very well, and I endorse all that the gentleman has said; but I know, too, that there are other projects. This City of Boston is full of projects, and other places are full of projects of different kinds, peculiar to themselves; and the representatives of all these projects would be glad to have seats upon this floor, and to introduce their projects to us. Individually, I am perfectly willing that Mr. DAY should talk with the members of the Convention, and sit here during our deliberations, and if the call embraced such projects as he and others represent, I should be perfectly willing that they should come in, under the call. But the call does not embrace anything of that kind, and we ought not to step beyond the limits prescribed by the Boston Board of Trade in calling this Convention. There is no reason why people should come in here as representatives of particular projects, unless they had been invited in the first instance. If they had been, they would have found seats assigned to them here. As it now stands, it seems to me a gross impropriety to open the door to any parties not embraced in the call of the Convention.

Mr. SOUDER, of Philadelphia: I agree with the gentleman last up. If Mr. DAY should be admitted, it would open the door for the admission of the representatives of various private interests, which certainly do not come within the scope of the call for this Convention. I therefore move to amend the motion, that Mr. DAY be allowed a seat on the floor, but without the privilege of voting or speaking.

A motion was made, and carried, giving Mr. DAY leave to address the Convention, in explanation of his position.

Mr. DAY: Living as I do in a village where we have no Board of Trade or Commercial Association, I have ventured to come here, feeling a very deep interest in the questions which are to come before this Convention. I have not come here to press any personal scheme upon the country; I have not come here to advocate my own private interests alone. Had that been my only object, I could have presented a communication to the Committee having charge of that subject, and I have no doubt it would have received full consideration from a Committee of an intelligent and eminent body such as this is. The gentleman from Cleveland does me great injustice. He bases his objection upon the proposition that I am here to advocate a particular scheme. It is very well known to many of the Boards of Trade in the West, and to some gentlemen of Boston, that I have been a consistent and earnest advocate of a system of communication for ships between the sea and the lakes — not alone a communication round Niagara Falls, for I look upon that as only one link in the great chain. I would have ships come up the river from New York and land in the upper lakes, without change of cargo. (Applause.) That is my object. The gentlemen from Buffalo and Cleveland have opposed me heretofore. They fear the success of my plan, and I expect their opposition; but I think it not fair that the vote should be placed upon that ground alone.

The question was put, and the amendment providing that Mr. DAY should not have the privilege of voting or speaking was carried; the motion was then passed, as amended.

A communication was then read by the Secretary from the Shipbuilders' Association of Maine, announcing the appointment of three delegates to represent them in the Convention: Messrs. N. G. HICHBORN, WASHINGTON RYAN and T. J. STEWART.

A motion was made that the same courtesy be extended to these gentlemen which had been extended to Mr. DAY.

A Delegate: Has this organization been invited to send delegates by the Boston Board of Trade?

The PRESIDENT: No, sir.

Mr. WOOD, of Philadelphia: I would ask if this organization is not an organization for general purposes, representing a large commercial interest in the State of Maine?

The PRESIDENT: I understand so.

Mr. TOBEY, of Boston: I would suggest that we may with propriety hear one of the delegates state their relation to the Convention. Mr. DAY was allowed to state his, and the motion is to allow these gentlemen the same courtesy.

Mr. HICHBORN, of Maine: Mr. President, allow me to thank the Convention for their courtesy in permitting me to state the facts in regard to the organization which we represent; and allow me further to say, before proceeding to state those facts, that I am not here to ask, individually, any courtesy of the Convention. A year ago, seeing that the commercial interest was suffering great depression in the State of Maine, we organized the Shipbuilders' and Shipowners' Association. I happen to be the President of that Association, and I am here to represent that interest, not in its narrow sense, but in its broadest application to all the interests of the country. I had supposed, under the call, that we had a right to come here. And you will further allow me to say, that having taken some interest in this subject during the last year, I have watched the effect of this call, and have been in consultation in regard to it, and it did not occur to me that we did not have a right to come here, under the call, inasmuch as commerce is named. I repeat, I ask nothing for myself; I only ask you to extend this courtesy to my State, which is struggling with you in this common cause, desirous as we all are, that the conclusions to which we shall arrive may benefit our common country by benefitting each and all of its interests.

Mr. Atkinson, of Boston: I move to amend the motion, to invite the delegates to take full part in the proceedings of this Convention. These gentlemen who come here from the Shipbuilders' Association, certainly represent a commercial association; and I think I can say, although not one of the Committee of Arrangements, but simply a member from Boston, that they would have been invited had it occurred to the Committee to extend them a formal invitation. I suppose if there were any Western Board of Trade or Chamber of Commerce, technically, to whom a formal invitation had not been extended, they would be welcomed upon this floor. The danger of this Convention is, I fear, that we shall neglect the interests of commerce, and therefore I hope and trust that the Shipbuilders' Association of Maine may be represented upon the floor.

Mr. Hatch, of Buffalo: I have read with very great interest the address of this Shipbuilders' Association of Maine, and every person, I think, must be familiar with the fact, that it is necessary that something should be done in this country to relieve the shipbuilding interest from its present depressed condition. We all know, that under the legislation of Congress, or from some other cause, our tonnage on the ocean has been rapidly decreasing. I think it has decreased at least one-half in three years; and it is proposed in certain quarters to abolish the navigation laws and the registry laws. Now, sir, if that is done, our tonnage on the ocean will not only be reduced, but our vessels engaged in inland commerce will be swept from our inland seas. This is one of the great subjects which must come before the Convention, and it is entitled to very grave consideration. I am in favor, therefore, of admitting these gentlemen from Maine to full participation in the proceedings of the Convention.

Mr. Tobey: Before this question is put, I desire to explain what seems to me to be the difference between the case of Mr. Day and the case of the gentlemen now under consideration. I ask attention to the terms of the call. It states here, that one of the subjects to be brought before this Convention is "the restoration of the foreign commerce of the country from its present greatly depressed condition." This is a topic distinctly recognized in the call, and must of necessity come before the Convention. These gentlemen come here not to represent a particular enterprise, even though it might be of national importance, like that in which the gentleman from New York (Mr. Day) is engaged; but they come here to represent a great branch of national industry, all-pervading in its extent;

hence the discrimination between their case and that of Mr. DAY. I ought to say, that in the case of Mr. DAY, I abstained from voting, quite willing to leave the question to be settled wholly by the vote of gentlemen from other parts of the country.

The question was then put on the amendment proposed by Mr. ATKINSON, and it was carried, and the motion in that form passed, giving the gentlemen from Maine full admission to the Convention.

Mr. WALBRIDGE, Chairman of the Committee on Permanent Organization, submitted a list of officers for the Convention, as follows:

PRESIDENT,

E. W. FOX, of Missouri.

VICE-PRESIDENTS,

AT LARGE,

| | |
|---|---|
| SAMUEL V. MERRICK, of Penn. | GEORGE F. BAGLEY, of Michigan. |

BY STATES,

| | |
|---|---|
| F. P. SAGE, of New York. | T. C. HERSEY, of Maine. |
| GEO. H. THURSTON, of Penn. | A. DEWITT, of California. |
| I. Y. MUNN, of Illinois. | G. G. LOBDELL, of Delaware. |
| J. Y. LEIGH, of Virginia. | CHARLES G. NAZRO, of Mass. |
| C. A. KING, of Ohio. | R. BLAKELEY, of Minnesota. |
| A. W. FAGIN, of Missouri. | T. W. BARHYDT, of Iowa. |
| M. B. MEDBERY, of Wisconsin. | JULIUS DORN, of Kentucky. |

SECRETARIES,

| | |
|---|---|
| HAMILTON A. HILL, of Mass. | THOMAS ALLMAN, of Penn. |
| JOHN T. BEATY, of Illinois. | J. C. SAGE, of Ohio. |
| JASON PARKER, of New York. | EDWARD BETTS, of Delaware. |

Mr. WALBRIDGE: I have the honor to say, that the report was the unanimous result of the deliberations of the Committee, and I move its acceptance and adoption.

Mr. MUNN, of Chicago: It seems to me that the list of Vice-Presidents from the various States is a kind of buncome addition to the officers necessary to run this Convention. We have come here for business, if there is any business to do, and I do not like to have this thing loaded up with a great many officers. We want men who will work, and I move that that part of the report be stricken out, leaving the President and two Vice-Presidents, that is about all we want.

Mr. WALBRIDGE: I will simply state the reason why the Committee acted as they did. At the first great Convention, held in the city which the gentleman has the honor to represent, in part, — and represents so ably too, — and at the Ship Canal Convention, this method was adopted. At the first National Commercial Convention, at Detroit, in 1865, the same course was pursued; and in order to facilitate our labors, we followed the example set by other Commercial Conventions, and we trust it will meet the hearty assent of this body.

Mr. STRANAHAN, of New York, moved the previous question, which was ordered, and the motion to accept and adopt the report was carried.

Mr. WALBRIDGE and Mr. MCCHESNEY were appointed a Committee to conduct the President elect to the Chair.

On assuming his official position, Mr. FOX said:

GENTLEMEN OF THE NATIONAL COMMERCIAL CONVENTION OF THE UNITED STATES:

Standing almost in sight of Bunker Hill, and, by a felicitous combination of art and good taste, almost in the living presence of the father of our country, deliberating at the home of Webster, surrounded by his associates, and in the presence of the solid men of the nation, it ill becomes me to say a word further in regard to the objects for which you are convened, especially after the practical and eloquent manner in which the President of the Boston Board of Trade presented those objects, and the eloquent manner in which your venerable President from the State of Pennsylvania has enforced them. (Applause.) Gentlemen of the Convention, if I understand the object of your work, it is to unite the great powers of agriculture, manufactures, and commerce by a bond of common interest. (Applause.) If you shall so well succeed in your deliberations as to advance one step in that direction, you will command the good will of the people and the blessings of Divine Providence. Thanking you, gentlemen, for the honor which you have conferred upon the West, upon St. Louis, and upon the St. Louis Board of Trade, over which I have the honor to preside, and invoking your kind indulgence for any errors that I may commit in the decisions which I may make, in which

I shall endeavor to exercise what little common sense I have, in order to forward promptly the objects of your meeting, I have to announce that the next business in order is to hear the report of the Committee on Rules.

Mr. DORE, of Chicago, Chairman of the Committee on Rules and Regulations, presented a report, recommending the adoption of the rules of the United States House of Representatives for the government of the proceedings of the Convention, with the following exceptions:

1st. No person shall speak more than ten minutes upon the same question without first obtaining the leave of the Convention.

2nd. No person shall speak more than once upon the same subject without express leave of the Convention.

3rd. The members of this Convention shall vote on all questions submitted to them *per capita.*

4th. In the appointment of Committees composed of a representative from each delegation, the different delegations shall designate their own representatives.

5th. On rising to address the Chair, members shall give their names and the names of the bodies they represent.

Mr. GANO, of Cincinnati: I move to amend the report by providing that the basis of voting shall be one vote for each fifty members of the association represented.

A Delegate: I would like to inquire how many millions of people that would allow Chicago to vote for? This is a very important matter, and I hope the amendment will not be adopted by the Convention. Each Board was invited to send delegates here on the basis of fifty voting members to each organization, and we have come together on that basis; the Committee, in recommending that the voting should be done *per capita*, thought they would thus avoid a great deal of contention that might arise in regard to the number belonging to each Board, and that we should be able to enter more promptly upon the duties before us. The Board which I have the honor to represent have a rule in reference to voting which is not adopted in other Boards, and it would be a very great hardship to some Boards if that plan should be adopted. I hope the report of the Committee will be adopted.

Mr. WETHERILL: An objection strikes my mind which it seems to me has some force. In my own Board we have say, six hundred firms in our membership, but if we take the names of all the individuals in these firms we should run it up to fifteen hundred. How can we get at it? It seems to me that the amendment would so complicate the question that we could never get at just the right number. I hope the report of the Committee will be adopted, as presented.

Mr. HINCKEN, of New York: The delegation from New York are willing to have a vote of eighteen. Under the amendment proposed by the gentlemen, we should be entitled to two hundred and fifty or sixty votes. The delegation do not claim that. They are satisfied that they can represent the interests of New York, and they are willing to submit to that representation. (Applause.) If you call on us to vote according to the number of our respective bodies, we have twenty-five hundred men in the Produce Exchange, and here are four or five men from the Chamber of Commerce, who will vote for another two thousand. And many of these men are duplicated; many of the members of the Produce Exchange are members also of the Chamber of Commerce. We all represent the interests of the City of New York, and we are willing that the interests of New York should be guided by the representatives of all the country. (Applause.)

Mr. GANO: It seems to me that the plan proposed will exactly meet the case. We want to represent the mechanical and manufacturing interests of the country, and I see no way in which it can be better done than in the way I have proposed. If New York happens to have so many more, I see no injustice, for my part, in her having a corresponding number of votes. Before the vote is put, I would like to have these gentlemen explain what they mean by voting *per capita*; I do not understand it.

Mr. SLOANE, of Sandusky: The Committee did not consider the basis they recommended entirely equitable; but they thought it the best that could be reported. The gentleman's amendment is impracticable. It involves the necessity of another Committee, to ascertain how many members constitute the different Boards of Trade represented on this floor. This resolution which was adopted by the Committee, and which is now before the house for its adoption, is probably as equitable as any plan that could be devised. If this Convention propose to send any communication to Washington, to influence the Members of Congress, their action will carry with it a direct and positive influence, if determined in the manner proposed by the Committee, which would not be obtained if the capital of the country in the great cities were to be represented against the smaller cities and towns, scattered all over the Middle States, the West, and the North-West. I am opposed to the amendment, and in favor of the report of the Committee.

The question was put, and the amendment rejected. The report of the Committee was then accepted and adopted unanimously.

Mr. WALBRIDGE: I move that a Committee of nine be appointed by the Chair, on each of the subjects submitted for the consideration of the Convention by the Boston Board of Trade, except the Committee on Currency, which Committee shall consist of fifteen members.

Mr. FRALEY: I move to amend, so as to provide that each of the Committees on these several subjects embraced in the call, shall consist of one delegate from each Board or organization represented in the Convention, and that each delegation shall name its own member of the Committee.

Mr. WALBRIDGE: I accept the amendment.

Mr. BRYSON, of St. Louis: I wish to say, in regard to this amendment, that inasmuch as we have already decided that we will vote finally *per capita*, I do not see the necessity of recognizing again the element of different associations. If we do, these Committees will consume a very large amount of time, and we shall not have a report for two or three days. I think Committees of ten would be large enough. Let them be comprised of members from the different sections, and then, when they make their reports, if there is any change desired by the different sections, let them vote for it here. I do not see the necessity of again bringing up this question of associations. Let the vote be *per capita* in the Committees, as it is *per capita* in the final action.

Mr. FRALEY: I believe that the questions which this Convention are to consider are so important, that upon every one the opinion of the different delegations should, in Committee, have a fair chance of expression. (Applause.) In no other way than the one I have proposed can such an expression of opinion be obtained. The questions are broad in their nature. They reach to the very roots of society; they strike at the foundations of all our prosperity; and, unless there be such an examination of them as will go to the roots, the examination is worthless. Now, a Committee of fifteen, to consider the question of the currency, as suggested by my friend from New

York, would approach very nearly to what I propose for the other Committees. Upon that great question of the currency, I hold that each Board of Trade and commercial organization represented in this Convention should have a vote. There are very great differences of opinion upon this subject. We have not only differences of individual opinion upon this subject, but there are sectional differences upon it, which are to be reconciled, and we cannot expect or hope to reconcile them upon this floor in speeches of ten minutes each. In such a Committee, constituted as proposed, each section would have its sectional voice, each commercial representation would have its commercial voice; and we might expect that reports coming from Committees so constituted, and in which these subjects had been fully discussed, would meet with the same unanimous approbation as the reports of the Committees upon which we have acted this morning, which Committees were constituted precisely in the same way that I propose these general Committees shall be. It is perfectly fair, that upon these questions, the Committees should be so constituted. The Chairman, impartial as he may be, trustworthy as he may be, and as I concede him to be, has no personal knowledge of the members of the Convention, such as will enable him to make his selections as he would if he knew us all personally; but we, in our respective delegations, know each other; we know to what extent gentlemen in our respective delegations have attended to these various questions; we know the feeling of our several constituencies upon them; and we can present in such Committees those feelings and those views, and have them properly and thoroughly discussed and compared; and when such Committees as I propose we shall have upon these subjects come to report, I am satisfied their reports will meet with the unanimous approval of this house, as we have found to be the case this morning. If a Committee of fifteen be right on the question of the currency, a Committee of fifteen would certainly be right upon the question of foreign commerce, and would be equally necessary upon the subject of taxation, and its bearing upon the tariff question.

I think, sir, that I have said enough to convince the Convention that the constitution of the Committees in this way is the fair way to constitute them, and that they ought to agree to the proposition.

The question was then taken, and the motion carried.

Mr. ATKINSON, of Boston: I move a reconsideration of that vote. I think gentlemen are not aware that there are thirty-two different bodies represented here, and the vote will therefore require that each Committee consist of thirty-two members. If these Committees are to cut and dry the work of the Convention, and decide what it shall do, perhaps it would be well to have them consist of thirty-two or more members each; but if not, if the Convention is to do something itself, they should be simply Business Committees, to systematize the business, and aid the Convention in its work.

Mr. Tobey, of Boston: If that vote is adhered to, we shall find that our work is to be nearly doubled in this Convention. We come here as a commercial body, and we are tenacious, as a commercial body, of the saving of time. Now, I submit, that if we put thirty-two men on each of these Committees, we must expect minority reports from each one of them, and a great deal of time will necessarily be consumed in discussing them. I submit, that any nine gentlemen, chosen in a fair way, are competent to bring before us the consideration of any question. When it is here, it is within the control of the Convention, and can be acted upon as we see fit, and much time will be saved. We cannot do injustice to any section of the country, when a Committee makes a report, and when that report is fairly discussed and acted upon.

Mr. Stranahan, of New York: I apprehend that the very liberal views of the Convention will not embarrass us at all. The Committees are to judge of the matters brought before them, and each Committee will have the sagacity to see the value of time, and will appoint Sub-Committees to take charge of the different matters, and I apprehend we shall get along very well.

Mr. Potter, of Philadelphia: I will inquire of the Secretary the number of organizations represented in the Convention?

Mr. Hill: Less than thirty, so far as reported.

Mr. Potter: There will be no difficulty in having Committees constituted of from twenty-six to thirty members. The object is to have these Committees collect facts and digest business, and present it in more tangible form; and a large Committee is quite as competent to do this as a small one. The whole object is to obtain information and present it in the best possible form, in order that those who are in this body may be able to come to such a decision as will make the best impression upon the public mind, and bring about the best state of things in regard to all these measures. I think there are no difficulties in the way of having the Committees as proposed by my colleague, (Mr. Fraley,) and I hope the reconsideration will not prevail.

The question was then put, and the motion to reconsider was lost.

On motion of Mr. SHEPPARD, of Albany, it was voted, that when the Convention adjourn, it be to meet at ten o'clock, to-morrow.

Mr. BAGLEY, of Detroit: I move that the Committee of Arrangements, appointed by the Boston Board of Trade, be invited to take seats on the floor.

Carried.

Mr. ADAMS, of Wilmington, Del.: I move that the matter of internal taxation be referred to the Committee on Currency.

Mr. ROPES, of Boston: I hope that will not be done. It strikes me that the Committee on Currency have one of the most difficult and important questions to consider, and it is not worth while to saddle them with this question of taxation. I move to amend, that there be a Special Committee formed in the same way as other Committees, on the general subject of taxation.

Mr. FRALEY: In one of the calls for this Convention, there was just such a proposition as my friend from Delaware has referred to, and it formed a part of the text from which I spoke this morning. "Third. The relief of our manufacturing and other great producing interests, by reducing the burdens of taxation."

The PRESIDENT: That has a scope sufficient to embrace the gentleman's proposition.

Mr. ADAMS: Allow me to say, that is not the call upon which we are assembled here this morning.

The Secretary, by request of the Chair, read the official call.

Mr. FRALEY: I read from a late number of the *Commercial Bulletin:* "In the article published in our columes two or three weeks ago, there were two or three things omitted." Then follows the list of subjects, and the third is this — "The relief of our manufacturing and other great producing interests, by reducing the burdens of taxation." Now, that is a perfectly simple proposition, one that claims the attention of this body, and, in my judgment, one of the most important of all of them, and I hope that a Committee will be raised upon it, and that it will be considered as included in the call.

Mr. TAYLOR, of St. Paul: At the Detroit Commercial Convention, one of the most useful Committees of that body was the

Committee on Finance, and by common consent, that Committee was made competent to consider every question bearing upon taxation, as well as currency. It seems to me that if the Standing Committee we have designated as the Committee on Currency was designated as the Committee on Finance, it would be a very proper Committee for all questions bearing upon that subject.

Mr. CHAMBERLIN, of Cleveland: It appears to me that this matter may be very easily disposed of. Some gentlemen seem to be afraid of burdening this Committee on Currency by referring this question to them; but it appears to me that this proposition belongs properly to that Committee, and if they embrace the two subjects, they can appoint a Sub-Committee for each, and combine their reports, without any trouble at all.

Mr. TOBEY: I find in the call this sentence — "And such other subjects, not of a local or political character, as may properly come before the Convention." It is, therefore, for the Convention to determine what may properly come before it. The gentleman has made his motion that this subject of taxation be considered by the Convention. We have accepted that, and the question is, how shall we act upon it? I submit, that the Committee on such a broad national subject as that, should be selected in the same way as every other Committee has been selected.

Mr. STRANAHAN: It is quite evident that there will be many questions introduced here outside of the four or five propositions stated by the Board of Trade of this city. I would suggest, therefore, whether it would not be wise to appoint a Committee to whom all such questions should be referred. It will save a great deal of time. Let the Committee be appointed in the usual mode, and consist of a member from each body represented here upon this floor. If you have such a Committee, then all these questions may be referred to it, and it will facilitate the proceedings of the Convention, I make no doubt.

Mr. WETHERILL, of Philadelphia: I think this subject is of sufficient importance to have a Special Committee, and I do hope the gentleman from New York will not load the Committee down with any thing else. If you refer any other outside matter to the Committee, I do not believe they can consider it at all. Let us appoint a Special Committee for it, and for it alone, and then the motion of the gentleman from New York will be in order, that there be a Committee appointed to whom all other subjects may be referred. I do hope that this Conveution will give us a Special Committee on so important a subject.

Mr. HATCH, of Buffalo: I would like to ask the President of the Board of Trade of Boston, whose name is attached here, and who seems to be responsible for the classification of the subjects which are to be presented to the Convention, to explain what I would call the sort of a scoop-net which is attached to the call—"And such other subjects, not of a local or political character, as may properly come before the Convention." We should like to have some idea as to what is contemplated by this section, and I would ask the President of the Board of Trade for an explanation of it. We want to know something what it means. (Calls of "Question," "Question.")

The amendment proposed by Mr. ROPES, providing for the appointment of a Special Committee on the general subject of taxation, was accepted by Mr. ADAMS, and the motion, in that form, passed.

Mr. THURSTON, of Pittsburgh: I notice by the call, that the subject of "the restoration of the foreign commerce of the country from its present greatly depressed condition" is to be considered by this Convention. It seems to me, and to others, that there are other interests in this country than "foreign commerce," that are now in a depressed condition, and I would move that there be a Committee on the enhancement of the agricultural and the restoration of the manufacturing interests of the country.

Mr. SLOANE, of Sandusky: There will probably be other questions submitted for consideration than those already named, and if we appoint a Committee for every subject that may be presented for consideration, we may have a hundred different Committees. I would move, therefore, as an amendment, the appointment of a Committee to be called the Miscellaneous Committee, to whom may be referred such other incidental matters as may be referred to the Convention.

One other matter. It is proposed that the names of these Committees be reported at ten o'clock to-morrow morning. Now, many of the delegates desire to get through with the business of this Convention, if practicable, within a reasonable period of time—say two or three days. I apprehend that many of the gentlemen here understand the very great importance of the action contemplated, and the reports of the Committees will be arrived at only after a great deal of labor. If it is the object of this Convention to have any influence upon the legislation of this country, the action of the Committees should be well considered, and presented clearly for the consideration of the legislative bodies of the nation. It seems to me that the delegations should announce their Committees before we adjourn, and I think those Committees should meet to-morrow morning. We who do not live in your great cities are in the habit of going to work early in the morning, and we might meet at eight or nine o'clock, and be ready to report when the Convention meets.

Mr. THURSTON: It seems to me that the depressed condition of the manufactures of the country is as worthy of consideration as the depressed condition of our foreign commerce. The interests of agriculture, manufactures, and commerce are so intertwined, as has been ably and eloquently said by several gentlemen here, that whatever benefits or depresses one, benefits or depresses all. I hope that this Convention will not refuse to order a Committee on two such interests as the agricultural and the manufacturing. It is not a merely local question. It is a question that concerns the whole country, in every shape and form. I am sure that upon the agricultural and manufacturing interests depend in large measure the interests of our foreign commerce.

Mr. WARD, of Detroit: Before the question is put, I hope gentlemen will consider the very important subject now before the Convention. As the gentleman says, no subject has or probably will come up of so much importance to the national interests as the subjects of taxation and of manufactures. Upon these two subjects the prosperity of this country now and hereafter must depend; and, in my judgment, all other subjects that are here before the Convention are of minor importance to these. Taxation is weighing heavily upon all parts of the country, and especially on the West. Money is scarce there. The manufacturing interests of the country are certainly very much depressed, both at the East and the West. The Eastern manufacturers are suffering because the West has but little money, and cannot buy their goods and pay for them. The subject of taxation is one that affects the whole nation. In my judgment, the importations into this country are so large that we must lessen them, or suspend specie payments for all time to come. We send all our specie to Europe—for what? To buy the labor of Europe. We are talking about a return to specie payments. It is a mere myth. It is utterly impracticable. Our importations have been so large, that they have taken all our cotton and corn, and all our other exports, and twelve hundred millions of coin, and probably fifteen or sixteen hundred millions of state and national securities, to pay for the trade between this country and Europe. If this subject is not one of sufficient importance for this Convention to consider, I certainly do not know what is. We never can reach specie payments while all our gold goes to other countries to pay for commodities which we import; it cannot be done. We never can pay our national debt while our manufactures are prostrate; it is impossible. The industry of the country is the only means through which wealth can be procured, and it is the only means through which we can ever pay our national debt. The Western people are as honest as any in the world; but if you drive them to the wall, you may endanger your national debt and your national bonds. (Hisses.)

Mr. BRYSON, of St. Louis: I move that the motion for the appointment of a Miscellaneous Committee be laid upon the table, until this motion of the gentleman from Pittsburgh can be acted upon. I think the question is a very important one, and that it should have a special committee. Then let the gentleman come in and have an omnibus committee, if he wishes.

Mr. POTTER, of Philadelphia: I think it would be better to vote down the proposition with regard to an omnibus or miscellaneous committee, and also for a Committee on Manufactures. We have commenced preparations for doing business, and an arrangement has been made for the appointment of Committees covering all the subjects embraced in the call. Now, if there are any other subjects besides those, it is a very easy matter to bring them in by resolution, and have them referred to one of these Committees. There will be abundance of time on some of these Committees to consider other subjects than those specified under a particular head in the call. I think, therefore, the better course is to stop with what we have done to-day, and after we have had these Committees announced at the next meeting, then we can see whether there is a necessity for making any addition to these Committees or not.

The question was then put on the amendment of Mr. SLOANE, and it was lost. The original motion of Mr. THURSTON was carried.

Mr. WETHERILL offered the following resolution, which was, on his motion, referred to the Committee on Currency:

*Resolved*, That the Committee on Currency be requested to inquire into the propriety of memorializing Congress to abolish the Usury Laws.

Mr. LINCOLN, Chairman of the Committee of Arrangements on the part of the Boston Board of Trade, was then introduced, and said:

MR. PRESIDENT: — In behalf of my colleagues of the Committee of Arrangements, I would express our great obligations for the courtesy extended to us in inviting us to seats upon this floor.

The gentlemen who are here are very well aware, that for such a Convention it is necessary to make some arrangements, and the Board of Trade has appointed a Committee for that purpose. We shall endeavor not to interfere at all with the business of the Convention, but we have supposed that you would have some leisure hours in which there would be opportunity for free social intercourse between the citizens of Boston and the members of this Convention. Acting upon this supposition, we shall extend to you these courtesies, which we hope you will receive in the same spirit in which they are tendered. (Applause.)

The time is already so far spent that the arrangements for this afternoon may be somewhat interfered with, and I will not trouble the Convention with any further remarks. I will, however, go over a brief programme, that you may know what our plans are.

To-day, we propose, after the Convention adjourns, to take a sleigh ride in the suburbs of our city. It will occupy an hour and a half or two hours, and we shall be able to bring you back to your respective hotels in time for dinner.

We understand that quite a number of the gentlemen have brought their ladies with them, and we shall be very happy to give them an excursion also; it is proposed by the Committee that to-morrow the ladies shall have a sleigh ride. (Applause.)

This evening, there is to be a Concert at the Music Hall, to which all the members are entitled to tickets. Our friends will meet at this Concert — which is to be a sort of Promenade Concert — many of the ladies and gentlemen of the city, and they will have an opportunity of making acquaintances there.

To-morrow evening, the Convention will, it is hoped, accept the invitation of the City of Boston, to a banquet at the same Hall.

On Friday evening, the new Masonic Hall will be open for inspection by the members of the Convention; and at half-past eight o'clock, there will be a reception by the Board of Trade at the American House, where you will meet most of the business men of the city.

It has been suggested that some delegates, — we hope a great many, — will remain here on Saturday, and in anticipation of this, the gentlemen who are interested in the factories at Lawrence, have given an invitation to the members of this Convention to make an excursion to Lawrence, so that they may see the Pacific Mills, and some of those other large manufacturing establishments which have done so much for New England.

A telegraphic despatch was read from Mr. CHAPIN, President of the Boston and Albany Railroad, inviting the Western delegates to return by that road and its connections westward, free of charge.

The Convention then adjourned, to meet Thursday morning at ten o'clock.

## SECOND DAY.

THURSDAY, FEBRUARY 6, 1868.

---

The Convention met at half past ten o'clock, and was called to order by the President.

Prayer was offered by the Rev. CHANDLER ROBBINS, D.D., of Boston.

On motion of Mr. MORGAN, of St. Louis, the reading of the record of yesterday's proceedings was dispensed with.

Mr. VERMILYE, of New York, called for the reading of the list of delegates; it was read by the Secretary from Chicago, (Mr. BEATY,) and various corrections were made.

Mr. PORTER, of Louisville: I understand that Mr. E. M. BARNUM, of Oregon, representing the "Randall Steamer Construction Company of New York," is in the city, and desires to occupy a seat upon the floor. I move that he be admitted.

The motion was carried.

A communication from the Natural History Society was read, inviting the members of the Convention to visit the rooms of the Society at such time as might suit their convenience.

On motion of Mr. WETHERILL, of Philadelphia, the invitation was accepted, and the thanks of the Convention were tendered to the Society for the courtesy.

Mr. HILL, one of the Secretaries, presented a communication, which had been received from Mr. A. WATSON, of Washington, in relation to "storm signals," and suggested that it be referred to some Committee.

On motion of Mr. FIELD, of Detroit, the communication was referred to the Committee on Commerce.

Mr. GANO, of Cincinnati: I move the appointment of a Committee of one from each delegation as a Committee on Order of Business.

Mr. FIELD: A Committee was raised yesterday for that purpose, (the Committee on Rules and Regulations,) and if we raise a second Committee, it will occupy the time and attention of the Convention, and it occurs to me that it will be useless. I move, therefore, that instead of raising a second Committee, all new matter be referred to the same Committee, which consisted of one from each commercial body represented upon the floor.

Mr. GANO: I do not understand that Committee to have been appointed for that purpose.

The PRESIDENT: The Chair does not understand that there was any Committee appointed on Order of Business.

Mr. McLAREN, of Milwaukie: I would like to ask whether the Committee on Rules and Orders is still in existence, or whether it is considered as discharged?

The PRESIDENT: The Committee has been discharged.

Mr. McLAREN: Then I favor the motion.

Mr. FIELD: I will withdraw my motion.

Mr. PORTER, of Louisville: I move that the Committee on Rules be revived.

Mr. STRANAHAN, of New York: That Committee having performed its duty and been discharged, it is quite as well to make up a new Committee. I think that is the shortest way of disposing of the question altogether.

Mr. ALEXANDER, of St. Louis: There is an objection to reviving that Committee. The member of the Committee from the St. Louis delegation has been placed on another important Committee, on which we want him to act. Therefore, if you revive that Committee, you have no member from this delegation. Other delegations may be situated in the same way, and for that reason I should prefer having a new Committee.

The question was then put, and the motion of Mr. GANO was adopted.

Mr. WETHERILL presented the following resolutions, which, on his motion, were referred to the Committee on Agriculture and Manufactures:

WHEREAS, The true market for the farmer is the factory, and these two important interests are thus intimately connected, and the advance of the one is an advantage to the other; and

WHEREAS, It is an imperative duty to protect and encourage American manufactures by recommending such a just and equitable reädjustment of the laws as shall give to the skilled labor of this country a fair remunerative profit for the work performed; and

WHEREAS, It is unwise to place the American mechanic on a footing with the ill-paid and suffering laborer of the old world; therefore

*Resolved*, By this Convention, that the Committee on Manufactures and Agriculture be instructed to take into consideration the subject of a proper reädjustment of the laws regulating the tariff, and to prepare a memorial to Congress, setting forth its importance, and to present the same for the action of this Convention.

At this point, the proceedings were interrupted by the entrance into the hall of a Committee of both branches of the Massachusetts Legislature, which had been appointed to wait upon the Convention.

The Committee were invited to seats upon the platform, and after they had been introduced severally to the President, their Chairman, the Hon. WILLIAM SCHOULER, presented a communication, which was read by one of the Secretaries, (Mr. HILL,) as follows:

COMMONWEALTH OF MASSACHUSETTS.

STATE HOUSE, SENATE CHAMBER,
BOSTON, February 6, 1868.

*To the* Hon. E. W. FOX, *of St. Louis,*
*President of the Commercial Convention:*

SIR, — The undersigned have the honor to forward by a Committee of the two branches of the Legislature, to the President of the Commercial Convention, now in session in Boston, the following copy of an Order which passed unanimously both Houses, yesterday, February fifth.

ORDERED, That the President of the Senate and the Speaker of the House of Representatives be requested to invite the delegates now in Convention in Boston from the various Boards of Trade in the chief commercial cities of the Union, to visit the State House and be introduced to the members of the two branches; and that a Joint Committee be appointed to convey the invitation to the Commercial Convention, and to receive their answer; and Messrs. SCHOULER, CRANE, and TWEED are appointed on the part of the Senate.

Sent down for concurrence.

S. N. GIFFORD, *Clerk.*

HOUSE OF REPRESENTATIVES,
February 5, 1865.

Concurred; and Messrs. NASH, of Boston, JACKMAN, of Newburyport, TILTON, of Boston, HOUSE, of Bolton, SHERBURNE, of Charlestown, BROWN, of Marblehead, and HUGHES, of Somerville, are joined.

W. S. ROBINSON, *Clerk.*

In performing the pleasant duty assigned us, we would express not only our own feelings, but those of every member of the Legislature of Massachusetts, when we express the hope that the invitation may be accepted, and that the Senators and Representatives of this ancient Commonwealth may have the honor of receiving in the capitol of the State the distinguished representatives of the great commercial interests of the nation.

We have the honor to be, most respectfully,

Your obedient servants,

GEO. O. BRASTOW,
*President of the Senate.*

HARVEY JEWELL,
*Speaker House of Rep.*

Mr. WALBRIDGE, of New York: I move that the invitation be accepted, and that the President be authorized to return the thanks of the Convention for the same, and to speak on its behalf on the occasion of the visit.

The motion was adopted.

The PRESIDENT: The hour of two and a half o'clock, on Friday, has been arranged as the time for the Convention to call upon the Legislature.*

The PRESIDENT: The first business now in order is to hear the announcement of the Standing Committees.

Mr. McLAREN, of Milwaukie: I move that the reading of the list be dispensed with.

Mr. ALEXANDER, of St. Louis: It seems to me that the whole Convention should know the members of the several Committees. Each delegation knows its own members upon the Committees, but does not know the members from other delegations. I would like myself to hear who are upon the Committees from the other delegations. It seems to me that the best plan is to carry out the resolution passed yesterday, that the President announce the Committees this morning.

The motion of Mr. McLAREN was lost, and one of the Secretaries (Mr. SAGE) proceeded to read the lists of the Committees; but as the reports of several delegations had not been properly classified, the reading was suspended, and, on motion of Mr. NELSON, of Chicago, the Committees had leave to retire for the purpose of organization.

---

* The following is a copy of the official reply sent in acceptance of the invitation.

NATIONAL COMMERCIAL CONVENTION,

BOSTON, February 6, 1868.

*To the* Hon. GEORGE O. BRASTOW, *President of the Senate, and the* Hon. HARVEY JEWELL, *Speaker of the House of Representatives of the Commonwealth of Massachusetts:*

GENTLEMEN, — I have the honor to acknowledge in behalf of the Commercial Convention your communication of this date, received by a Joint Committee of both branches of the Legislature, in which you convey a copy of the Order passed yesterday by your honorable bodies, inviting the Convention to visit the State House, and to be introduced to the members.

I beg to say in reply, that the members of the Convention are deeply impressed with the courtesy which you have thus extended to them, and that they accept the invitation with great pleasure and cordiality.

I beg further to say, that as arranged with your Committee, the Convention will wait upon the Legislature, on Friday, the 7th inst., at half past two o'clock, P. M.

I have the honor to subscribe myself, Gentlemen,

Your obedient servant,

E. W. FOX, *President of the Convention.*

Mr. BRUNOT, of Pittsburgh, offered the following resolution, and moved its reference to the Committee on Manufactures:

*Resolved*, That in view of the probable reduction of the premium on gold, and the fact that a return to specie payment will be equivalent to a reduction of the duties on articles of foreign production to less than the standard required by revenue, it is expedient to adopt a sliding scale by which the duties on foreign productions shall be augmented *pari passu* with the decline of the gold premium.

The resolution was referred to the Committee on Manufactures.

Mr. BRYSON, of St. Louis, offered the following resolution:

*Resolved*, That all communications presented shall be referred to the appropriate Committees, without being read. (Cries of "No," "No.")

Mr. BRYSON: Allow me to make an explanation. I offer the resolution because I am fully aware that there will be a great many communications presented to this body, to be referred to the appropriate Committees. Many of them will be very lengthy; of that I am fully informed; and if we are to sit here and hear these read in full, we need no Committees at all. We shall be as fully prepared to act without the intervention of any Committee as with such intervention. I think it is customary and usual in all deliberative assemblies to have such communications referred by reading merely the title. I know it is customary in our Legislature and in Congress. I am afraid we shall squander our time by reading every communication that comes before us.

Mr. HATCH, of Buffalo: I think the gentleman is somewhat mistaken in his views of the facts. I think it is usual in public bodies to have the communications which are presented read, but the reading can be dispensed with if the body sees fit. We may desire to hear some particular communication read, and I think, therefore, it would be unwise in the Convention to adopt an arbitrary rule on the subject.

The question was then put, and the motion of Mr. BRYSON was lost.

Mr. BUZBY, of Philadelphia, offered the following resolution:

*Resolved*, That this Convention recommend to the Congress of the United States the adoption of a free banking law, under whose provisions the circulation of the several banks shall be based on the national securities, and the number of banks and amount of banking capital be regulated by the natural law of supply and demand, the details of the system to be similar to those controlling the administration of national banks, with such improvements as experience has shown to be necessary.

Mr. BUZBY moved a reference of the resolution to the Committee on Currency.

Mr. SLOANE, of Sandusky: It seems to me that the resolution is not in order. If I understand the call of this Convention, no questions of a political character are to be introduced. (Laughter.)

The PRESIDENT: The Chair decides that the resolution is in order.

The question was put, and the resolution was referred in accordance with the motion of Mr. BUZBY.

Mr. WARD, of Detroit, presented the following resolution:

*Resolved*, That the Congress of the United States be and hereby are requested to pass an act declaring that all contracts which are specifically made payable in gold or gold coin, by the parties thereto, shall be payable in gold, according to the tenor of the same.

The PRESIDENT: To what Committee does the gentleman desire the resolution referred?

Mr. WETHERILL: I hope that the resolution will not be sent to a Committee. I think we can act upon it without a reference.

Mr. WARD: I move that it be referred to the Committee on Currency.

This motion was adopted.

Mr. GANO: I move that the name of the Committee on Currency be changed to the Committee on Currency and Finance.

Carried.

On motion of Mr. LYONS, of Cleveland, the name of the Committee on the Measurement of Grain was changed to the Committee on Weights and Measures.

Mr. CANBY, of Philadelphia: I move that when the Convention adjourn, it be to meet at four o'clock this afternoon.

An amendment was offered to substitute ten o'clock to-morrow morning for four o'clock this afternoon.

Mr. WETHERILL: I have the honor to be upon the Committee on the establishment of a National Board of Trade, and we certainly can be ready to report upon that subject this afternoon.

The amendment was lost, and Mr. CANBY'S motion prevailed.

Mr. ATKINSON offered the following resolutions, and moved their reference to the Committee on Taxation, which motion was adopted:

*Resolved*, That no revision of the revenue system of the United States can be considered complete which does not involve an adjustment of the taxes which are imposed under the name of a tariff of duties upon imports, and that such adjustment should be made for the purpose of securing the largest revenue from such a tariff with the least injury to the productive power of the people.

*Resolved*, That in such adjustment of the tariff all private or special legislation should be avoided, and the only object aimed at should be the public good.

The Committee on the Order of Business was then announced, as follows:

### COMMITTEE ON THE ORDER OF BUSINESS.

| | | |
|---|---|---|
| Charles G. Nazro, | Board of Trade, | Boston. |
| William S. Preston, | Board of Trade, | Albany. |
| N. G. Hichborn, | Maine Shipbuilders' Asso'n, | Augusta. |
| William D. Sewall, | Board of Trade, | Bath. |
| Avery Plumer, | Corn Exchange, | Boston. |
| Elmore H. Walker, | Board of Trade, | Buffalo. |
| Ira Y. Munn, | Board of Trade, | Chicago. |
| A. T. Goshorn, | Chamber of Commerce, | Cincinnati. |
| Philo Chamberlin, | Board of Trade, | Cleveland. |

| | | |
|---|---|---|
| Moses W. Field, | Board of Trade, | Detroit. |
| George A. Owen, | Board of Trade, | Louisville. |
| W. P. McLaren, | Chamber of Commerce, | Milwaukie. |
| J. S. T. Stranahan, | Chamber of Commerce, | New York. |
| W. W. Wickes, | Produce Exchange, | New York. |
| D. W. C. Brown, | Board of Trade, | Ogdensburgh. |
| F. B. Lathrop, | Board of Trade, | Oswego. |
| E. A. Souder, | Board of Trade, | Philadelphia. |
| S. L. Ward. | Commercial Exchange, | Philadelphia. |
| George H. Thurston, | Board of Trade, | Pittsburgh. |
| T. C. Hersey, | Board of Trade, | Portland. |
| C. A. Ropes, | Board of Trade, | Salem. |
| Rush R. Sloane, | Board of Trade, | Sandusky. |
| Alfred DeWitt, | Chamber of Commerce, | San Francisco. |
| James P. Fiske, | Board of Trade, | St. Louis. |
| William Wallace, | Union Merchants' Exchange, | St. Louis. |
| James W. Taylor, | Board of Trade, | St. Paul. |
| E. W. Harris, | Board of Trade, | Toledo. |
| Charles Eddy, | Board of Trade, | Troy. |
| Francis Barry, | Board of Trade, | Wilmington. |

Mr. WARD, of Boston: Although a motion has been passed with regard to the adjournment, fixing the hour of meeting at four o'clock, this afternoon, I wish to make a suggestion in regard to that matter. Here are seven Committees, consisting of some thirty-five members each, thus taking about the whole of this Convention. Now, let us suppose that one-half of these Committees shall be ready to report at four o'clock, the other half will be engaged upon their work, and therefore, if we meet at four o'clock, we shall probably have not more than half our number. I am sorry that it is so, but the system which has been adopted of forming the Committees by the selection of one member from each delegation, absolutely necessitates either our meeting with but a small portion of our members, or an adjournment until all the Committees shall have substantially completed their labors. I suggest, therefore, whether it would not be better to adjourn over until to-morrow morning, at ten o'clock. I will move a reconsideration of the vote whereby the Convention voted to meet this afternoon, at four o'clock.

The motion was carried, and Mr. WARD then moved that the Convention, when it adjourn, adjourn until ten o'clock, to-morrow morning. The motion was adopted.

The Standing Committees were then announced, as follows: *

## COMMITTEE ON CURRENCY AND FINANCE.

| | | |
|---|---|---|
| Frederick Fraley, | Board of Trade, | Philadelphia. |
| Frank Chamberlain, | Board of Trade, | Albany. |
| N. G. Hichborn, | Maine Shipbuilders' Asso'n, | Augusta. |
| B. C. Bailey, | Board of Trade, | Bath. |
| William Endicott, Jr., | Board of Trade, | Boston. |
| Samuel G. Bowdlear, | Corn Exchange, | Boston. |
| E. P. Dorr, | Board of Trade, | Buffalo. |
| R. McChesney, | Board of Trade, | Chicago. |
| James Espy, | Chamber of Commerce, | Cincinnati. |
| A. Hughes, | Board of Trade, | Cleveland. |
| Moses W. Field, | Board of Trade, | Detroit. |
| H. Lowry, | Board of Trade, | Dubuque. |
| W. W. Alcott, | Board of Trade, | Kalamazoo. |
| John Tait, | Board of Trade, | Louisville. |
| P. D. Armour, | Chamber of Commerce, | Milwaukie. |
| John A. Stevens, Jr., | Chamber of Commerce, | New York. |
| William Blanchard, | Produce Exchange, | New York. |
| O. C. Lee, | Board of Trade, | Ogdensburgh. |
| George B. Sloan, | Board of Trade, | Oswego. |
| George L. Buzby, | Commercial Exchange, | Philadelphia. |
| George W. Cass, | Board of Trade, | Pittsburgh. |
| A. K. Shurtleff, | Board of Trade, | Portland. |
| Rush R. Sloane, | Board of Trade, | Sandusky. |
| Alfred DeWitt, | Chamber of Commerce, | San Francisco. |
| George Coray, | Board of Trade, | Scranton. |
| John R. Lionberger, | Board of Trade, | St. Louis. |
| M. L. Pottle, | Union Merchants' Exchange, | St. Louis. |
| Russell Blakely, | Board of Trade, | St. Paul. |
| George W. Davis, | Board of Trade, | Toledo. |
| Thomas Coleman, | Board of Trade, | Troy. |
| Edward Betts, | Board of Trade, | Wilmington. |

* The Chairmen of these Committees were chosen by the Committees respectively; their names are placed first in the text, for convenience of reference.

## COMMITTEE ON TAXATION.

| | | |
|---|---|---|
| Erastus B. Bigelow, | Board of Trade, | Boston. |
| William H. Taylor, | Board of Trade, | Albany. |
| B. C. Bailey, | Board of Trade, | Bath. |
| Edmund W. Clap, | Corn Exchange, | Boston. |
| Israel T. Hatch, | Board of Trade, | Buffalo. |
| Murray Nelson, | Board of Trade, | Chicago. |
| William Resor, | Chamber of Commerce, | Cincinnati. |
| J. H. Clark, | Board of Trade, | Cleveland. |
| E. B. Ward, | Board of Trade, | Detroit. |
| Julius Dorn, | Board of Trade, | Louisville. |
| John Bradford, | Chamber of Commerce, | Milwaukie. |
| Martin Bates, Jr., | Chamber of Commerce, | New York. |
| Isaac H. Reed, | Produce Exchange, | New York. |
| D. W. C. Brown, | Board of Trade, | Ogdensburgh. |
| F. B. Lathrop, | Board of Trade, | Oswego. |
| Henry Winsor, | Board of Trade, | Philadelphia. |
| H. S. Hannis, | Commercial Exchange, | Philadelphia. |
| D. McCandless, | Board of Trade, | Pittsburgh. |
| Woodbury S. Dana, | Board of Trade, | Portland. |
| Washington Ryan, | Maine Shipbuilders' Asso'n, | Portland. |
| Rush R. Sloane, | Board of Trade, | Sandusky. |
| Moses Ellis, | Chamber of Commerce, | San Francisco. |
| Martin Collins, | Board of Trade, | St. Louis. |
| Nathan Cole, | Union Merchants' Exchange, | St. Louis. |
| James W. Taylor, | Board of Trade, | St. Paul. |
| C. A. King, | Board of Trade, | Toledo. |
| Charles Eddy, | Board of Trade, | Troy. |
| John H. Adams, | Board of Trade, | Wilmington. |

## COMMITTEE ON INLAND COMMUNICATION AND TRANSPORTATION.

| | | |
|---|---|---|
| Edward D. Holton, | Chamber of Commerce, | Milwaukie. |
| James McMartin, | Board of Trade, | Albany. |
| B. C. Bailey, | Board of Trade, | Bath. |
| Solomon R. Spaulding, | Board of Trade, | Boston. |
| Harrison E. Maynard, | Corn Exchange, | Boston. |
| Elmore H. Walker, | Board of Trade, | Buffalo. |
| John C. Dore, | Board of Trade, | Chicago. |
| S. Lester Taylor, | Chamber of Commerce, | Cincinnati. |
| Philo Chamberlin, | Board of Trade, | Cleveland. |
| Edmund Trowbridge, | Board of Trade, | Detroit. |

| | | |
|---|---|---|
| W. W. Alcott, | Board of Trade, | Kalamazoo. |
| J. J. Porter, | Board of Trade, | Louisville. |
| L. J. N. Stark, | Chamber of Commerce, | New York. |
| Paul Worth, | Produce Exchange, | New York. |
| George A. Eddy, | Board of Trade, | Ogdensburgh. |
| D. G. Fort, | Board of Trade, | Oswego. |
| Samuel T. Canby, | Board of Trade, | Philadelphia. |
| Robert Ervein, | Commercial Exchange, | Philadelphia. |
| C. B. Herron, | Board of Trade, | Pittsburgh. |
| Samuel J. Anderson, | Board of Trade, | Portland. |
| Washington Ryan, | Maine Shipbuilders' Asso'n, | Portland. |
| W. P. Phillips, | Board of Trade, | Salem. |
| Rush R. Sloane, | Board of Trade, | Sandusky. |
| M. A. Bryson, | Board of Trade, | St. Louis. |
| George Pegram, | Union Merchants' Exchange, | St. Louis. |
| James W. Taylor, | Board of Trade, | St. Paul. |
| William T. Walker, | Board of Trade, | Toledo. |
| Perry E. Toles, | Board of Trade, | Troy. |
| E. T. Warner, Jr., | Board of Trade, | Wilmington. |

## COMMITTEE ON FOREIGN AND DOMESTIC COMMERCE.

| | | |
|---|---|---|
| Edward S. Tobey, | Board of Trade, | Boston. |
| James McMartin, | Board of Trade, | Albany. |
| N. G. Hichborn, | Maine Shipbuilders' Asso'n, | Augusta. |
| William D. Sewall, | Board of Trade, | Bath. |
| Avery Plumer, | Corn Exchange, | Boston. |
| Israel T. Hatch, | Board of Trade, | Buffalo. |
| B. F. Culver, | Board of Trade, | Chicago. |
| Robert Hosea, | Chamber of Commerce, | Cincinnati. |
| A. Hughes, | Board of Trade, | Cleveland. |
| George B. Dickinson, | Board of Trade, | Detroit. |
| John B. Green, | Board of Trade, | Louisville. |
| M. B. Medbery, | Chamber of Commerce, | Milwaukie. |
| S. D. Babcock, | Chamber of Commerce, | New York. |
| John H. Boynton, | Produce Exchange, | New York. |
| D. W. C. Brown, | Board of Trade, | Ogdensburgh. |
| D. G. Fort, | Board of Trade, | Oswego. |
| George N. Tatham, | Board of Trade, | Philadelphia. |
| Seneca E. Malone, | Commercial Exchange, | Philadelphia. |
| Felix R. Brunot, | Board of Trade, | Pittsburgh. |
| M. N. Rich, | Board of Trade, | Portland. |

| | | |
|---|---|---|
| John C. Osgood, | Board of Trade, | Salem. |
| N. W. Warne, | Board of Trade, | St. Louis. |
| W. W. Sanford, | Union Merchants' Exchange, | St. Louis. |
| Joseph A. Wheelock, | Board of Trade, | St. Paul. |
| John B. Carson, | Board of Trade, | Toledo. |
| James Forsyth, | Board of Trade, | Troy. |
| Francis Barry, | Board of Trade, | Wilmington. |

## COMMITTEE ON AGRICULTURE AND MANUFACTURES.

| | | |
|---|---|---|
| James I. Bennett, | Board of Trade, | Pittsburgh. |
| William H. Taylor, | Board of Trade, | Albany. |
| William D. Sewall, | Board of Trade, | Bath. |
| George L. Ward, | Board of Trade, | Boston. |
| Calvin M. Winch, | Corn Exchange, | Boston. |
| Elmore H. Walker, | Board of Trade, | Buffalo. |
| E. W. Blatchford, | Board of Trade, | Chicago. |
| Henry Pearce, | Chamber of Commerce, | Cincinnati. |
| R. T. Lyon, | Board of Trade, | Cleveland. |
| Thomas McGraw, | Board of Trade, | Detroit. |
| George A. Owen, | Board of Trade, | Louisville. |
| James S. Peck, | Chamber of Commerce, | Milwaukie. |
| J. S. T. Stranahan, | Chamber of Commerce, | New York. |
| A. H. Philips, | Produce Exchange, | New York. |
| W. L. Proctor, | Board of Trade, | Ogdensburgh. |
| A. H. Failing, | Board of Trade, | Oswego. |
| Thomas Potter, | Board of Trade, | Philadelphia. |
| Philip B. Mingle, | Commercial Exchange, | Philadelphia. |
| George W. Woodman, | Board of Trade, | Portland. |
| J. O. Safford, | Board of Trade, | Salem. |
| W. H. Pulsifer, | Board of Trade, | St. Louis. |
| A. W. Fagin, | Union Merchants' Exchange, | St. Louis. |
| Russell Blakely, | Board of Trade, | St. Paul. |
| R. Cummings, | Board of Trade, | Toledo. |
| Charles Eddy, | Board of Trade, | Troy. |
| Samuel Bancroft, Jr., | Board of Trade, | Wilmington. |

## COMMITTEE ON A NATIONAL CHAMBER OF COMMERCE.

| | | |
|---|---|---|
| Hiram Walbridge, | Chamber of Commerce, | New York. |
| William S. Preston, | Board of Trade, | Albany. |

| | | |
|---|---|---|
| William D. Sewall, | Board of Trade, | Bath. |
| T. J. Stewart, | Maine Shipbuilders' Asso'n, | Bangor. |
| Joseph S. Ropes, | Board of Trade, | Boston. |
| T. Albert Taylor, | Corn Exchange, | Boston. |
| P. S. Marsh, | Board of Trade, | Buffalo. |
| W. H. Low, | Board of Trade, | Chicago. |
| John A. Gano, | Chamber of Commerce, | Cincinnati. |
| J. H. Clark, | Board of Trade, | Cleveland. |
| George F. Bagley, | Board of Trade, | Detroit. |
| H. Lowry, | Produce Exchange, | Dubuque. |
| J. J. Porter, | Board of Trade, | Louisville. |
| W. P. McLaren, | Chamber of Commerce, | Milwaukie. |
| W. H. Harris, | Produce Exchange, | New York. |
| O. C. Lee, | Board of Trade, | Ogdensburgh. |
| A. H. Failing, | Board of Trade, | Oswego. |
| John P. Wetherill, | Board of Trade, | Philadelphia. |
| John H. Michener, | Commercial Exchange, | Philadelphia. |
| George H. Thurston, | Board of Trade, | Pittsburgh. |
| T. C. Hersey, | Board of Trade, | Portland. |
| W. J. Dill, | Board of Trade, | Sandusky. |
| J. H. Britton, | Board of Trade, | St. Louis. |
| H. C. Yaeger, | Union Merchants' Exchange, | St. Louis. |
| Joseph A. Wheelock, | Board of Trade, | St. Paul. |
| M. D. Carrington, | Board of Trade, | Toledo. |
| Thomas A. Tillinghast, | Board of Trade, | Troy. |
| George G. Lobdell, | Board of Trade, | Wilmington. |

## COMMITTEE ON WEIGHTS AND MEASURES.

| | | |
|---|---|---|
| C. J. Hoffman, | Commercial Exchange, | Philadelphia. |
| A. K. Shepard, | Board of Trade, | Albany. |
| T. J. Stewart, | Maine Shipbuilders' Asso'n, | Bangor. |
| Charles G. Nazro, | Board of Trade, | Boston. |
| Otis Munroe, | Corn Exchange, | Boston. |
| Jason Parker, | Board of Trade, | Buffalo. |
| T. P. Lawrence, | Board of Trade, | Chicago. |
| Thomas H. Foulds, | Chamber of Commerce, | Cincinnati. |
| R. T. Lyon, | Board of Trade, | Cleveland. |
| H. J. Buckley, | Board of Trade, | Detroit. |
| H. Lowry, | Produce Exchange, | Dubuque. |
| Julius Dorn, | Board of Trade, | Louisville. |
| C. Holland, | Chamber of Commerce, | Milwaukie. |

| | | |
|---|---|---|
| William H. Guion, | Chamber of Commerce, | New York. |
| J. Hobart Herrick, | Produce Exchange, | New York. |
| W. L. Proctor, | Board of Trade, | Ogdensburgh. |
| J. W. Pitkin, | Board of Trade, | Oswego. |
| George N. Allen, | Board of Trade, | Philadelphia. |
| George W. Hailman, | Board of Trade, | Pittsburgh. |
| Charles H. Haskell, | Board of Trade, | Portland. |
| C. A. Ropes, | Board of Trade, | Salem. |
| W. J. Dill, | Board of Trade, | Sandusky. |
| R. W. Crittenden, | Board of Trade, | St. Louis. |
| H. R. Whitmore, | Union Merchants' Exchange, | St. Louis. |
| Russell Blakely, | Board of Trade, | St. Paul. |
| Frederick Bissell, | Board of Trade, | Toledo. |
| Thomas A. Tillinghast, | Board of Trade, | Troy. |
| George G. Lobdell, | Board of Trade, | Wilmington. |

Mr. WALBRIDGE: I ask the unanimous consent of the Convention to print a speech which I have prepared, upon the subject of inland transportation.

No objection was made, and the Chair stated that leave was granted.

A gentleman of Detroit read a despatch from Mr. H. E. SARGENT, General Agent of the Michigan Central Railroad, tendering the Western members a free passage home over the several lines connecting with the Eastern roads at Suspension Bridge and Buffalo.

Mr. SLOANE, of Sandusky: Yesterday we adopted a rule limiting speakers to ten minutes, but we have just granted Mr. WALBRIDGE leave to print his speech; we do not know the subject of it, nor how extended it may be. It may be a most brilliant speech—I have no doubt it is—almost every thing is that emanates from the distinguished gentleman who has made the request; but I object to it at this stage of the proceedings, as conflicting with the rule which we have adopted, limiting speeches to ten minutes.

Several voices: The objection is too late.

Mr. SLOANE: The Convention has established a rule, that no member shall be permitted to discuss any subject before the Convention for its consideration, more than ten minutes. Now, here is a request made by the gentleman from New York, that he have leave to print a speech which otherwise he would deliver to this Convention.

As a member of this Convention, I am not willing to allow any remarks to be printed, until I know at least the subject to which those remarks relate. You have limited the time that gentlemen can occupy in addressing the house to ten minutes; the gentleman's speech may occupy an hour.

Mr. HATCH, of Buffalo: I rise to a point of order. I do not understand that there is any motion before the Convention.

Mr. WARD, of Boston: I move that the rule which limits speakers to ten minutes be repealed. (Cries of "No," "No.")

Mr. SLOANE: I move a reconsideration of the vote.

Mr. WETHERILL: It strikes me the gentleman is out of order. I do not know how he voted; but I know he objects.

The PRESIDENT: There was no formal vote. No objection was made, and the Chair stated that the request was granted by unanimous consent.

Mr. BARNUM, of Oregon: I move that every member of the Convention have the same privilege which has been granted to the gentleman from New York. I make the motion to enable the gentleman from Ohio to proceed, but I shall vote against it.

Mr. WETHERILL: I move to amend, by adding, "and assess the expense thereof upon each delegation."

Mr. SLOANE: There is something more in this question than the mere granting of the privilege to print a written speech.

Mr. HATCH, (interrupting:) I rise to a point of order. After the Convention has given unanimous consent to the gentleman to write out his speech, I think we cannot reconsider the motion.

Mr. BARNUM: I am satisfied that the gentleman will make a very able and eloquent address, but when I consider the results to which it will lead, I deprecate the granting of his request. I know the gentleman is an eloquent man, but this Convention has met for the purpose of transacting business. It passed a rule that debate be limited to ten minutes, in order that the time might not be occupied with spread-eagle speeches, but with short business speeches. (Applause.) I propose to cast no reflections upon the gentleman for his request, but there are other gentlemen in this Convention who, I have no doubt, could spread upon the printed record of the proceedings as able and eloquent speeches as the gentleman from New York. I hope that the resolution which I have made will be voted down; I made it for that purpose; and I hope that it may carry with it a withdrawal of the request of the gentleman from New York.

Mr. WALBRIDGE: The reason for making the request was, that at the Convention at Detroit, when we found ourselves pressed for time, that rule was adopted. The speech relates to the transportation of freight through the country, and embraces a great many facts and figures, with which I did not wish to bore the Convention. If I had proposed to make an eloquent speech, I should not have made the request, for I trust I can speak without committing my speech to paper. I have given a great deal of care and attention to the subject, and I thought the facts could be spread before the community in this way. That is the only reason for my making the request. I hope other gentlemen will have the same privilege, if they desire it.

Mr. McCHESNEY, of Chicago: I presume that Mr. WALBRIDGE can take the same course that Mr. WARD, of Detroit, has done, and publish his speech at his own expense. I object to any speech being printed without knowing what it is, and without an opportunity to have it answered.

Mr. STRANAHAN, of New York: Gentlemen do not seem to understand the facts of the case. The speech which Mr. WALBRIDGE proposed to make is upon the desk of the Secretaries, and it is as much beyond the power of this house to take it back, as it would be if he had made his speech without committing it to paper. You cannot recall it. One word more. If any gentleman has a speech prepared, and is ready to put it upon the table, I say, let him present it. And I say one thing further: it is a very cheap way of getting rid of long speeches and long speech-makers.

Mr. BARNUM: I will withdraw my motion, if some gentleman will make a motion to refer that speech to the appropriate Committee.

The PRESIDENT: If the object is to take the speech out of the business record of the Convention, it cannot be done by the motion of the gentleman from Ohio.

Mr. SLOANE: Then I will withdraw my motion, and second the motion of the gentleman from Oregon. If this privilege is to be conceded to the able gentleman from New York, I ask that every gentleman upon this floor may have the same privilege. There are other questions to be considered here of vital importance, as well as the question of inland transportation which the gentleman discusses.

Mr. BARNUM'S motion did not prevail.

## REMARKS OF THE HON. HIRAM WALBRIDGE,

### OF NEW YORK.

Mr. President, and Gentlemen of the Convention:

The subject of intercommunication by internal improvements, so as to bring the interests of all sections of the United States into closer and cheaper connection in trade and travel, has been justly presented to the American people as one of the most important matters that can occupy the consideration of a National Convention like this which is here assembled — composed of delegations representing the views and interests of Boards of Trade and Chambers of Commerce located in most of the prominent cities of the Union.

As the supply and value of nearly every article of necessity and luxury are affected by the means and cost of transportation, and as the productions of some sections, like the farming products of the great West, are largely excluded from the Atlantic markets, while various articles of the seaboard are similarly debarred from profitable distribution through the interior States, the interests of every section of society and of the country are directly connected with and essentially affected by this branch of our inquiries.

### RAILWAYS AND WATER-COURSES.

The natural and artificial water-ways on the main routes of trade — embracing the great lakes and rivers, and the canals connecting those waters with each other as well as with the Atlantic — certainly deserve and should receive ample and enduring consideration. They should be fostered always as matters of increasing national importance in all the connections of peace and war. Every practicable facility should be afforded for improving existing connections in our inland navigation, and also for making additional connections wherever required, as for instance at Niagara Falls, and between the Mississippi and Lake Michigan, for enabling vessels to traverse freely all practicable routes of water communication between the seaboard and the regions tributary to our great lakes and rivers.

But it is nowise derogatory to the importance of our internal navigation to say that the subject of improving the means and cheapening the cost of trade and travel over our railway system is worthy of at least equal consideration — especially when we consider that some of the proposed improvements in railway management may render the existing tracks vastly more efficient in promoting the rapid and steady interchange of commodities between different sections, and at the same time largely reducing the cost of transportation while essentially promoting the legimitate interests of railway stockholders.

Still more important must the railway question appear, when we reflect on the fact that railroads are fitted to meet the wants of broad regions that are either meagrely supplied with, or wholly deficient in, the navigable facilities of lakes, rivers and canals — like most of that largest division of the Union lying between the Mississippi and the Pacific Ocean.

When, in this connection, it is also considered that the railways already constructed extend nearly forty thousand miles, and that the wants of rapidly increasing settlements, especially between the Mississippi and the Pacific, will soon require double that amount of railway accommodation, it may readily be conceded that no one interest in the nation deserves more prompt, careful and persevering attention from all classes of the business community — from the farmer, the mechanic, the manufacturer — from the merchant, the miner, the trader — and also from faithful legislators and practical statesmen.

As the price of almost every article of trade and commerce is dependent on the cost of transportation, and as the railways must always furnish the greatest means of transit between the widest extent of country, — vast portions of which lie far beyond reach of canals, rivers or lakes, and far distant from seacoasts — the question of railroad improvement is therefore most eminently *national*, and thus falls within the powers constitutionally vested *exclusively* in the National Government for regulating trade and commerce between the American people in their various localities, as well as between them and foreign nations. Hence the great and peculiar importance of the movement now made to procure national legislation concerning the regulation of the railway system, which thus directly or indirectly concerns the welfare of every human being dwelling on American soil.

### PROPOSED NATIONAL RAILROAD SYSTEM.

The consideration of the railroad question is not merely optional with this Convention. It is measurably compulsory on us, as representatives of a large portion of the men engaged in the trade and commerce of the United States. The fact that public sentiment is now strongly turned upon questions of railway reform and improvement — that three national railroad bills have been brought before Congress by senators from different regions — that a National Railway Reform League has obtained auxiliaries all through the United

States — and that a large portion of the members of both branches of Congress and the governors of several States have publicly avowed their opinions on the subject — indicates the degree of importance attached to the subject of immediate and thorough reformation in the railway system. All these and many other considerations, it is repeated, render it not merely optional, but absolutely obligatory on this National Convention to meet the question promptly, to discuss it fully, and to express such opinions concerning it as the intrinsic greatness of the subject and the peculiar circumstances of the times imperatively demand.

The fact that the subject of "internal improvement" is justly set forth as the primary object for consideration in the published call for this Convention, is in itself sufficient to justify and require that our earliest attention shall be paid to this great question, which concerns the people and the public interests, as well as the interests of railroad companies, in every section of the United States.

On the ground of nationality and far-reaching consequences, the action upon railroad policy must and will form one of the strongest characteristics of the National Commercial Convention now assembled to consider the interests of the community generally in connection with the means and cost of intercommunication for freight and travel through all portions of our wide-spread States and Territories.

## NECESSITIES OF THE INTERIOR REGIONS.

The rapid extension of settlements through all portions of the new regions, especially through the country between the Mississippi and the Pacific, renders railroad reform peculiarly important at the present time. We have now reached a point where public experience connected with the railways may be most profitably employed, not only in reforming evils on the present lines, but also in guiding the construction and management of the new railways required to facilitate intercourse between the interior regions and the older settlements. The immense regions between the Mississippi and the Pacific, remarkable as are their features in other respects, are not less remarkable for the scantiness of navigable facilities compared with the country between the Mississippi and the Atlantic. The map of the United States is in nothing more remarkable than in this important feature; and the lesson it teaches is pregnant with admonition concerning the proper organization of the railroad system, so that the benefits of that system may produce the greatest good to the greatest number of the American people, now and through all time. For reasons connected with the geographical condition of the territory west of the Mississippi, therefore, as well as for the greater extent of that region as compared with the territory between the Mississippi and the Atlantic, the former has necessities for railway facilities even greater than the latter.

### COMMERCE OF EUROPE AND ASIA.

Superadded to these considerations are the circumstances in which our country is placed concerning the prospective trade and travel across this continent connected with the intercourse between Europe and Asia, which we all hope to see flowing ere long across the United States. Cheapness and regularity of transportation are indispensable for such a world-wide trade. In this view alone, the railroad question assumes immense importance. The railway organization required for this single purpose would form one of the noblest objects for commercial enterprise, for practical statesmanship, and for enlightened legislation. Attention cannot be too early or too earnestly directed towards this prominent feature in the world's commercial necessities.

The completion of a single-track railroad to the Pacific, for which we all look anxiously in the year 1870, — remarkable as that event will be in the history of these times, — will probably be equally remarkable for its effect in arousing public attention to the *insufficiency* of that enterprise, and to the necessity of greater exertions somewhat commensurate with the commercial necessities which that solitary single-track will signally fail of supplying.

### GREAT RAILWAYS ACROSS THE CONTINENT.

Even for the local accommodation of the rapidly increasing population in different sections of the regions between the Mississippi and the Pacific, three great double-track east-and-west railways would not be more than sufficient to meet the necessities of the Southern, Central and Northern portions of that vast expanse, as those necessities will exist in 1870 when the solitary single-track shall be completed on the Central route. And in constructing and organizing those several roads, the importance of providing ere long for four tracks on each route should be promptly considered — so that the ponderous matters of trade and commerce on each route could flow to and fro over one double-track, while the other double-track should be appropriated to passengers, mails and expresses, and such costly freight as could afford to pay high charges for rapid transit.

The single-track road now rushing towards completion in 1870 will indeed form a remarkable feature in the history of American progress; but it is nowise derogatory to its importance to say that, in view of the vastness of the field and the requirements of commerce and travel, that solitary single-track, from which so many people expect so much, is comparatively what a California statesman pronounced it to be, — "A mere pismire's track, compared with the extensive railway facilities required even now for trade and travel across this continent."

All the great double-track railroads of the Atlantic regions are very properly arranging to connect with that Central Pacific single-track, and multitudes of people are indulging in visions of the instantaneous effect on trade and commerce which is expected by them to follow its completion. But a moment's reflection may satisfy any one that that pioneer track will be utterly insufficient even for the satisfactory accommodation of the throng of passengers and fast-freight paying high prices to meet the most pressing *local* necessities along that single route. The high rates of freight upon its unfinished sections already indicate the absurdity of supposing that it can accommodate any considerable portion of the trade which we hope ultimately and ere long to see flowing across America between Europe and Asia. Some specimens of costly silks and teas, along with some precious metals and international mails, will be able to pay the high freight on this single-track; but the supposition that such an incomplete and insufficient roadway can have much effect beyond measurably accommodating local traffic and travel, seems to be one of the wildest visions of this practical age and country.

These remarks are made in no unfriendly spirit towards any of the pioneer Pacific Railway projects. *The very reverse is the case.* What is here said is influenced only by an earnest desire to aid in arousing attention to the great national necessity of promoting the rapid extension of double-tracks on each of the three great routes now in progress for crossing the continent — the Southern and Northern, as well as the Central routes — the Northern route claiming additional consideration from the fact of its connection with the westerly end of Lake Superior — a point of vast importance connected with our immense inland navigation, which there makes its nearest approach to the waters of the Pacific world. And it may be here added that the legislative and other arrangements for these great purposes should be such as would ultimately and ere long secure *four* tracks on each of those three routes; so that trade and commerce may flow freely to and fro over one double-track on each route, while the other track could be devoted to passengers, mails, expresses and fast freight that could pay largely for rapid transit.

In this one point alone — touching the communications between the Atlantic and Pacific — the national railroad question assumes a degree of importance worthy of the prompt and zealous consideration of the business men of the United States — justifying and requiring the fullest examination and the most energetic action of the people generally, as well as of the various Boards of Trade and Chambers of Commerce represented in this Convention. The necessities of the case — social, commercial and political necessities — forbid any delays in turning the public mind and the action of legislators and capitalists, toward expediting the facilities for intercommunication on several routes across our continent, as matters of the highest value to the interests of the American people and to the trade and commerce of the world.

### IMPROVEMENT IN RAILWAY MANAGEMENT.

Intimately connected with this specific application of railroad facilities across the newly-opening settlements between the Mississippi and the Pacific Ocean, is the policy of improving the management of the railway system which has its ramifications over nearly forty thousand miles between the Mississippi and the Atlantic Ocean. And the importance of improvement on this field of enterprise is increased by the consideration that all improvements made on the existing railroads will of course produce corresponding effects on the whole network of railroads that is now having its commencement between the Mississippi and the Pacific Ocean.

Investigations and statements lately made, and to which the public attention has been widely attracted by popular movements and by the introduction of the several bills in Congress for establishing a national railway system, present the proposed improvements in a light that deserves respectful attention on an occasion like this.

Among the multitude of intelligent citizens who approve the proposed reforms, there appear the names of a large portion of the members in both Houses of Congress; and we also find that several governors of States have given emphatic sanction, as the result of mature consideration. Governor PEIRPONT, of Virginia, has actually gone so far as to recommend these proposed improvements as being essentially important to the success of the newly-projected railway across the Virginias, between the Chesapeake Bay and the Ohio River — where he considers the cheapening of transportation vitally necessary to the projected acquisition of a large trade on that route between the interior States and the Atlantic seaboard.

The importance of the subject, and the respectability of the source, render it proper to quote some of the statements of Governor PEIRPONT, which present matters in a mode so concise and emphatic, as to command the attention of thoughtful men, and to require formal examination in a National Convention which has "Internal Improvements" placed first in the catalogue of subjects for its consideration.

### PROPOSED NATIONAL THOROUGHFARE BETWEEN EAST AND WEST.

Let delegates from all sections of the Union mark the several highly important points to which Governor PEIRPONT has emphatically invited the public attention. The argument in favor of an improved and nationalized railway system comes, at this time, with peculiar interest from the Executive of the State of Virginia.

Speaking of the proposed railway between the Chesapeake and the Ohio, Governor PEIRPONT says:

"This route" [through the States of Virginia and West Virginia] "ought to be a *national thoroughfare*,—created by the nation for accommodating the commerce of the great sections of the country. Ohio, Kentucky, Indiana, Western Tennessee, Arkansas, Missouri, Illinois, Wisconsin, Minnesota, Iowa, Kansas and Nebraska, have, in fact, as great an interest in this work as Virginia and West Virginia."

### OWNERSHIP OF PROPOSED NATIONAL RAILWAYS.

And now for a few words respecting the single point on which Governor PEIRPONT differs from some other distinguished men as well as from the National Cheap Freight League.

On that point, it is desirable to be distinctly understood; especially as the opinions of Governor PEIRPONT, however warmly appreciated in all other respects, are not sustained in reference to *governmental ownership*, either by the National League, or by the railway bills in Congress. That single point, however, is so very important, and gives rise to so much opposition, even among those who favor all the features which Governor PEIRPONT sustains in common with the National League and the Congressional bills, that justice to the latter requires that the matter shall be clearly understood; and hence the originators of the Cheap Freight organization promptly and emphatically expressed their dissent on this single point from the worthy Governor of Virginia, whose views on other matters are in cordial unison with their own, concerning the general reform and improved management of the railway system.

### LAKE, RIVER AND CANAL NAVIGATION.

It is proper that the precise objects of the League should be definitely stated, because a pamphlet has just appeared, from the pen of a well-known citizen of Oswego, concerning the "Commerce and Transportation of the great lakes and rivers of the northwest," in which the author erroneously asserts, at the commencement of his essay, that the National League is actually urging that railroads shall be "*owned and constructed* by the National Government."

Without underrating the value of the trade and commerce on the "great lakes and rivers of the northwest," it is not irrelevant here to notice the fact that the navigation of those waters is suspended by ice for about five months out of the twelve, during which enormous evils arise from the present deficient means and increased cost of transportation on the railways as now managed, and likewise from the opportunities which this state of things affords for systematic and gigantic operations of speculators, by collusion with railway managers and otherwise, for controlling the supplies of breadstuffs and other necessaries of life during the long season, when those lakes and rivers are embargoed by our northern winters,—while trade and commerce, and the interests of farmers, mechanics, manufacturers, and all others in the community, except the speculators aforesaid, strongly require that great avenues of intercommunication shall be open, and operative throughout every month of the whole year.

It so happens, too, that the great lakes and rivers are chiefly in the northerly regions most fettered by ice during that long portion of the year; while the railroads, even as they now exist, can be arranged, under the proposed Cheap Freight system, so as to furnish supplies to and fro during the wintry season, in a manner that will greatly promote trade and commerce, and largely relieve the people from the extortions to which they are now subjected, particularly during the long period wherein our great lakes, rivers, and canals are mostly obstructed by ice.

The Erie Canal, the most important of our commercial waterways, frozen about five months in the year, and moving its freight at the slow average of about one mile and a half per hour during its seven months navigation, has such limited freight capacity, that one double-track freight railroad, with trains at *equal speed* of ten miles per hour, (or more than six times the canal speed, and that through all the twelve months of the year,) could transport *fourfold* more freight during the year, than even that justly celebrated waterway.

### NATIONALITY OF THE RAILROAD SYSTEM.

In this connection, a few words and some relevant statistics may be properly submitted, concerning the extent to which railways are already constructed, or are being extended, through the United States — showing that the interests we are now considering are eminently *national* in their bearings, and impartially affect all sections and neighborhoods throughout our common country — freed from the interruptions which winter produces on the navigation on the great canals, rivers, and lakes of the northern and northwestern regions.

The Bureau of Statistics has just furnished a summary statement of the length and cost of the railroads completed and in progress throughout the United States, at the close of the year 1867:

| States, &c. | Miles. | | Cost of Roads and Equipment. |
|---|---|---|---|
| | Total. | Complete. | |
| Maine, - - - - | 638.29 | 512.57 | $18,039,779 |
| New Hampshire, - - | 667.36 | 687.36 | 22,230,337 |
| Vermont, - - - | 601.74 | 588.74 | 24,459,893 |
| Massachusetts, - - | 1,479.50 | 1,400.60 | 71,731,934 |
| Rhode Island, - - | 151.74 | 119.24 | 4,973,682 |
| Connecticut, - - - | 793.20 | 637.30 | 14,097,741 |
| New York, - - - | 3,830.34 | 4,182.59 | 169,508,176 |
| New Jersey, - - - | 984.77 | 911.29 | 64,550,741 |
| Pennsylvania, - - | 4,628.72 | 4,192.81 | 221,917,857 |
| Delaware, - - - | 177.40 | 160.40 | 5,417,484 |
| Maryland, - - - | 855.35 | 606.69 | 37,106,685 |
| West Virginia, - - | 586.75 | 364.75 | 22,972,154 |
| Virginia, - - - | 1,073.32 | 1,494.18 | 49,365,194 |
| North Carolina, - - | 1,367.54 | 1,000.42 | 20,089,040 |
| South Carolina, - - | 1,109.17 | 1,007.17 | 26,961,091 |
| Georgia, - - - | 1,750.60 | 1,547.90 | 34,352,624 |
| Florida, - - - | 606.60 | 439.60 | 9,416,000 |
| Alabama, - - - | 1,507.00 | 850.00 | 27,268,295 |
| Mississippi, - - - | 897.90 | 897.90 | 25,508,404 |
| Louisiana, - - - | 872.50 | 333.25 | 14,386,557 |
| Tennessee, - - - | 1,508.85 | 1,326.35 | 44,386,387 |
| Kentucky, - - - | 1,012.10 | 634.90 | 23,719,404 |
| Arkansas, - - - | 1,921.23 | 113.00 | 4,400,000 |
| Texas, - - - - | 2,590.75 | 495.25 | 15,200,000 |
| Ohio, - - - - | 4,726.46 | 3,397.84 | 147,540,950 |
| Indiana, - - - | 2,606.08 | 2,306.05 | 87,560,722 |
| Illinois, - - - | 3,607.49 | 3,224.49 | 149,000,657 |
| Michigan, - - - | 1,851.88 | 1,062.82 | 45,043,870 |
| Wisconsin, - - - | 1,467.70 | 1,036.50 | 40,960,182 |
| Minnesota, - - - | 1,646.00 | 419.50 | 11,250,000 |
| Iowa, - - - - | 2,146.00 | 1,109.00 | 49,191,450 |
| Nebraska, &c., - - | 988.70 | 555.00 | 25,000,000 |
| Missouri, - - - | 1,494.48 | 984.75 | 55,754,105 |
| Kansas, - - - | 835.00 | 484.00 | 22,500,000 |
| California, - - - | 1,093.50 | 382.50 | 27,090,000 |
| Nevada and Utah, - - | 545.30 | 30.00 | 2,000,000 |
| Oregon, - - - | 250.50 | 19.50 | 500,000 |
| Aggregate, - - - | 54,325.85 | 38,605.81 | $1,654,050,799 |
| Aggregate last year, - | 51,606.54 | 38,896.26 | 1,592,464,085 |
| Increase over 1866, - | 2,719.31 | 1,709.55 | $61,586,714 |

### NEW YORK CENTRAL AND ERIE RAILWAYS.

With the views already expressed, let us particularly examine some few facts now suggested for the improvement of our railway system, and glance at what are considered some of the leading defects in the present management of even our most prominent railroads.

Without dwelling on evils that have too largely affected and too frequently disgraced such a vast range of railway enterprises, beset, as they were, with many difficulties usually connected with the various interests involved in new projects of such diversified character as now compose the American Railroad system, let us seek some prominent practical exemplifications of errors which now most seriously affect the management of the iron thoroughfares, with the purpose of seeing how those errors may be abated or remedied, and the efficiency of the railroad system vastly increased, for the mutual benefit of the people and the railroad corporations.

### EFFECTS OF BAD MANAGEMENT.

Take, for example, the operations of the two great railways through the State of New York, connecting the Atlantic waters with the northwestern lakes and rivers. The Erie Railway and the New York Central, from their position and magnitude, may be considered fair samples of railroad management in the United States; and how have these great corporations improved or neglected the cultivation of their great advantages?

Examination of the sworn returns from those two railroads, embodied in the documents of the New York legislature, has enabled the National Cheap Freight League to present those great thoroughfares as "prominent exemplars of errors alike injurious to their stockholders and the public." The defects thus referred to are of specific and practical character, which it is in the power of either or both companies to remedy. The errors thus particularized, and which are independent of any other defects in those corporations, are briefly specified as consisting, in their present mode, of "freight and passenger transportation, with *mixed trains of varying speed.*"

Never before were the affairs of any railroad companies analyzed in a clearer manner, than has been done by the author of that paper in the publications of the National League. His statements, thus founded on the official returns from the above-named companies, carry with them a degree of authority that may well challenge and defy criticism. His is the logic of facts, sustained by the logic of "figures that cannot lie" in this case, unless we suppose that the officers of both companies have deliberately falsified their own sworn returns to the New York Legislature.

### NO ANTAGONISM TO EXISTING RAILWAYS.

Let it not be overlooked, for it is an important feature of the proposed Railway Reform, that the parties who are most zealous in sustaining the policy proposed by the several national railroad bills now pending in Congress, are emphatic in declaring that they would gladly see such improved arrangements made by existing railroads as will render congressional intervention less important, if not wholly needless, in regions where railroads already exist; though a *general National Railway Law* would still be desirable, to authorize railroad companies to extend their routes wherever they find the public wants require such extensions, substantially in the same way that the National Government lately passed *a General Telegraph Law*, allowing telegraphers to spread their lightning lines, wherever required, *throughout the United States.*

It is for the managers of existing roads on the great thoroughfares, to show by their course that they will take immediate measures for adopting some such improvements, to *facilitate the transit*, while *lessening the cost* of freight. Hence, as before stated, there is "no necessary antagonism between the friends of reform and the present railway managers." If the energies of those managers shall continue to be directed, as they are too frequently directed, to speculations in stocks and other sharp practices, instead of reforming the errors and adopting the improvements which experience has demonstrated, the necessity for new lines will be generally recognized by the public. As a specimen of the prevailing opinions on these matters, we may quote a brief passage from a report submitted to the New York State Constitutional Convention, now in session, by one of its most valued members,—the Hon. FREEMAN CLARKE,—a well-known banker, who was formerly in Congress, and more recently the Controller of the national currency. That distinguished gentleman,—than whom few can be better fitted to express correct opinions on such subjects,—warmly approves of the cheap freight policy proposed by the National League, and embodied in the bills before Congress; and, in a report on the financial condition of the State, he refers to the internal improvements, for the purpose of saying that the public necessities demand just such cheap freight railroads as are now proposed; adding that, if existing railroad companies will not promptly comply with the popular requirements for better and cheaper freight arrangements, "there is *capital enough ready* to establish a new railway line on the cheap-freight system between New York and Lake Erie — to be continued ultimately to the Pacific Ocean."

### HOW AN IMPROVED RAILWAY POLICY MAY BE INTRODUCED.

There is less difficulty than many people may suppose in preparing some of our great railways for adopting some of the principal features of the proposed improvements. The Erie Railway and New York Central, for instance, could, in a short time and with moderate expense, provide themselves with an additional double-track on the portions of their respective routes where they have now only one double-track. On the New York Central, a double-track between Albany and Syracuse is all that would be needed to secure this great result — as the Company owns *two* double-tracks between Syracuse and Buffalo. The Erie Railway requires an additional double-track *only* between New York and Corning — owning or controlling two or more double-tracks between the latter place and the lakes. Here, then, is a comparatively easy way to introduce the proposed reform. The "mixed" way of running freight and passenger trains, with *various speed* on the same tracks, is most pernicious to the companies owning both roads, as well as to the public. The course of each road is suicidal. The struggle for passengers causes both roads to make the freight trade secondary to the travelling — although it is from freight that both roads derive the profit which enables the Central to work almost for nothing in conveying passengers, while the Erie Railway *actually loses money largely* on its passenger traffic — as shown by an analysis of the sworn returns from both companies. "The freight business of the Erie and Central, which produced a net revenue last year of $5,132,289, must necessarily continue cramped, and remain but partially developed, so long as the running of freight trains is regarded by railway managers as of secondary importance to the passenger trains." "Just think of twenty-five thousand (25,000) freight trains being switched on to side-tracks of these two roads during the year, to allow passenger trains to dash a-head!" says Mr. F. H. STOWE, an eminent statistician. And what was the pecuniary result? Why, only a profit of eighty-seven thousand dollars ($87,000) to the Central, on all its large passenger business, while the Erie Railway staggers under the suicidal infliction of an *actual loss* of one hundred and twenty-one thousand dollars ($121,000) upon the passenger business, for which it madly neglected the freight trade — on which latter it has to rely for all its profits, and for enough to pay its actual losses on its passenger traffic! Such folly and madness would be wholly incredible, were it not actually proved by the sworn returns of the managers of both roads. But a dawn of hope is furnished by the recent elections in both companies—and to the newly-chosen managers, the public at large, as well as their own stockholders, must and will look for a system of management less injurious to the companies themselves and less pernicious to the people at large.

### POLICY OF THE CONGRESSIONAL RAILWAY BILLS.

In considering proposed arrangements for improving the railway system, it is proper to inquire whether we should or should not act in conformity with the principles embodied in the several Congressional bills, which are the pioneer measures in a proposed national system of intercommunication. If the movements for railway reform, which have caused the introduction of those bills, should progress in popular favor in the future as in the past, any arrangement that ignored the principles of those bills would probably prove unsatisfactory and short-lived. That the management of the railway system is to be brought under a combination of improvements, whereby its power may be largely increased and its cost greatly lessened, is quite certain. That freight tariffs, under proper organization and economy, may be reduced more than fifty per cent., is now the settled conviction of many of the best business men who have investigated the subject in all its bearings. The people are becoming more and more satisfied that the odious feature of monopoly in the carrying of freight and passengers is injurious to the Commonwealth, and oppressive to all the producing interests.

It is therefore a public necessity, whether or not it be the choice of railway managers, that an almost complete revolution shall be effected in the management of a system so intimately connected with the interests of the people in every branch of society and in every section of the land.

### SUBSTANCE OF THE CONGRESSIONAL BILLS.

And now let us turn to the Congressional bills on the railway question, that their precise nature may be fully understood. These bills are all founded on the proposed "cheap-freight anti-monopoly plan."

One of them, introduced by Senator HENDERSON, of Missouri, is for a route connecting with the Pacific road in Kansas, and thence running through Arkansas and Texas, to the Gulf of Mexico.

Another enterprise, for which Senator NYE, of Nevada, introduced a bill, is designed for a coal thoroughfare from the Pennsylvania mines to the eastern shore of New Jersey, on the navigable waters of the harbor of New York.

A third bill, submitted by Senator HARLAN, of Iowa, proposes encouragement for a freight thoroughfare from the Mississippi to the Atlantic, with termini at New York, Boston, Philadelphia and Baltimore; with ultimate design to extend the same from the Mississippi to the Pacific.

Other bills of similar character are said to be in preparation by Congressmen from different sections; but the three above-named are the only ones actually before Congress.

These bills are all substantially identical in reference to principles, plan of construction, and management — as likewise to the proposed financial arrangements and proprietorship. So that a quotation from one of them — say the HARLAN bill, with which the others will be made to conform, if they are not already in strict conformity, will enable all readers to judge of the characteristics of the whole.

The two preliminary sections in each bill are occupied with designating the location and the corporators; about two hundred persons, residing in all parts of the Union, being named now in the three bills, with more to be added, so as to have all interests and all sections represented in the proposed corporations. Then follows:

"SECTION III. *Be it further enacted,* That the principle and plan upon which said railway and branches shall be constructed and managed, shall be as follows, viz.:

"*First.* The railway shall be a double track, well graded, ballasted, and substantially laid with rails adapted to heavy freights, together with all necessary bridges, culverts, turn-outs, depots, etc., and in width of gauge shall correspond with the most numerous class of roads to be accommodated in transporting over the same.

"*Second.* Said railway and branches shall be open to free competition for all persons, companies, or other corporations, who may desire to put passenger, mail, or freight trains thereon, or to engage in transporting on or over said railway and branches; such persons, companies, or corporations to pay such reasonable tolls as may be prescribed by the company hereby incorporated, or by Congress, for the privilege of transporting over said railway.

"*Third.* For the purpose of giving to said railway its greatest carrying capacity, as well as to avoid difficulties in management and liability to accident, there shall be adopted a moderate and uniform rate of speed for all trains of whatsoever description passing over said railway; such rate of speed to be prescribed with reference to economy in fuel and the preservation of the railway and rolling stock; and said company hereby incorporated shall have full power to make all necessary rules and regulations as to the quality of rolling stock to be placed or admitted on said railway, and the management of the same, and to compel compliance with said rules and regulations, and in case of non-compliance to exclude any person, company, or corporation, so refusing to comply, from transporting over said railway. * * * * *

"SECTION VI. *Be it further enacted,* That the United States, and the respective States and incorporated cities, when duly authorized by the laws of the State wherein situated, shall be privileged to take stock in said railway and branches, to the extent, in the aggregate, of three-fourths of the entire stock, by paying into the treasury of said company in gold or its equivalent, *the same as other stockholders;* and when said United States, or any State or incorporated city shall have become stockholders as aforesaid, they shall have a voice in the election of directors and officers corresponding to the ratio which their respective shares shall bear to the whole of the shares of said company: *And it is further provided,* That said company is, and shall be authorized to receive, take, hold and convey any donations in land or other property which may be made by the United States, or by any State, company, corporation, or individual, for the purpose of assisting to carry out the enterprise authorized by this act."

### IMPORTANT PRINCIPLES INVOLVED.

The principles contained in the Congressional bills, and in the memorials on which they are founded, aside from the proposed management of the railway trains, are no less important than the increased freight capacity and cheapening of freights. The foundation of this proposed national railway system is made to rest on solid principles of legislative rectitude and commercial integrity. If this new system is carried out into practice, it will revolutionize the whole machinery of corrupt legislation and profligate railway management. Its effect will be to destroy the plans and practices whereby false capitalization, and dividends on fictitious stock, have too frequently and too largely plundered the stockholders, oppressed the people, and disgraced the railway system. The provisions of the Congressional bills, concerning the financial operations in railroading, indicate the integrity which characterizes this railway reform movement, and are worthy of the warmest popular approbation.

And in this connection it is proper to quote the sentiments of a leading organ of the existing railroad interests, in which that journal advocates the real interests of honest stockholders as contra-distinguished from the corrupt profits of scheming railway managers. The *American Railroad Journal,* after warmly commending the proposed mode of running trains so as to expedite and cheapen freight transit on the roads, says:

"There is another provision in the bills before Congress which requires that the roads shall be *capitalized on cash* and *built for cash,* and no share of stock to be issued unless there be paid into the treasury of the company one hundred dollars in gold, or its equivalent, therefor; and *no bonds or mortgages* on the road, or franchise, *to be allowed. This cuts off all chances for watered stock, or dividends on fiction.* The public will not be very likely to object to this, while the strikers and jobbers about Congress, if any, will have a poor show for fictitious shares to be divided out for services in passing the bills. The example in the British Parliament will hardly be followed, wherein it was alleged, a few years since, that four hundred and eighty thousand pounds (nearly two and a half millions of dollars) were absorbed in parliamentary expenses, in nine years, on a single railway. There are other provisions of a novel character, betokening much forethought in guarding the bills, in order to avoid imposition on the public."

### FINANCIAL CHARACTER OF THE NATIONAL RAILWAY REFORM.

In this connection, it is due to the high importance of the subject, and also to the friends of reform who are sustaining the Congressional railway bills, that the emphatic declarations of the National League shall be quoted in reference to the financial character of the movement:

"And here let it be distinctly understood," says an Address from that League, "that this anti-monopoly cheap-freight railway movement relies for success only on its intrinsic merits, on the intelligence of the people, and on the integrity of the legislators. It will nowise provide means for hiring 'the lobby,' or buying (if it were possible to buy) congressional or legislative votes. No person whatever — not even the corporators named in the Congressional bills — have, or can have, any greater interest in the new railways than a share of the common benefits which the system may confer on the people generally. There are no bonuses or bribes — no fat contracts for favorites — no ficticious stock for speculators. By a rigid financial policy, combined with provisions for securing equal rights to all forwarders who will pay tolls on the roads, and by showing how railways can be made to transport *vastly more freight at far less cost,* this new railway system seeks to secure popular favor and legislative authority for its establishment and support. Like the original project of the great Erie Canal, this cheap-freight railway system must succeed by the strength of its own merits among the people, whose interests it will largely promote."

### DUTIES OF THE CONVENTION IN REFERENCE TO RAILWAY REFORM.

Justice to the multitude of citizens, in all sections of the Union, who are united in the movement for railroad reform, so as to promote better management of the railroad system in ways that may provide increased means of interchanging commodities, as well as travelling at less cost than at present — justice to the great number of prominent men, including a large portion of the members of both branches of Congress, who have endorsed the cheap-freight policy as "the most effective agency that can be adopted to secure the prosperity of the people" in all parts of the land — justice to the various Boards of Trade and Chambers of Commerce which have sent their delegates from all parts of the nation to examine and discuss the best means proposed for promoting intercommunication by the different means of internal improvement — justice towards one of the greatest questions of national policy ever presented in any country — requires that this National Convention shall fully consider, with the view of expressing definite opinions upon, the important matters involved in the Congressional bills so eminently national in their connection with the public welfare in every section and neighborhood throughout our wide-spread Union.

Hence the extent and explicitness with which I have endeavored to ascertain and present the leading features of the improvements proposed by the National Cheap-Freight League and by the pending Congressional railway bills. Whatever we may individually think about some of the features or about the general scope of the policy proposed in those bills, every consideration of propriety seems to require that this Convention shall devote to such matters a full share of the time and attention which we are expected to bestow on the important topics included in the call which has brought us together— first and foremost in that call being the subject of "internal improvements" in their connection with the welfare of all portions of the community and with the vital interests of the commercial section of that community which we as delegates have been sent here to represent.

With a view, therefore, of causing proper action on the various important topics to which attention is invited, I submit the following resolutions in accordance with the leading considerations which have influenced the expressions of opinion embodied in the foregoing remarks; and I now move that the same lie upon the table, to be first in order for the action of the next National Commercial Convention.

## RESOLUTIONS ON THE SUBJECT OF INTERNAL IMPROVEMENTS.

1. *Be it Resolved*, That this Convention fully recognizes the universality and justice of the popular demands from all parts of the Union for such amendments and extensions of internal improvements, by land and water, as will suitably accommodate the great and rapidly increasing public wants for better and cheaper means of intercommunication, as a vital necessity among all portions of the American people — such improvement and cheapening of facilities for intercommunication ranking next in importance only to the great subject of national reconstruction.

2. *Resolved, therefore,* That this Convention earnestly recommends the most liberal policy from the National Government towards all companies that are laboring to improve our vast internal water-communications, so as to increase, to the greatest practicable degree, the advantage of connections between the whole range of the great lakes, rivers and canals, in such way as to render our inland navigation most serviceable to the people through all the vast regions connected with our inland navigation.

3. *Resolved, also,* That immediate measures should be taken by existing railroad companies, especially on the great routes of trade and travel between the Northern lakes and the Southern Gulf coast, and between the Atlantic and Pacific Oceans, to organize their respective railways — so that, as soon as possible, two double-tracks shall be provided on each of the leading routes between those important points — so as to remedy the evils and losses resulting from the present practice of transporting freight and passengers in trains of *different speed* over the same tracks.

4. *Resolved, further,* That this Convention, in view of existing evils and deficiencies, earnestly recommends that the existing railroads on the aforesaid great routes of trade and travel, shall meet the popular requirements for safety, cheapness and increased freighting facilities, by so combining their operations that some one or more of those double-tracks shall be devoted wholly to transportation of general freight, in trains running with *equal speed,* at such velocity (say ten miles per hour) as may secure the greatest amount of freight transportation, with greater speed and regularity, and at lower prices, than at present — including with their freight-trains, on the cheap-freight railways, such passenger cars as may accommodate the multitudes who would prefer moderate speed with increased safety, at far lower cost — freed from dangers of collision and other accidents always largely existing on tracks where mixed trains of freight and passengers are run with varying speed.

5. *Resolved, also,* That this Convention recognizes the propriety of immediately devoting some of the above-mentioned railroads to the exclusive transit of passengers, mails, expresses, and such costly freight as can afford to pay high prices for the most expeditious transportation; so that life and property shall be no longer sacrificed by the collisions and other difficulties resulting from the pernicious mode of running mixed trains of freight and passengers with *different velocities* on the *same track.*

6. *Resolved, further,* That, in the opinion of this Convention, such arrangements for separating travel and traffic would result in trans-

porting vastly greater amounts of freight and passengers with greater safety, regularity and cheapness than by the present mode of railway management; especially as it is demonstrable that one double-track road, with *trains running at equal speed* of ten miles per hour, could transport three or four times more freight during a year than the great Erie Canal, and eight or ten times as much freight as either the Erie Railway or New York Central now transports through their "mixed" arrangements for travel and traffic between the East and West.

7. *Resolved,* That, inasmuch as the facts deduced from official sworn returns of such railroads as the Erie Railway and New York Central, prove that "mixed traffic" of freight and passenger trains at *various velocities* over each track, vastly impairs the freighting facilities, while at the same time leaving no adequate profit to those companies on their *passenger* traffic, it be respectfully recommended that each of the above-named companies shall consider the propriety of making a new double-track on the Central route between Albany and Syracuse, and on the Erie route between New York and Elmira, westward of which places the respective companies have several tracks on different routes connecting with the great lakes and the Western railroads, which comparatively small additions to their present tracks would enable each of those companies to devote a double-track on each route to freight and passengers, running at moderate regular speed and low prices, while the other double-track on each route would be devoted to travellers, mails, expresses, and costly freight, that can afford to pay high prices for rapid transit.

8. *Resolved,* That, in contemplation of the world-wide trade expected to flow across our continent between Europe and Asia, as well as in reference to the domestic trade and intercourse between the rapidly increasing population of Western America and the residents of other portions of our National Union; and as the single track Central Railroad now rushing toward completion in the year 1870, (however valuable as a pioneer measure,) will be utterly inadequate for the necessities of advancing civilization in this age and country; it is the opinion of this Convention, that the highest social, commercial and national considerations imperatively demand that the strongest immediate efforts of government and capitalists shall be directed toward the speedy completion of double-track railways on each of the three leading routes across the United States,—with ultimate provision for a second double-track on each route, so that *cheap freight and travel, at moderate equal speed,* may occupy one double-track, while the other double-track can be devoted to

*fast travel, mails, expresses and costly freight,* paying "fast" prices; one of which great railways being additionally required by the interests of our immense inland navigation, from the fact of its connection with the upper end of Lake Superior,—the most westerly point where lake navigation approaches the Pacific Ocean.

Laid on the table.

On motion of Mr. FRALEY, the Convention adjourned, to meet on Friday, the 7th inst., at ten o'clock, A. M.

## THIRD DAY.

FRIDAY, FEBRUARY 7, 1868.

---

The Convention met at a quarter past ten o'clock, in the forenoon, the President in the chair.

Prayer was offered by the Rev. WILLIAM R. NICHOLSON, D.D., of Boston.

By vote, the reading of the Journal of yesterday was dispensed with.

On motion of Mr. FRALEY, leave to retire was granted to the Committee on Commerce.

Mr. HATCH, of Buffalo, offered the following resolution, which, on his motion, was laid on the table, informally:

*Resolved*, That inasmuch as the commerce upon the canals of the State of New York is national, and the people of all the States are interested in cheap transportation — the food consuming States of the Atlantic and the food producing States of the West — this National Commercial Convention do recommend Congress, after the usual survey and report of the Government engineers before expenditure of public money, to appropriate sufficient money to improve these transit lines of inland commerce to their utmost capacity for the transportation of Western products in the cheapest and shortest time to our seaboard cities. Provided: that the people of the State of New York shall, through the Legislature, enact in their laws or adopt in their Constitution a section, that, after the payment of all debts contracted for the construction or maintenance of their canals, thereafter they will levy no more or greater tolls upon property transported upon their canals than shall be necessary for their repairs and further improvement.

Mr. NAZRO, of Boston, from the Committee on Order of Business, submitted a report, recommending that the several questions to be considered be called up in the following order:

1. National Chamber of Commerce.
2. Weights and Measures.
3. Transportation.
4. Foreign Commerce.
5. Taxation.
6. Agricultural and Manufacturing Interests.
7. Currency and Finance.
8. Miscellaneous.

The report was adopted.

Mr. HILL read a communication from Mr. OTIS KIMBALL, General Agent of the Southern Michigan Railroad Line, tendering to the Western delegates a free passage over that road and the Lake Shore road.

On motion of Mr. WETHERILL, the invitation was accepted, and the thanks of the Convention were ordered to be returned to Mr. KIMBALL for his civility.

Mr. HILL also read a communication inviting the members of the Convention to inspect an improved freight car at the Lowell Railroad station, which was referred to the Committee on Transportation.

Mr. WALBRIDGE presented the following report from the Committee on

## A NATIONAL CHAMBER OF COMMERCE.

Your Committee, to whom has been referred the consideration of a plan for the organization of a National Chamber of Commerce, beg to present a paper on the general subject, prepared by Mr. HILL, of Boston, as introductory to the recommendations which they desire to make to the Convention.

## MR. HILL'S PAPER.

The Detroit Convention of 1865, just before its final adjournment, passed two resolutions, upon the recommendation of a special committee, the one of which urged the importance of the immediate organization of a new department of the General Government, to be known as the Board of Trade, and to have the oversight and care of all questions relating to our agricultural, manufacturing and commercial interests; and the other, requested the Boston Board of Trade to mature a plan for a National Chamber of Commerce, to have no organic connection with the Government, but to concentrate and give expression to the views of the merchants of the country upon all questions relating to trade and finance.

The division of the manifold duties devolving upon the Secretary of the Treasury, which it was hoped in 1865 would soon be made, has not yet been acted upon at Washington, and that official is still charged with the care of the commercial interests of the country in all their variety and diversity, in addition to the vast responsibility which attaches to the management of the public finances and the collection of the national revenues. It is hoped that the Commercial Convention of 1868 will again bring this subject to the attention of Congress, and that it will authorize a memorial in its behalf, asking for the immediate establishment of a Department of Trade, for reasons which were set forth at length in a report submitted to the Detroit Convention.

But whether such a department be established, or otherwise, the time would seem to have fully come for the formation of a National Chamber, composed of the business men of the nation, whereby they may be enabled to take counsel and to act together for the promotion of the great material interests which belong to them in common. Within a few months past, attention has been given by some of the members of the Boston Board of Trade to the proceedings of an association in Great Britain, which will illustrate perhaps what the merchants of the United States may imitate with advantage to themselves. Notwithstanding the existence of a Board of Trade as a branch of the English Government, the efficiency and value of which, to British industry and enterprise, it would be difficult to estimate, the merchants of that country, or rather the local Chambers of Commerce, judged it for their interest a few years since to establish what is called "The Association of Chambers of Commerce of the United Kingdom," the object of which, as succinctly stated in its Constitution, is "to attain those advantages by united action (where that is practicable,) which each Chamber would have more difficulty in accomplishing, in its separate capacity." Its organization is simple, the officers consisting only of a Chairman, two honorary Secretaries, a paid agent in London, and a Standing Committee of ten. It holds a meeting annually; and special meetings as these may be called for. As indicating the position which it has gained, it is interesting to know that last spring her Majesty's Government requested it to depute some of its members to visit Russia, in order to see what could be done to improve the existing commercial relations between that empire and Great Britain, and, accordingly, Mr. ATKINSON, of Hull, and Mr. WRIGLEY, of Huddersfield, made a tour of thorough investigation, the results of which are given in carefully elaborated reports, which have appeared in print. The Association was not in existence when Mr. COBDEN was engaged in negotiating the commercial treaty now in force between Great Britain and France, or its assistance would then, undoubtedly, have been in requisition; but the representatives of several of the local Chambers were invited to lend their coöperation during the progress of those negotiations, and to supply the particulars on which action should be based. These facts show the feeling of the British Government toward the local and the associated Chambers. An extract from the speech of a member of Parliament on a recent occasion will show the feeling of individual members of that Government. At a dinner at the Westminster Palace Hotel, Mr. BERKELEY spoke to the following effect:

"For thirty years past, during which period he had represented Bristol, he had found that the creation of local Chambers of Commerce was not only of the greatest advantage to himself and any gentleman who happened to be his colleague, but was also productive of the greatest benefit to the towns in which they were established, and to the commercial community generally. He also considered that the organization of these Chambers, which allowed their forming part of one general association, was productive of great benefit. As far as he was personally concerned, he could only say that a great weight had been taken off his shoulders by the assistance he had received from the Chamber connected with the city which he had the honor to represent."

As further illustrating what the relations of such an association may be to the Government under which it exists, we quote from another speech on the same occasion, by Mr. LLOYD, the Chairman:

"The object of associating these different Chambers together was to endeavor to attain that harmony of opinion which would give their expressed opinions some weight with the Legislature of the country, a weight they could not have if they were not united. They endeavored to give their views and opinions the requisite maturity, before they ventured to ask the Government to act upon them; and the means they employed was mutual discussion. Therefore he contended that if the opinion of a Chamber of Commerce was of more weight than the opinion of an individual merchant, the matured opinions of an association of Chambers, some of them comprising perhaps three hundred members, must be of still greater importance, because the views adopted and advocated were the result of deliberate and long continued discussions, extending perhaps over two or three years before any representation was made to the Government. The object of the Association was, therefore, to obtain such advantages as could not be attained by individual Chambers, and he believed that both the last and the present Government gave much more weight to an expression of opinion on the part of the Association, than they would to that of a single Chamber."

It is difficult to conceive why, in the United States, a somewhat similar association, simple in its organization and elastic in its workings, should not be equally useful in watching over industrial interests, and equally influential with the government. With us also, no doubt, an expression of opinion from such an association would carry more weight than one coming from any local body, and, from the very conditions under which it would be reached, it would be entitled to do so. Members of Congress frequently desire to know the judgment of merchants, bankers, and others, upon measures in which they are especially concerned; and the information they would be likely to receive from a National Chamber of Commerce would be more mature, more impartial, more comprehensive, than that which would be supplied by individuals, and, perhaps, even by local chambers. The business men, constituting a National Chamber, would be two removes distant from personal and special considerations; first, by their membership in the local body comprising manifold branches of industry; secondly, by their presence in a chamber representing not only various industries, but various localities. The results, therefore, of their deliberations, could not fail to be received with attention and with respect; and to the extent to which these would reach, they would obviate the necessity for that personal and persistent pressure of particular interests at the seat of government, which is so annoying to representatives, so trying to merchants, and so prejudicial to a sound and well balanced system of legislation.

## ORGANIZATION.

Your Committee further beg to propose the following resolutions for the adoption of the Convention:

*Resolved,* That the following plan be adopted for the preliminary organization of a National Board of Trade:

1st. This Association shall be designated as the "Associated National Board of Trade."

2nd. Its object shall be the promotion and harmonizing of the industrial and commercial interests of the country.

3rd. It shall consist of one delegate from each incorporated Board of Trade, Chamber of Commerce, or similar commercial body in the United States, which shall join the Association, and agree to appoint such delegate. Each such designated body having one hundred members, shall have an additional delegate; any such body having five hundred members, shall have a third delegate; and any having one thousand or more members, shall have a fourth delegate.

4th. It shall hold at least one session annually, at such time and place as shall be designated, and may hold special meetings as may be directed in its By-Laws.

5th. The Association shall adopt a Constitution, shall determine and elect its own officers, and establish such By-Laws as may be requisite for its proper working.

6th. The Boston Board of Trade is requested to take measures to carry out the above plan, and to call a meeting of the delegates at such time and place as may seem best.

*Resolved*, That this Convention strongly recommend to the delegates composing the National Board of Trade, that the basis of the Constitution shall be the plan prepared by Mr. GANO, of Cincinnati.

## MR. GANO'S PLAN.

In order to promote the efficiency and extend the usefulness of the various Produce, Corn and Commercial Exchanges, Boards of Trade and Chambers of Commerce in the United States; to secure unity and harmony of action in reference to commercial usages, customs and laws, and especially in order to secure a fair consideration of questions that pertain to the financial, commercial, and manufacturing interests of the country at large, this Association, hereby designated and to be known as the National Chamber of Commerce of America, is formed.

### ARTICLE I.

*Section* 1. Each local Board of Trade, Chamber of Commerce and Produce, Corn, or Commercial Exchange in the United States that is or may be chartered under State or National laws, and that shall comprise fifty active members, shall be entitled to membership in the National Chamber of Commerce, to be represented by four delegates, one to be chosen annually, and each delegate to serve four years.

*Sect.* 2. Delegates selected to represent the constituent members for the first year, or fraction of a year, shall, amongst themselves, by lot or otherwise, determine which one of their number shall serve for the various terms of one, two, three and four years.

*Sect.* 3. Honorary members may be elected by the Chamber, on the proposal of any one of the local organizations represented herein; but shall have no voice in its affairs, or in disposing of its business; though they may, on leave, address the Chamber, or submit questions for consideration.

### ARTICLE II.

*Section* 1. Voting on questions submitted for the action of the Chamber, shall be on the following ratios, namely: Each constituent Association, through its delegates, shall have,—

One vote for 50 to 150 members.

Two votes for 150 to 300 members.

Three votes for 300 to 500 members.

Four votes for 500 members, and upwards.

*Sect.* 2. The basis of representation shall be determined on a statement of the number of members of each local Association represented, certified by the President and Secretary, accompanied by a copy of the charter of the Association, proposing membership.

### ARTICLE III.

*Section* 1. The government of the affairs of the Chamber shall be vested in an Executive Board of nine members, to be selected by registered ballot at each annual meeting.

*Sect.* 2. The members of the Board shall, immediately after their election, select from their number a President, a Secretary, and a Treasurer, and may from time to time employ such assistants or clerks as shall be necessary.

*Sect.* 3. The Secretary and Treasurer may receive such special or annual compensation as the Chamber shall grant.

*Sect.* 4. In case of the removal, resignation or death of any member of the Executive Board, his place for the unexpired term shall be promptly filled by the constituent Association that delegated him.

### ARTICLE IV.

*Section* 1. It shall be the duty of the Executive Board:—

1st. To keep (or provide for) full and accurate records of the proceedings of the Chamber, and of its own meetings.

2nd. To submit to each annual meeting a report of the doings of the Chamber, and of their own official acts, as well as a statement of what new or unfinished business may require the attention of the Chamber.

3rd. To make full statement as to the finances of the Chamber to the annual meetings, and to other meetings when called on to do so.

4th. To apportion to each Association represented, its assessment for the expenses of the Chamber, as provided elsewhere.

5th. To make such recommendations as they may deem to be necessary for the welfare and to promote the objects of the Chamber.

*Sect.* 2. The President shall serve as Chairman of the Chamber, and of the Board; in his absence one of the other members of the Board shall serve as Vice-President.

*Sect.* 3. The Secretary shall conduct the official correspondence of the Chamber, and shall make and have charge of the records of the Board and of the Chamber.

*Sect.* 4. The Treasurer shall receive and account for all moneys belonging to the Chamber, collect assessments and fines, but shall pay out no money and dispose of no property of the Association, except on a warrant of the Secretary, countersigned by the President.

### ARTICLE V.

*Section* 1. Meetings of the Chamber shall be held in the City of Philadelphia, on the third Tuesday in September of each year; and at other times on the call of five members of the Executive Board, or on the written call of twelve lay members of the Chamber.

*Sect.* 2. The attendance of twenty members shall constitute a quorum.

*Sect.* 3. Circular notice of the annual or other meetings shall be served by the Secretary on each constituent Association, at least thirty days before the time appointed for assembling. The notice shall state the object of the meeting, and the questions to be considered.

*Sect.* 4. Meetings of the Executive Board shall be held annually on the day preceding the day of the yearly meeting of the Chamber, and at such other times as may be provided in its By-Laws.

### ARTICLE VI.

*Section* 1. The necessary expenses for managing the affairs of the Chamber shall be borne in equal proportion by an assessment to be made by the Executive Board on each local Association represented herein, according to the ratio of officially reported membership.

ARTICLE VII.

*Section* 1. When any constituent Association shall desire to present a paper for the consideration of this Chamber, it shall be its duty to transmit an authenticated copy of it to the Secretary of the Chamber at least sixty days previous to the annual meeting.

*Sect.* 2. Questions or resolutions may be submitted to any irregular or informal meeting of the Chamber by the members thereof, but final action shall not be had on them excepting at an annual meeting.

ARTICLE VIII.

*Section* 1. Any constituent Association charged with a violation of the laws of this Chamber may, after formal complaint thereof in writing, on a vote of two-thirds of all the delegates of the other local Associations represented herein, be expelled; but it shall not be exempted from the payment of assessments levied for the year current.

*Sect.* 2. Any constituent Association may withdraw from membership in the Chamber on submitting a formal request to that effect at an annual meeting, and on full payment of all dues.

ARTICLE IX.

*Section* 1. These laws may be revised, amended or repealed by the members in annual convention, notice of the proposed revision, amendment, or repeal having first been submitted to the Secretary by a member at least sixty days previous to the meeting, at which the same is to be considered, and transmitted by the Secretary in circular copies to each member, at least thirty days before said meeting.

ARTICLE X.

*Section* 1. When the majority of the Boards of Trade, Chambers of Commerce and Produce, Corn, or Commercial Exchanges in the United States which number five hundred members and upwards, shall have given their formal assent to this Association by filing written notice thereof with the Secretary of the Boston Board of Trade, the National Chamber of Commerce shall be regarded as formally constituted, and these laws as binding on them for the uses and purposes named.

*Sect.* 2. When the Association is completed, as provided in Section 1 of this Article, the Secretary of the Boston Board of Trade shall give the constituent Associations thirty days' notice of a time for the delegates to meet for organization.

Mr. WALBRIDGE : I move the acceptance and adoption of the report.

Mr. NAZRO : I would merely suggest whether it would not be expedient, in recommending this plan, to say that the Annual Meeting shall be held in the City of Washington, instead of leaving it to be called by the Boston Board of Trade, at any place designated by them.

Mr. WETHERILL : I would say, in reply to that, that the very moment you open that question, the gentlemen from Philadelphia will make the same request, and the gentlemen from New York, Boston, and every other large city will do the same thing; and the Committee therefore deemed it best to leave the entire matter to the gentlemen of Boston.

Mr. GOSHORN, of Cincinnati: It seems to me that the Committee have not reported according to the instructions given them by this Convention. It was their duty to report a plan of organization. They have given us suggestions, and have unanimously resolved that the plan submitted by Mr. GANO is a proper one. It seems to me, sir, that it is highly proper that there should be no further delay, and that this Convention should adopt a Constitution and a plan for the permanent organization of the Association. As it is now, it is left just where it was by the Detroit Convention.

Mr. WALBRIDGE : This report provides for the organization of a National Chamber of Commerce at once, and the suggestion that Mr. GANO's plan should be adopted, is merely made for the consideration of the delegates, when they shall assemble. The paper is decisive upon the question of having a National Board of Trade.

Mr. GOSHORN : We ought to have a definite understanding before we separate as to the plan of this organization. The plan submitted by Mr. GANO, as I understand, is only a suggestion by the Committee; the Convention have no knowledge of it. I would therefore offer the following resolution, as it seems to me the delegates to this Convention were sent here for the express purpose of forming a Board of Trade:

WHEREAS, The Detroit Convention affirmed the necessity of the establishment of a National Board of Trade, and empowered the Boston Board to take proper steps to bring about the organization; and

WHEREAS, The present Convention has been called for the specific purpose "to organize a National Board of Trade," and the members have been delegated by their respective Boards with a special view to the accomplishment of this object; therefore

*Resolved*, That the report of the Committee on a National Board of Trade be recommitted, with instructions to report a Constitution for such Association, and temporary officers for the same, who shall make the necessary arrangements for the first meeting of the National Board, and who shall hold office till the election of successors at said meeting.

Mr. WETHERILL: I differ very much indeed from the gentleman from Cincinnati, because I conceive that the Committee having this matter in charge have fully accomplished their entire work, and on the adoption of that report, we shall have done exactly what we were authorized to do. The Convention will then have organized a National Board of Trade. We give its name; we state its objects; we specify its ratio of representation; and we allow it, as I understand, very properly, to form its own By-Laws. It would hardly be in good taste for this Convention to undertake to dictate to a different body what its Constitution and what its By-Laws should be. We shall not, in all likelihood, be delegates to the National Board of Trade, and when others than we shall meet, it does seem to me that for us to have said what their Constitution and their By-Laws shall be, would be highly improper.

Now, sir, we have examined this subject in all its aspects, and we believe that to accomplish this object, and make it effective and satisfactory, the simplest plan the plainest, and that which is most easily understood, is the proper and most effective one. Suppose we had offered a set of By-Laws, and suppose we had fixed, for instance, the day of meeting. Why, there are not ten gentlemen in this room who could agree as to that day. The gentlemen in the Eastern part of the country would want to meet, for instance, in October; that would not suit the gentlemen in the West; and so, sir, upon that one point, we should probably spend this entire day arguing as to the proper time for this Convention to meet.

As to the place. We have already heard from Boston—they would prefer Washington. The delegates from Pennsylvania would prefer Philadelphia; and so all the States of the West and of the North would contend that the National Convention should meet in the city of their preference; and it would take another day, probably, to discuss and settle that question. We leave these questions to be settled by the gentlemen who are to direct and control the National Board of Trade—and how proper that is. We give its name, as I said before; we state its object; we fix the ratio of representation; and we require the Association to meet at least once a year, and as much oftener as the necessities of the case demand; and what more do we want? If, I repeat, we desire to make this organization effective, we must make it simple. The Committee believe their plan will be effective, and I hope the Convention will endorse their report.

Mr. McLAREN, of Milwaukie: As a member of that Committee, I agree with the main points of the report; but if I understand the English language rightly, we have not fulfilled our duty. We have not "organized a National Board of Trade." If the gentlemen will refer to the call which brought them here, they will find this specific topic is named: "The organization of a National Board of Trade, or Chamber of Commerce," and it seems to me, as the gentleman from Cincinnati has said, we are leaving the matter exactly where we found it. The Boston Board of Trade were authorized and requested to call a Convention to form a National Board of Trade; they have done this; and now we simply vary the basis of representation, and then ask the Boston Board of Trade to call the delegates together again to form the National Board. It seems to me we should form the Constitution and elect the officers, and then we should have done something. I would not propose to go into the making of By-Laws, but I would like to see a Constitution adopted, and temporary officers appointed, who would take the matter in charge, and then, I repeat, we should have done something.

Mr. ROPES, of Boston: I do not think that the Committee or the Convention were so bound by the call of the Boston Board of Trade,—which was intended to be of the most general character,—as to preclude us from acting on our best judgment. If this Convention deems it wise to adopt this report, instead of forming a Constitution and appointing officers, it is perfectly competent to do so. The Committee have come to the conclusion that it is best to advise the Convention to take that course, instead of undertaking, at this session, (which must necessarily be brief, and which has seven important subjects before it, of which this is only one,) to do the whole work which ought to be done by the National Board itself. It is according to the principles of our government, that all bodies should govern themselves, and that "governments derive their powers from the consent of the governed." Now, sir, a National Board of Trade, with officers appointed by this Convention, which is *not* the National Board of Trade, would be somewhat of an anomaly. The object with us now is not to have a National Board to-morrow or next month, but to start the machinery which will inevitably put it in motion; and I submit that this report accomplishes that object. Therefore, I am now in favor, — although at first I was not, — of this simple plan for putting the machinery in operation; and the National Board, for which we have provided all that is necessary — given it its name, fixed the basis of representation, and laid upon the Boston Board of Trade the duty of calling it together and of fixing the time and place, — then, I say, it is the business of the National Board of Trade to organize itself and start itself. I submit, that we have more important business before us than to go into all these details, on which no ten men could agree.

Mr. WALBRIDGE: I desire to state, that after a full discussion of the question by the Committee, they unanimously instructed me to make the report, and I regret that any member of the Committee should come in here with objections to it. I say, upon my honor, we unanimously agreed to that report in Committee.

Mr. NELSON, of Chicago: While I agree entirely with the report, which I think will accomplish the good that we anticipate from the organization of a National Board of Trade or Chamber of Commerce, it seems to me of the utmost importance that we fix the time and place. The other details must necessarily be arranged by the Board when it meets; but we must, as every gentleman here will see, leave a large amount of unfinished business, which will just be started. We want to go home and discuss these matters with our people, with the understanding that they will come before this National Board of Trade when it is organized; and I think that this report might be recommitted to the same Committee, with instructions to report the time and the place. The only motion I have to make in answer to the gentleman from Philadelphia is to cover the ground with regard to one Western city. I move, as the sense of this Convention, that Philadelphia be the place appointed for the first meeting of the National Board of Trade, and that the time be the 5th of January, 1869.

Mr. McLAREN: I rise to a personal explanation. I did not vote for the report in the Committee. On the contrary, I opposed it all through.

Mr. WALBRIDGE: It is proper to say, that that was so; but, upon the final vote, it was unanimous.

Mr. McLAREN: I was not present.

Mr. STRANAHAN moved the adoption of the report, and demanded the previous question.

The previous question was ordered, and the report was adopted.

Mr. HOFFMAN, of Philadelphia, submitted the following report:

## ON WEIGHTS AND MEASURES.

Your Committee on Weights and Measures beg leave to report, that in their opinion the interests of the country at large demand an uniform standard of weights and measures which will apply to each State of our Union; and they have concluded to report and recommend for your adoption, the following:

*Resolved*, 1st. That the cental system for the measurement of all the products of the soil is best adapted to the requirements of the trade of the country, and is in harmony with our decimal currency.

*Resolved*, 2nd. That it be recommended that on and after the first of August, 1868, each association represented in this Convention, adopt the cental system in the sale, storage, and transportation of said products.

*Resolved*, 3rd. That we recommend that on and after the first of August, 1868, two hundred pounds shall constitute a barrel of flour or meal.

*Resolved*, 4th. That this Convention recommend the enactment by Congress of such laws as are necessary to carry into effect the foregoing resolutions as a national measure, and to extend the cental or decimal system to all weights and measures.

*Resolved*, 5th. That as Congress has now under consideration the subject of the measurement of spirits and other liquids, with a view of collecting the revenue on the same, this Committee do not deem it necessary to take any action in regard to that matter.

On motion of Mr. SHEPARD, of Albany, the report was accepted, and was adopted unanimously.

Mr. BENNETT, of Pittsburgh, from the Committee on Agriculture and Manufactures, stated that the Committee, after deliberation, had agreed unanimously to report the following resolution :

## AGRICULTURE AND MANUFACTURES.

*Resolved*, That the natural market of the agriculturist is the home market, and that all the interests of this great and growing country should be so arranged as to harmonize, and that in a revision of the tariff laws the duties should be so adjusted as to keep the balance of trade in favor of this country, and at the same time afford the greatest protection to domestic labor and production, by placing upon those articles in which labor constitutes the greatest proportion of cost, the highest duties, thus encouraging the importation of the laborer, instead of the completed fruits of his labor.

Mr. ATKINSON, of Boston : I want to say a word; and in order that I may do so, I move to amend by adding, " that the home market be considered the market of the world." I also move that the report be recommitted, in order that the Committee may define what they mean by " the balance of trade." I will withdraw these two motions, and move that when the vote be taken, it be taken by tellers, and the Chairman of each delegation report the vote of his delegation.

Mr. WETHERILL : I should like very much to know the reasons why this report should not be acted upon in the usual way. I hope the gentleman will give his reasons for making this an exception.

Mr. HINCKEN, of New York : The gentleman from Philadelphia wants to know why a different course should be pursued from that which has been taken with other reports. This report contains within it a mighty matter; and is this Convention, supposed to be composed of the business men of the United States, to adopt such a report as that? I know that some on my side of the house believe that the balance of trade should represent our profit; and if that balance of trade is against us, we are doing a bad business. Therefore I think the gentleman from Boston is right in asking the Committee to define what they mean by " the balance of trade." If I send abroad one hundred dollars, and get ninety back, the balance of trade is against me; but still, some gentlemen, I believe, think it is in my favor. I will support the motion of the gentleman from Boston, that the report be sent back to the Committee, to define precisely what they mean.

MR. FORSYTH, of Troy: I have not troubled the Convention, thus far, with any remarks, and have only a few to make now. This report I regard as unusual in its form. I would ask, therefore, leave to second the motion of the gentleman from Boston, to recommit for the definitions called for; or else, that the question be divided, and the vote taken on the several propositions contained in it. I do not know what the Committee mean by "the balance of trade": and there are other propositions in this report which I should like information upon, before I vote. I second the motion, therefore, for its recommittal; and if that motion should not prevail, I give notice of a motion to subdivide the propositions contained in the resolution, in order that the Convention may act intelligently upon the several propositions contained therein.

Mr. STRANAHAN: With your permission, sir, I wish to state a simple fact, which will be found within the experience of every Committee appointed by this Convention. We had our difficulties, such as each gentleman on this floor can suggest; and we made our report in the form of a resolution, general in its terms, purposely avoiding all hard words, and all difficult questions which gentlemen might raise touching the question of a tariff. Now, I hope that the house can do better than the Committee. If it can, I shall hail with pleasure its success. But I do beg to say, that if you undertake to divide this question, you will find difficulties more easily suggested than surmounted.

Mr. ROPES, of Boston: I am uncertain in what shape to put an amendment which I desire to offer. I agree entirely with the gentleman from Troy, that either we must have a recommittal, or a vote *seriatim*. There are two things, at least, which I would wish to see stricken out; one is the passage which speaks of making the balance of trade in favor of this country, and the other the passage that speaks of "encouraging the importation of the laborer, instead of the fruits of his labor." I would much rather import tea and silks from China, than import the Chinese; and I would rather import a great many other things from foreign countries, than import the half-starved laborers,—as they are sometimes called,—who are engaged in producing them. I do not wish to be turned out of house and home by foreign laborers, any more than I wish the balance of trade turned against this country. In old times, it was supposed that gold and silver formed the one great object for which trade was carried on. Any nation that could export so much more of its finished productions than it imported of the productions of other countries as to bring back gold, was supposed to have gained a great advantage. But, now that we are producing gold to the extent of I do not know how many millions annually, in California and elsewhere, is it proposed that we shall keep it all in this country forever, and that we shall go on importing gold from other countries? That is what "the balance of trade" means. Are we ready to take that position? The whole thing is superannuated. We do not want any such language as that put into a report by live men to-day. I hope, instead of that, the idea will be adopted that has been endorsed by both political parties of the country, that the object of a tariff is to obtain as large a revenue as possible, and at the same time to protect industry. These are two tangible things, which we all understand and approve; and I want to see these two things stated, and nothing more, in the reports which are sent forth from this Convention. The idea that we should import laborers, instead of the fruits of their labor,—the idea that we should want the balance of trade, in 1868, in our favor,—I trusted that such ideas were done with long ago. I move the recommitment of the report, with instructions to strike out the obnoxious phrases.

Mr. BENNETT: I would withdraw the report, and favor its recommitment.

Mr. FRAZAR, of Cincinnati: I see that this is one of those questions that will excite a great deal of debate, which I think will result in very little good. We must necessarily have a high tariff to raise revenue. It is, therefore, unnecessary to discuss the question here further. I move, therefore, that the whole subject be laid upon the table.

Lost.

Mr. POTTER, of Philadelphia: I want to say a word in opposition to the motion to recommit. I had the honor to be a member of the Committee. If I understand the object of the recommittal, it is to obviate the objections which have been raised against the report, because it contains certain objectionable words. The subject contained in this resolution was very thoroughly and carefully discussed by the gentlemen constituting the Committee, coming from various sections of the country, and representing all the various views which are entertained on the subject of a tariff or no tariff; and the resolution which has been reported was supposed to be sufficiently conservative — (I do not like that word "conservative;") I would rather say, so catholic in its enunciation of principles as to meet the entire approbation of this Convention, as it met with the entire approbation of the Committee. The report did not contemplate dictating to Congress what should be its action on this question of a tariff. The report in its recommendation, leaves the whole question of the tariff to be settled by the constituted authorities whose duty it is to settle such questions. It makes no pretence of dictating to Congress, on the subject of the readjustment of duties in any particular form. It is general in its expressions. It recognizes the fact, that the duties on imports must be maintained for many years in order to meet the requirements of the Government; and it simply expresses the desire that those duties should be so adjusted as to protect that class of manufactures in this country upon which labor is so largely expended. Who can object to the propriety of such a recommendation as that? Can any man who is opposed to a tariff for protection, object to a resolution recommending Congress to discriminate in favor of those branches of manufactures in the country which require skilled labor? This meets the objection that is raised here, that this report recommends that we should import labor. No such recommendation is contained in the resolution. It is simply an expression of what would be the result of the adjustment of taxation, as it is proposed to be adjusted; namely, that upon those branches where skilled labor is required, duties of a higher class should be imposed. The result of that would be, that instead of the importation of the articles, the skilled labor which produces those articles in other countries would be brought into our country; and labor is the basis of all wealth and of all prosperity. This resolution looks to the interests of the whole country, and of all branches of industry. Who can object to it, recognizing as it does that there is an union of interests between the agriculturist and the manufacturer? As I, in my way, expressed it in Committee, both are sailing in the same boat, and the current which gives prosperity to the one gives prosperity to the other, and the adverse winds which wreck and ruin the one will cause the wreck and ruin of the other. All the interests of our country, agricultural, manufacturing and commercial, are bound up together and go together, and the prosperity of one is the prosperity of the others. This resolution recognizes that fact, and recommends that this Convention should so declare by its adoption. Its recommittal would not avail to change, in a single iota, the recommendations which it contains. It is broad; it is national; it is based upon common sense and propriety, and looks to the best interests of the country; and I hope the motion to recommit will not prevail, but that the resolution, perfect as I believe it is, — as perfect as it can be made, — will pass this body, and stand as the recommendation of this Convention; a catholic resolution, looking to the interest of all branches of industry, east, west, north and south.

The question was then taken on the motion to recommit, and it was lost. The motion to accept and adopt the report then passed.

Mr. WETHERILL offered the following resolution, and moved its adoption:

WHEREAS, The cities of Boston, Philadelphia, Cincinnati and St. Louis, have, through their Boards of Trade, desired a change in the laws regulating foreign importations; therefore

*Resolved*, By this Convention, that in our opinion Congress should, by necessary legislation, secure such change in the laws regulating foreign importations as shall authorize invoices of merchandise arriving at one port, but designed for another, to be directly forwarded from the ship's side to the ultimate ports and custom houses for entry, and without bonding, warehousing or other detention at the port of arrival.

Mr. HINCKEN, of New York: I have, perhaps, more familiarity with the practice of the Government in relation to importations than many of the gentlemen here, and it is my desire that the Convention should not adopt such a resolution. It would be laughed at by the authorities at Washington as impracticable, and I hope that the good sense of this Convention will prevent the adoption by it of any suggestions except such as are reasonable and can be carried out. The idea that the Government of the United States will permit goods intended for the interior cities to be transported to those cities without bonds, without any protection, is absurd. They will not let them go, even from the ship to the warehouse without bond. They are under bond when they are transported from the ship to the Government warehouse; and do you suppose that a Government so jealous of all these points, will permit goods to be transported thousands of miles from the port of importation, before they are even examined? I think the thing is impracticable, and therefore the Convention should not adopt it. My experience, and I think every importer here will agree with me, teaches me that the thing cannot be done without a change of the entire revenue system of the United States, and I do not think we are prepared to make such a change.

Mr. Fox, of St. Louis,—(Mr. BAGLEY, of Detroit, in the Chair): I stand on the floor to second the resolution offered by the gentleman from Philadelphia. The resolution is an important one to the interior cities of this country. For many years we have collected our customs under revenue laws calculated and managed for the cities on the seaboard, and they have spread the commerce, the wealth, and the business of the country in the interior. Within twenty-four months, the trade of the East will come by way of the West; the trans-continental lines of railway will be established within that time, from ocean to ocean. The West comes here to-day, Mr. Chairman, and desires some change in the laws for the collection of customs. All we ask is a simple change, which the Treasury Department at Washington is not prepared to dispute by argument. We simply ask for the benefit of the great steamship lines that run into the ports of New York, Baltimore, Boston and Portland, that the most expeditious and economical method may be adopted for the purpose of transporting foreign merchandise from the vessel to the car, without unnecessary delay, without unnecessary expense, and without the intervention of the superior knowledge of a New York broker. (Applause.) I intend no disrespect to New York or to any other city on the seaboard; but gentlemen importing well know the delays incident to the importation of merchandise. They well know that it takes a month, sometimes, to get eight or ten packages through the Custom House at New York; and that, with large expense for carting, warehousing, etc., and for the employment of a broker, competent and expert in doing business with the Government agents at New York. (Laughter.)

This, with the West, is a practical question; and all we ask now is, to have the law so simplified, that with regard to all kinds of imported goods, the cities of Chicago, Cincinnati, St. Louis, Louisville, and all those large centres of trade inland may have the same facilities for doing business that you who reside on the seaboard now have. To state it in a few words, it will be simply this: To so amend the laws for the collection of revenue that property may be transferred from the vessel to the railroad car, or, if at New Orleans, to the river steamboat lines, a proper officer of the Government superintending the transfer, and checking the merchandise on the bill of lading, and the railroad or steamboat transportation lines giving a bond that they will deliver it to the surveyor of the port to which it is destined in the order and condition in which it is received, leaving the examination of the packages, the appraisement, and the collection of duties, to the sworn officer of the Government residing in the interior. (Applause.) Now, sir, the only objection that Mr. GUTHRIE, the gentleman who presides with so much dignity and such long experience over that department of the Treasury at Washington could offer to the proposition which we of the West made, was that there was danger that Uncle Sam would be cheated out of the duties. I put this question to the gentleman, whether the Government was any better secured by the carman in New York who moved the merchandise three or four miles on his dray to the bonded warehouse, where it is received by a gentleman who is paid fifty or sixty dollars a month to watch it, than it would be by the bond of the New York Central Railroad Company and its employees, or of the Erie Railway, or of the Baltimore and Ohio Railroad Company, or of the Pennsylvania Railroad Company agreeing in good faith to deliver that freight in like good order as received, to the cities of the interior? (Applause.) I asked the gentleman if, under that reasoning, he would have issued United States bonds or greenbacks, because they might be counterfeited? He did not offer many arguments in opposition to this proposition, and I came away feeling that Mr. GUTHRIE would use his influence towards obtaining the privileges which the cities of the West were asking at the hands of the Government.

Mr. Chairman, I thank the Convention for the opportunity of offering these few remarks upon the question, and I would like to see the men of the seaboard shake hands with the men of the West, and adopt the resolution unanimously. (Loud applause.)

Mr. OSGOOD, of Salem: I believe it costs now about twenty-five per cent. to collect the revenue of the Government, and under this proposed plan, I think it would cost one hundred per cent., and there would be nothing left for the Government. We must have a Custom House at every interior town, and a collector in every district to collect the revenue. There would be nothing left. I would sooner go for free trade.

Mr. NAZRO: It seems to me that the gentleman from Salem entirely misconceives the proposition. If I understand the resolution correctly, it is that the goods shall be landed and sent to their place of destination, but that place must be a port of entry; otherwise, they might have to be sent to every city and town. Instead of causing greater expense, it will reduce the expense very much. (Applause.) I think it will obviate one of the greatest difficulties that has been experienced in the importation of goods. I think it will save the sending of goods outside the United States by the Grand Trunk route, and in other directions, as is done now, to prevent the very delay that is complained of; and I believe, sir, that so far from any greater frauds being committed, the goods will be quite as safe on the lines of railroad, as has been suggested, in charge of United States officers, as they would be in any other position after their arrival in the country. I have not given the subject much thought, never having been directly interested in it, but the plan proposed commends itself highly to my judgment. I believe it will be one of the most fruitful sources of benefit to the great business interests of the country, East and West, that could be devised. It is true, it may affect some local interests injuriously; undoubtedly it will. It may affect us here in Boston. Possibly there may not be so many goods sent to Boston, or Philadelphia, or New York; but that is a local interest, which, as a member of this Convention, acting for the whole country, I should certainly waive. (Applause.) I should be very glad to see any measure initiated which would be likely to benefit the West, for, as I had the honor to state the other day, I believe that any measure which enures to the benefit of any portion of our great country will eventually enure to the benefit of the whole. If we on the seaboard have any local interest that would lead us to desire to retain the present revenue system, I believe we should waive it, in view of the great benefit that I believe will result to the whole country by the adoption of a system permitting imported goods to be sent to their place of destination without this great delay. And I believe the Government, directly as well as indirectly, — and indirectly much more largely than directly, — will reap great pecuniary gain, and that the saving of expense will be enormous. I was astonished to hear the remark of the gentleman from Salem, that this would increase expenses. I do not believe we are so corrupt. I do not believe that, even if people are trusted, there is going to be so great an amount of fraud committed, as he seems to anticipate; and certainly, if it be fairly and honestly carried out, no gentleman can say that it will not be the means of reducing the expense. And I believe that it will be carried out honestly. I had the honor to be present at the conference of the Committee on Taxation of our Board with the authorities at Washington, and it was suggested, that if our plan were adopted, the people would cheat the Government. I said I believed that the people were not so dishonest; and so I believe now. The great mass of the business people of this country are essentially honest. I believe, therefore, that these goods can be transported in the way proposed, and that within twelve months after the enactment of the law, the whole country will acknowledge the great benefit which will have resulted from it.

Mr. BABCOCK, of New York: Whatever may have been thought of the action of the Convention on previous days, I think gentlemen will all admit that we are making very good time this morning. If I understand the resolution passed a few moments ago, it virtually tends, if carried out, to stop the foreign trade of the country; and the resolution now before us is of the same character. You seek to set aside the tariff laws imposed by Congress, under which no New York importer, or any other importer, can obtain his goods without the delay incident to the operation of the law; and while, for one, I would gladly favor any project which would do away with these cumbersome regulations, I suppose there is no way in which it can be done. Even with these stringent regulations, in the City of New York, and probably elsewhere, stupendous frauds are practised upon the Government. Large amounts of goods are brought in, upon which no duty is paid, or very much less than is due. I would gladly favor any project under which the people of the great West could receive their goods direct from the ships; but I see no way in which the resolution that has been offered can be carried out. You virtually say to us, "Would that we were altogether like you, except these bonds." I believe that is not exactly the language of the Apostle Paul, but somewhat like it. Now, as to your getting goods without bonds ——

A Delegate: We don't ask it.

Mr. BABCOCK: If I understood Mr. FOX correctly, he spoke as if he understood that the carman took charge of the goods from the ship to the warehouse, and that the Government took the risk of the honesty of that carman. Such is not the fact. Not a package of goods is discharged from any vessel in the City of New York until a bond has been signed and approved by the proper authority at the Custom House; and with such restrictions, there is not an importer in the City of New York who would not vote that every Western importer should have the same opportunity to obtain his goods that he has.

Mr. FOX: I did not state that the goods were not bonded while being transported to the warehouse. We do not ask to have the law any different for us than for the Eastern importers. We wish to give bonds, or to have the railroad companies give bonds to deliver the goods safely at the port of entry inland.

Mr. BABCOCK: I understood the gentleman to say that the carman had the custody of the goods from the vessel to the public store, and that during that time the risk of his fidelity was taken by the Government, which is not the case. If you can get Commodore VANDERBILT to say that he will give a bond every time you want one, and that the agents of the New York Central Railroad shall go to the vessel and get the goods that are to be transported over that line, I shall be glad to have you do it. I want you to have every facility possible.

A delegate from Philadelphia stated that the Pennsylvania Railroad would agree to do this.

Mr. FOX: When we take the merchandise from the vessel to the cars, to go to the interior cities, we give a bond to the transportation line.

Mr. HERSEY, of Portland: I desire to say simply one word upon this matter, and that is, that we in the City of Portland are practically carrying out the very idea which is conveyed in this resolution; and, sir, if other cities,—allow me to say to the great West,—have not these facilities, the City of Portland has them. The goods by the English steamers are rolled into the Government warehouse, and rolled through it into the cars of the Grand Trunk Railway, without an hour's delay; and before they could get through other custom houses, those goods are delivered at the West. It is clear from this, Mr. President, that it is practicable to carry out this idea of giving facilities to the West, which ought to do a large business, and in order to do it speedily, facilities should be given them to do that business. (Applause.)

Mr. WALBRIDGE: I will ask Mr. FOX if he wants, for the cities of the West, any advantages over New York?

Mr. FOX: I will say, without hesitation, we do not.

Mr. WALBRIDGE: Then I support the resolution. In New York we live by our shipping, by our commerce; and we do not care anything about our Custom House regulations. The West should be put upon the same footing with ourselves.

The question was then put, and the resolution was adopted.

Mr. WALBRIDGE offered the following resolution, and moved its adoption:

*Resolved*, That in the judgment of this Convention, one rail inter-oceanic communication will not be adequate to the demands of foreign commerce and the traffic and travel of this country; and that Congress should at once provide for the construction and completion of two more lines of railway communication to the Pacific Ocean.

Mr. CLARK, of Cleveland, moved the reference of the resolution to the Committee on Transportation, and it was so referred.

Mr. BRUNOT, of Pittsburgh, offered the following resolution:

*Resolved*, That in any readjustment of the tariff laws, specific duties, whenever practicable, and home valuations, in cases where *ad valorem* duties are deemed important, are necessary, in order to secure to the Government its just dues, and to the industry of the country and to honest importers protection against the injuries they suffer in consequence of evasions of and frauds upon the home revenue.

Mr. BRUNOT: I move the adoption of this resolution; and I wish to say, that in offering a resolution of this character, I do it under the impression that the various delegations which have assembled here, have come, not for the purpose of constituting themselves a debating society,—not for the purpose of going back and discussing the subjects upon which we have had the precedent of congressional action for so many years, but that each gentleman has been sent here on account of his supposed fixed opinions upon certain subjects likely to come before us, upon which he is prepared to vote. We of the West (at least, so far West as I happen to come from,) have sent delegates here upon that idea; and, sir, while much might be said in favor of this resolution, I take it for granted that the facts which have been spread upon the records of the debates of Congress are in the minds of most of the members of this Convention. I propose, then, that we vote upon this resolution, without taking up the time of the Convention myself in discussing it, and hoping that there will be no discussion upon it.

The resolution was adopted.

Mr. BLATCHFORD, of Chicago, presented the following resolution, which was referred to the Committee on Currency and Finance:

*Resolved*, That as specie is the only sound, available, and universally recognized measure and standard of value, and as the restoration of this standard is essential to our industrial and commercial prosperity, it is most desirable that the resumption of specie payments be effected at the earliest possible moment consistent with the public good.

Mr. FORSYTH, of Troy, introduced the following resolution, and moved its reference to the Committee on Currency and Finance:

*Resolved*, As the sense of this Convention, that it is the duty of Congress, in all its legislation, to maintain a *constant tendency* toward the earliest possible resumption of specie payments; that such a tendency furnishes the only hope of ultimate and permanent relief to all the disordered relations of business; and that no disaster is now to be so much feared as further inflation, a little more tariff, and a few more subsidies.

Mr. WETHERILL: I move an amendment, that it be referred to the Committee on Miscellaneous Matters; for it seems to be of that character itself.

Mr. HINCKEN: To get rid of the question at once, and dispose of it as far as this Convention is concerned, I move the adoption of the resolution.

Mr. STRANAHAN: I wish simply to remark, that I would gladly vote for the resolution, if the last paragraph was stricken out. I think as it stands, it is not quite courteous.

Mr. WARD, of Boston: I move that the resolution lie upon the table; and I do so, because we have just adopted a resolution in relation to the resumption of specie payments, which was a broad resolution, upon which we could all agree.

Mr. NAZRO: I hope the motion will not prevail, but that the resolution will be referred to the Committee on Finance.

The question was then taken, and the resolution was laid on the table.

## REPORT OF THE COMMITTEE ON TAXATION.

Mr. Bigelow, of Boston, presented the report of the Committee on Taxation.

Whereas, Domestic products constitute the basis of nine-tenths of the internal trade of the country and furnish the means of sustaining its foreign commerce, thus rendering an extensive, varied and active domestic industry essential to its proper commercial prosperity; and

Whereas, The capital required to initiate and sustain industrial enterprise commands on an average double the rate of interest here that it does in the great industrial nations abroad, which higher rate of interest is inseparable from the condition of a country constantly absorbing capital in new settlements and improving virgin lands; and

Whereas, For similar reasons, as well as for the higher social and educational requirements of our industrial population, the rates of wages of labor inevitably rule comparatively high; and

Whereas, Our domestic industry cannot sustain itself in competition with the foreign production of commodities of easy transportation, unless placed upon an equality in the command of capital and labor, and exemption from internal taxation; or, unless the disparity against us in these respects is neutralized by suitable legislative provisions; therefore

*Resolved*, That while the General Government provides revenue for its support by duties on imports and tonnage duties, sound policy demands such an adjustment of these duties as to equalize the disparities in the cost of capital and labor between our own and competing nations, that thereby the industrial and commercial interests of the whole country may be promoted, labor and skill receive their just reward, and the arts, civilization and the civil power of the nation be extended.

*Resolved*, That as the present internal revenue tax on useful productions is depressing our domestic industry, shipping and transportation interests, and is absorbing the capital by which they are sustained, it should be speedily removed.

*Resolved*, That as a preliminary to a reduction of taxation the expenditures of the Government should be reduced in every practicable way, and effective measures be taken to insure the faithful execution of the revenue laws.

*Resolved*, That in our opinion the revenue received from import duties, from licenses, legacies and stamps, together with a tax that would not be oppressive, upon spirits, tobacco and other articles, denominated luxuries, would be ample to defray the expenses of the Government if economically administered.

*Resolved*, That Congress be and they are hereby requested to lay an internal revenue tax on such articles only as are indicated in the foregoing resolution.

The resolutions were adopted unanimously, with much applause.

Mr. TAIT, of Louisville, presented the following resolution, and moved its adoption:

WHEREAS, The speedy reduction of the taxes and the resumption of specie payments are the objects desired by the American people; and

WHEREAS, They can only be obtained by wise legislation, stimulating labor where it can be made most productive, and by practising a most rigid economy in all the departments of the Government; therefore

*Resolved*, That we respectfully but earnestly urge Congress to loan the Cotton-growing States $20,000,000 for one year, to be secured by a lien on the growing crop of the present year, or such other securities as may be deemed sufficient.

Mr. WETHERILL moved to lay the resolution on the table.

Mr. TAIT: It is known that the Southern States are not represented here to any extent. Once the South occupied a proud position in the legislature of the country; now she has no one to speak for her; and we appeal to your sense of justice, to your kindly feeling. We ask you to be kind to the South, as you have been kind to her delegates whom she has sent here. You are anxious to hasten the time when specie payments will be resumed, and you will need the productions of that fertile country to aid you in securing the resumption of specie payments. I know that our influence, at present, is limited; but as a conquered people, as a people whose fields have been laid waste, whose homes have been made desolate, and whose spirits have been crushed, we ask of this Convention the adoption of the resolution. If such aid could be extended, it would tend to soothe

the feelings of those who have not, perhaps, been yet soothed since the issue of the late war. I know that the subject embraced in the resolution has been considered by Congress, but I want an expression from this Convention. I want to know the sentiments of the merchants throughout the country. All the business that has been done here, thus far, has looked to the interests of the East or of the West; the Southern States have not been noticed. In the resolution lately adopted, Louisville was not named, in connection with the other great cities of the West. Why should she be so ignored? Kentucky is a State yet in the Union, and never was out; and I ask that you will at least compliment the delegates to this Convention from that State, by adopting this resolution.

Mr. BRUNOT: I appreciate the appeal which the gentleman has made from the Southern States. I appreciate the fact which he mentions, of the desolation of their fields, and of the terrible trouble which now exists there. I do not believe there was a man in the whole North who was more delighted to see those fields desolated than I was. I believe in the justice and the righteousness of all that has come upon them. But now, sir, when the conflict is all past, I believe in doing everything we can to bring back our erring brethren to the right. (Applause.) With that view I do not rise to advocate the resolution, but to ask that it may have a respectful reference to the proper Committee. I hope the gentleman will withdraw his motion to lay on the table, and permit the resolution to be referred.

Mr. ALEXANDER, of St. Louis: I do not want this Convention to pass this matter over without thinking about it. If the business men here will give this subject a careful consideration, they will find that it is one of the great questions that ought to come before this Convention. The war is over. The South is desolated; we all know it; or, at least, we do, in St. Louis. Many of our people have gone there and have attempted to raise cotton. We know what the effects of the efforts of the last two years have been. We know that the South cannot recuperate without help from somewhere. The capitalists of the North are not willing to send their money down there; they are not willing to risk similar losses to those they have suffered during the past two years. The people of the South are too poor to continue their cotton planting. Now, sir, I believe that the best thing this country can do, — the best investment that can be made, is to loan to the Southern States twenty millions of dollars. Throw such restrictions round it as are necessary to insure its coming back again. Something must be done to help the Southern people.

I have lived a long time in the southwest. I have never lived further south than Missouri, but I have been pretty thoroughly identified with the Southern people, and have a strong feeling of affection for them; and anything that I can do to help them out of their trouble, I will gladly do. I did all I could to put down the rebellion. I thought they were wrong in entering into it, and fought against them while they were in it; but now I will raise my voice and do all I can in every way to get them out of the trouble which they have got themselves into. (Applause.) I appeal to you to pass this resolution, saying to Congress that this Convention, representing all parts of this great country, feel that it is magnanimous and right for this people,—that is, the people of the United States,—to lend money to those who are "flat broke," and to help them out of the trouble they are now in, because they are our brothers.

Mr. NAZRO: I concur in the views that have been expressed by the preceding speakers. I most earnestly hope that this Convention will adopt a very liberal policy in regard to the South. As has been said by the gentleman on my right, we can say here in Boston,—and I presume this city does not need any endorsement on my part,—that we went forward as firmly and as strongly as any community in the land in putting down the rebellion. We determined to do all we could to put it down; but, as the gentleman has truly remarked, we want now to take a broad, comprehensive and liberal view. We want now to gather up the fragments, and to pass over as leniently as we can the errors, even the crimes which we think have been committed against the whole country. (Applause.) Sir, I am strongly in favor of pursuing some liberal policy in regard to them; but I do not know that I should be in favor of the particular resolution that has been offered. I hope that this Convention will not take up any resolution of such an important character and pass it in a crude form, or without due reflection. I think, therefore, that the proper course to be pursued in this case is to refer the resolution to the Committee on Currency and Finance. They will give it a full examination, and we shall have the results of their deliberations; and we can finally adopt it or reject it, as we please. I therefore move that it be referred to that Committee.

Mr. WARD, of Boston: I wish to offer an amendment to that proposition — that it be referred to a Special Committee of one from each delegation, and that the gentleman who offered the resolution be Chairman of the Committee.

Mr. SOUDER, of Philadelphia: I hope that will not be done. The appointment of a Special Committee will certainly cause delay. The Committee on Currency and Finance is really the proper Committee. With the exception of the portion in regard to loaning twenty millions of dollars, the resolution has already gone, in substance, to that same Committee; and I do hope the Convention will not create another Committee upon the subject.

Mr. ATKINSON, of Boston: If I were to make any motion with regard to the resolution, I should move its reference to the Committee on Agriculture. I look upon this attempt to obtain a loan for the South as the last struggle of the plantation system, which, in my judgment, was doomed by the war. Twenty millions would continue the barbarism of the South for part of a year, perhaps. I hope the resolution will have a respectful hearing; but I trust we shall soon come to a condition of things (which I hear is already the case in Georgia) when one man, with the capital of a spade and an acre of ground, may make four bales of cotton.

Mr. LIONBERGER, of St. Louis: As a member of the Finance Committee, I would state that that Committee has about as much as it can do. I would be glad if the matter could be referred to a Special Committee.

Mr. WETHERILL: The objection to a Special Committee would be this. It would probably defeat the resolution, on account of want of time, and then it would go forth that this Convention did not meet this question fairly and squarely in the face. The only question the Committee could inquire about, is whether the amount of twenty millions would answer the requirements of the South. We are just as much bound to ask, probably more, whether, in our present condition, we ought to lend the suffering South twenty millions of dollars. That is the simple question. A great deal has been said about the devastation of the South. With all respect to the gentleman from Louisville, I would say, that we too have suffered in the North; and that we cannot afford, in my opinion, to spend twenty millions in the way indicated, when the merchants of the North are to-day suffering, and do not know what the future will bring forth. We must be just before we are generous. When we recollect that the troubles at the South have left twenty-five hundred millions of debt upon us as a legacy,—when we recollect that agriculture and trade in every department are suffering,—it does seem to me that Northern men should be sectional in a case of this kind. Northern men should say, "Much as we pity and grieve over the South in her present position, still we do not think that the South should occupy any better position than we occupy at the West."

Mr. WARD, of Detroit: This subject has simmered down to this simple question. Is this Convention prepared to recommend that the people whom they represent shall be taxed twenty millions, for the purpose of lending the money to the South?

Mr. ROPES, of Boston: I should like to say just one word. This is not so much a question of lending twenty millions to the South, as a question simply of securing for our suffering brethren there a respectful consideration of their request, which one of the few representatives of that section of the country here present, has made before us. I hope we shall give it such degree of attention as is involved in the appointment of a Special Committee to consider it. It is very likely that such a Committee will not report the resolution recommending a loan of money to the South, but they will at least agree in sympathy, and will manifest the sympathy of this body, with the, it may be, deserved, necessary and retributive suffering and desolation of the South. I hope that the motion to refer to a Special Committee will prevail, and that we shall treat the mover, and the section he represents, with the respect involved in the appointment of such a Committee.

The question was then put, and the resolution was referred to a Special Committee, which immediately retired for the consideration of the subject.

Mr. WARD, of Detroit, offered the following resolutions, which were referred to the Committee on Taxation:

*Resolved*, That legislative and judicial power should be taken from the Commissioner of Internal Revenue and his subordinates, and questions between officers and tax-payers be tried in Federal Courts, so that the sacred right of jury trial may be respected, yet penalties kept severe, to imprisonment if need be, so that rigid justice be done to all.

*Resolved*, That the laws should be framed to oblige assessors to call for full information, and make strict investigations, before accepting sworn returns; and whenever such returns are accepted and passed, they should be final, unless fraud can be proved in a Federal Court.

On motion of Mr. WETHERILL, it was voted that the Convention take a recess to-day, from half-past two until a quarter past three o'clock, to enable it to accept the invitation of the Massachusetts Legislature.

Mr. COREY, of Scranton, offered the following resolution:

*Resolved*, That in order to carry out the recommendations of the Committee on Weights and Measures, this Convention recommend the repeal of all laws regulating the standard weight of grain, seeds, and cereals by measure.

Mr. LATHROP, of Oswego, moved to lay the resolution on the table. Lost.

A Delegate from Wilmington moved its reference to the Committee on Weights and Measures. Lost.

On motion of Mr. PRESTON, of Albany, the resolution was amended by the insertion of the word "flour" before "grain, seeds, and cereals," and it was then adopted.

Mr. HOLTON, of Milwaukie, presented the following report from the Committee on

## INLAND COMMUNICATION AND TRANSPORTATION.

The Committee to whom was referred the question of "the improvement of our inland and interior means of transportation," beg leave to report the following series of resolutions as embracing the results of their careful deliberations upon the subject submitted to them.

1. *Resolved*, That it is the highest duty of a nation to encourage all public enterprises looking to the development of its resources and the increase of its basis of taxation.

2. *Resolved*, That this Convention regards the facilities of transportation between the seaboard, the Mississippi valley and the Pacific coast, as indispensable to the highest development of the country and the surest bond of perpetual union.

3. *Resolved*, That this Convention earnestly recommends to the Congress of the United States as incident to its plenary power to regulate commerce with foreign nations and among the States, to coöperate with either or all of the governments of the States interested in measures which will make certain the opening of a ship canal ade-

quate to pass vessels of one thousand tons burden from the Atlantic coast by the channel of the great lakes to the Mississippi River.

4. *Resolved,* That those great rivers of the West whose channels and commerce are not exclusively within the limits of a State are as proper objects of national improvement as the ocean and the lake coasts which are the external boundaries of the country, and should receive an equal degree of consideration from the Government of the United States.

5. *Resolved,* That the aid to the Union Pacific Railway incurred in the midst of war as a great measure of national defence, is now vindicated by events as a most important agency for the development of the national resources, and that this Convention deems it but just that the same policy be extended in behalf of the national system of railway communication to the Pacific coast, which shall include lines central to the lake States and the Territories and States of Dacotah, Montana, Idaho, Washington, Oregon, and also to the States which adjoin the southern frontiers of the United States, whenever the development of the country shall warrant their construction.

6. *Resolved,* That Congress and the legislatures of the different States be requested to provide by law for the greater safety of travellers upon railroads.

7. *Resolved,* That Congress should provide by a general act for the manner in which railroad bridges may be constructed and maintained over navigable streams and other bodies of water.

8. *Resolved,* That it is important to the interests of inland transportation and the country at large that facilities at the terminal points of tide water should be so improved as to afford the cheapest and quickest transfer of property to and from shipboard.

WHEREAS, Navigation affords the cheapest of all known means of inland transportation; and

WHEREAS, Lake Ontario extends lake navigation nearly three hundred miles farthest eastward; therefore

9. *Resolved,* That a free ship canal around the Falls of Niagara is vitally essential to the public interests, and is a commercial necessity that demands the attention and the action of Congress.

10. *Resolved,* That in the opinion of this Convention no appropriation from the public treasury should be made for new works of public improvement in the present depressed condition of the national finances; and that all appropriations should be confined to the maintenance of works in existence or to the completion of works of the utmost national importance now in progress.

11. *Resolved*, That the example of the Commonwealth of Massachusetts in prosecuting a public work of the magnitude of the Hoosac Tunnel, for the purpose of facilitating Western communication, challenges the admiration of this Convention, and that it recommends it to the imitation of our sister States.

Mr. HOLTON moved the acceptance and adoption of the report.

On motion of Mr. ALLEN, of Philadelphia, it was voted that the resolutions be taken up *seriatim*.

On motion of Mr. CHAMBERLAIN, of Albany, the first resolution was amended by striking out the word "highest," and was then adopted.

The second resolution was adopted.

Mr. HINCKEN: In reference to the third resolution, I would ask the Chair if he can inform me what would be the length of the canal from the great lakes to that point on the Mississippi River where a vessel of a thousand tons can be navigated?

The PRESIDENT: I will state, for the information of the gentleman, that it will be about three hundred miles, if they do not use the Illinois River. The gentleman from Chicago, Mr. MUNN, is more familiar with the subject than I am, and I will ask him to state the facts in regard to it.

Mr. MUNN: From the City of Chicago to the Illinois River, the distance is about ninety-six miles. They would not, in all probability, make a canal more than sixty miles; then slack-water navigation.

Mr. HINCKEN: What would be the depth of water?

Mr. MUNN: Not exceeding seven or eight feet.

Mr. HINCKEN: I will state, for the information of the Convention, that a vessel of a thousand tons burden, loaded with the products of Europe or the West, would require a canal with from eighteen to twenty feet of water. You see, therefore, the magnitude of the undertaking you are recommending. If I understand the matter, you will have to go very near the lower end of the Mississippi before you will have water sufficient to carry out the recommendation.

Mr. MUNN: Allow me to say, for the information of the Convention, that a canal constructed from Chicago to the Mississippi, including the Illinois River, in my opinion, cannot be built to take vessels of the same construction and with the same tonnage that float upon the lakes. Vessels of the same amount of tonnage, constructed as we construct vessels for those rivers, could navigate the canal and the Illinois River. In order to sail vessels upon the lakes, you need depth, without any great breadth of beam; on canals and upon rivers you need breadth of beam, and less depth. I do not believe that vessels adapted to the lakes and to the ocean will be adapted to any canal you could make.

Mr. BRYSON: I have recently given considerable attention to this subject; and as within the last twelve days I have been in conversation with an officer appointed by the Government, some two years ago, to make these surveys, I will state the result of the conversation, which was in the presence of the Chief of the Engineering Bureau of the War Department. We came to the conclusion, unanimously, that the boats used upon the lakes could not be used upon the Mississippi River, even if they could be got there. We cannot, below St. Louis, safely calculate upon over seven feet of water at ordinary stages, and the canal which this officer made the surveys for, and which is calculated to accommodate vessels drawing six feet of water, requires nineteen millions of dollars. We came to the conclusion, that vessels upon the ocean and upon the lakes, must be vessels, as the gentleman from Chicago stated, of great draft, and of not so much breadth of beam; the vessels upon the rivers must be vessels of great breadth of beam and of light draft. I do not pretend to argue the question; I merely state these facts, and I think that any gentleman who is acquainted with the subject will substantiate the remarks I have made here.

Mr. HOLTON: I will state to the Convention some of the principles that guided the Committee. Upon this question, the same inquiry was made in Committee that has been made by the gentleman from New York. It was answered by those familiar with navigation, that it was not likely that the same bottom would perform the entire journey from the lakes to the Mississippi River, by any route that should be chosen.

We tried to avoid a multiplicity of words in our report, and to compact our resolutions as much as we could. Many of these questions were considered, and I would ask, therefore, that a liberal construction be put upon the language and terms of our resolution.

Mr. FRAZAR, of Cincinnati: I thought this was a Convention of practical business men; that we came here for practical results. Now, sir, if I recollect aright, one of the resolutions of the report says that it is inexpedient for Congress or the National Government at this time to engage, in any system of public improvements, beyond those already in progress. While, sir, I may not agree with the first resolution, at the same time, I think it is unnecessary for us to spend time in arguing a resolution providing for the construction of a work which we say afterwards we have not the means to build. Why should we spend our time in this kind of nonsense? I think we had better limit ourselves to such things as are practical. If ever the time comes when such a canal is necessary, if ever the time comes when our Government is so rich that it can engage in such an improvement, if ever the time comes when it is expedient, right and proper for the National Government to engage in such an improvement, then it will be time enough for us to discuss such a resolution. I think, therefore, we should lay aside all this pile of resolutions, and come to one that is practical, which I think is the ninth or tenth resolution. Let us adopt that, as a resolution embodying practical financial common sense. Having done that, it will be unnecessary for us to act upon this third resolution.

Mr. TAYLOR, of St. Paul: The Convention will have noticed the care with which the Committee, in presenting the various propositions, have endeavored to indicate a policy, for the consideration of the country, without attempting, at this time, to present anything in the form of instructions to Congress. I appreciate as much as the gentleman, the financial difficulties to which he alludes, and one of the resolutions to which he refers expresses an appreciation of those difficulties; but, sir, the Committee believed that the whole subject of inland transportation was referred to them, for the purpose of indicating a policy for the consideration of the Convention, and for adoption by the country at the proper moment, and at the earliest proper moment. We must make some progress in the investigation of the principles which are to bear upon the settlement of this question. If we are to abstain from all discussion upon the manner in which these great enterprises are to be conducted until the financial difficulty is settled fully to our satisfaction, we shall not make much progress; but we can make substantial progress in considering the merits of the whole question, and in determining what measures are possible, what are demanded by the public interests, and what are proper to be urged, at the right moment, upon the consideration of Congress and the country. We forbear to urge any appropriations for these works, but at the same time we invite the attention of the Convention to the propositions themselves, as shadowing forth a national policy for increasing our means of transportation which we must soon reach.

One word more. This very resolution has one important feature. While it recognizes, as I understand, the duty of Congress, as incident to its plenary power, to regulate commerce with foreign nations and among the States, to aid and encourage this great enterprise of a ship canal from the lakes to the Mississippi River, it at the same time expressly asks that Congress will give its coöperation to the commercial States which are greatly and immediately interested in this improvement. I trust that this discussion will go on, and that the great commercial bodies of the country will satisfy themselves, and be willing to declare, that this is an object proper to be undertaken at the earliest practicable moment. I therefore hope that the resolution, thus carefully guarded, will meet with the approbation of the Convention.

The question was put, and the third resolution passed.

The fourth and fifth resolutions were adopted without objection.

Mr. COVINGTON, of Cincinnati, moved to amend the sixth resolution, by the insertion of the words, after the word "railroad," "and on steamboats and other vessels navigating the rivers and lakes."

Mr. TROWBRIDGE, of Detroit: I would state that that is already provided for by law.

Mr. COVINGTON: Not fully. I understand this is merely a recommendation. I am aware there is a law, but it does not cover the ground yet.

Mr. NAZRO: I hope the gentleman will make it broader, and include the ocean, for we on the seaboard want protection as much as our Western friends.

Mr. COVINGTON accepted the suggestion of Mr. NAZRO, and the resolution was amended as proposed, and passed.

Resolutions seven and eight were then adopted.

Mr. ALLEN moved to strike out the ninth resolution, but the motion was lost, and the resolution was adopted.

The question being on the adoption of the tenth resolution, a New York delegate inquired if it did not conflict with the resolution already passed, which recommended that measures be taken to build two more lines of railroad to the Pacific.

Mr. HOLTON: It will be noticed that all these resolutions have reference to the means of the Government to meet these requirements. We announce that, in our judgment, there is no preparation and no readiness on the part of the Government to assume these expenses.

The tenth resolution was adopted, and the eleventh came up for action.

Mr. NAZRO: I fully appreciate the compliment paid to Massachusetts by the eleventh resolution; I am satisfied that the gentlemen who made that report intended it as a compliment; but, sir, allow me to say that there is a very great difference of opinion in Massachusetts with regard to the expediency of that expenditure. Some of us believe that it would have been much better if that project had never been undertaken. We further believe that it will never be completed. We believe it is a source of political corruption; and I, for one, am decidedly opposed to it. While, therefore, I appreciate the courtesy of the Committee, (I beg they will not understand me in any other way than that,) I will move that that resolution be stricken out.

Mr. HOLTON: Allow me to say, in behalf of the Committee, that this was hardly regarded as one of the regular resolutions of the series, but was offered in compliment to this Commonwealth, at the suggestion of some friend who appeared before the Committee, and we should be very happy to see it adopted, if deemed wise and well by the Convention.

The motion to strike out prevailed; and the report, as a whole, was then adopted unanimously.

The resolutions as adopted, are as follows:

1st. *Resolved,* That it is the duty of a nation to encourage all public enterprises, looking to the development of its resources and the increase of its basis of taxation.

2nd. *Resolved,* That this Convention regards the facilities of transportation between the seaboard, the Mississippi valley, and the Pacific coast, as indispensable to the highest development of the country, and the surest bond of perpetual union.

3rd. *Resolved,* That this Convention earnestly recommends to the Congress of the United States as incident to its plenary power to regulate commerce with foreign nations and among the States, to coöperate with either or all of the governments of the States interested, in measures which will make certain the opening of a ship canal adequate to pass vessels of one thousand tons burden from the Atlantic coast by the channel of the great lakes, to the Mississippi River.

4th. *Resolved*, That those great rivers of the West whose channels and commerce are not exclusively within the limits of a State, are as proper objects of national improvement as the ocean and the lake coasts, which are the external boundaries of the country, and should receive an equal degree of consideration from the Government of the United States.

5th. *Resolved*, That the aid to the Union Pacific Railway incurred in the midst of war as a great measure of national defence, is now vindicated by events as a most important agency for the development of the national resources, and that this Convention deems it but just that the same policy be extended in behalf of the national system of railway communication to the Pacific coast, which shall include lines central to the lake States, and the Territories and States of Dacotah, Montana, Idaho, Washington and Oregon, and also to the States which adjoin the Southern frontiers of the United States, whenever the development of the country shall warrant their construction.

6th. *Resolved*, That Congress, and the legislatures of the different States, be requested to provide by law for the greater safety of travellers upon railroads and on steamboats, and other vessels navigating the rivers, lakes and sea-coast.

7th. *Resolved*, That Congress should provide by a general and impartial act for the manner in which railroad bridges may be constructed and maintained over navigable streams, and other bodies of water.

8th. *Resolved*, That it is important to the interests of inland transportation, and the country at large, that facilities at the terminal points of tide water should be so improved as to afford the cheapest and quickest transfer of property to and from shipboard.

Whereas, Navigation affords the cheapest of all known means of inland transportation; and

Whereas, Lake Ontario extends lake navigation nearly three hundred miles farthest eastward; therefore,

9th. *Resolved*, That a free ship canal around the Falls of Niagara is vitally essential to the public interests, and is a commercial necessity that demands the attention and the action of Congress.

10th. *Resolved*, That in the opinion of this Convention no appropriation from the public treasury should be made for new works of public improvement in the present depressed condition of the national finances, and that all appropriations should be confined to the maintenance of works in existence, or to the completion of works of the utmost national importance now in progress.

Mr. TAIT, of Louisville, from the Committee to whom was referred the resolution in regard to a loan to the South, submitted the following resolution as their report:

## RELIEF TO THE SOUTH.

*Resolved*, That this Convention has heard with deep sympathy the accounts of the destitution and suffering existing at the South, and would earnestly express the hope that Congress, in its wisdom, may be able to devise such measures of aid and relief as will, without loss to the Government, stimulate the industry, and speedily and permanently restore the prosperity of that section of our common country.

Mr. ALLMAN, of Philadelphia: I would like to move as an amendment, the substitution of the words "in the Southern States of this country," for the words "at the South."

The amendment was accepted, and the resolution was unanimously adopted, amid great applause.

Mr. THURSTON: I have a resolution which I desire to offer, for the consideration of the Convention. There is now, I understand, a bill before the Senate of the United States, providing for a change of our coinage, to correspond with the French system. It seems to me, that if the measure is carried out as proposed in the bill, it will be a surrender of a portion of our nationality, which I do not feel disposed to relinquish without expressing an opinion thereon. I submit the following resolution, and move its adoption:

WHEREAS, A bill has been reported to the Senate of the United States, by the Hon. JOHN SHERMAN, Chairman of the Finance Committee of the Senate, to change the decimal coinage of the United States to correspond to the French system, and for the adoption of *francs* in this country instead of eagles and dollars; therefore be it

*Resolved*, That, in the judgment of this Convention, no change in the character of our national coins to the sacrifice of national originality or prestige should be entertained, until it is incontestably proven that the new system offers such greater commercial advantages as fully justify the abandonment of a system originating with our organization as a nation, and rooted in the habits and love of the people. The more especially since the proposed change will involve an expense of six hundred thousand dollars, at a time when every principle of national integrity demands the most rigid economy in all branches of the administration of the Government, to the end that the burden of debt may be lifted at the earliest period from off the people of the nation.

Mr. WOOD, of Philadelphia: I want to ask whether the law of Senator SHERMAN means to change the denomination of our coinage; means to pledge us to call a milled dollar a *franc?*

Mr. THURSTON: I believe there is, somewhere in the law, a passage which specifies that there is to be a medallion of the French emperor on one side, and on the other, a medallion of something else.

Voices: Oh, no. You are mistaken.

Mr. SLOANE: I think the gentleman misunderstands the character of the Senate bill for changing the currency. I understand that that bill is one deliberately and considerately prepared, based upon the labors of a special commission. This commission met delegates from the great powers of Europe, and this bill is merely for the purpose of equalizing and rendering uniform the gold and silver currency of the world. Now, sir, if this subject is to be considered by this Convention ——

The PRESIDENT: If the gentleman will allow me, I will state, that the motion is, that the resolution be referred to the Committee on Currency and Finance.

The resolution was so referred.

Mr. TAYLOR, of St. Paul, introduced the following resolution, which, on his motion, was referred to the Committee on Currency and Finance:

*Resolved,* That Congress should immediately direct the Secretary of the Treasury to redeem United States notes in gold and silver coin; and for that purpose, in addition to the present supply of specie in the Treasury of the United States, should vest the amplest powers in the Secretary to obtain whatever quantities of gold or silver may be necessary to support specie payments by the Government; and simultaneously with such resumption by the Government, the national banks should also be required to redeem their issues in specie or United States notes.

Mr. WALBRIDGE submitted the following resolution, and moved its adoption:

*Resolved*, That this Convention considers it important to the general interests of the people of the whole United States, that the national Government shall now promptly exercise the constitutional right exclusively vested in it to regulate the means of trade and commerce between the American people in all sections of the country, as it has always done in reference to trade and commerce between them and foreign nations; and, that holding these opinions, the Convention hereby recognizes the propriety of Congressional action in nationalizing the railway system in the way that it has lately nationalized the telegraph system, by authorizing companies to extend lines all over the United States, wherever and whenever the public interests may require such lines, without annoyances from any local legislation, whereby speculators have so frequently controlled State legislatures on railroad questions by throwing impediments in the way of business men and capitalists, who have striven and are striving to provide better facilities at lower prices for intercommunication between the people of various regions throughout the United States.

Mr. MUNN: I move its reference to the Committee on Transportation.

Mr. WETHERILL: I hope the matter will not be referred. The Legislatures of several of the States have had the matter under consideration, and I doubt whether, in a little while, any State in our union will dare to vote against a free railroad law. Therefore, it can do no harm for us to pass a resolution of this kind. It is a popular movement, and one that will do us good. It is a movement that will benefit every one, and I hope the resolution, as offered by the gentleman from New York, will be adopted.

Mr. WALBRIDGE: I call the previous question.

Mr. BRYSON: I ask the gentleman to grant me one moment.

Mr. WALBRIDGE: With pleasure, sir.

Mr. BRYSON: I am not willing to place myself upon the record as voting for that resolution in its present shape, because it states there, in specific language, that we recognize "the constitutional right of Congress to regulate means of commerce between the States." I know of no such grant of power to Congress. I know there is a grant of power to regulate commerce, but not *the means* of commerce. I know the Constitution provides that the States shall not tax transportation between one State and another, but it does not give Congress the power to charter a road through any State; and when we asked for power to put a canal through a State, Congress could not give it, although the Government was to pay for it; they had to ask the privilege of the State of Iowa.

The question on ordering the previous question was then put, and it was lost.

Mr. BRYSON moved that the resolution be referred to the Committee on Internal Transportation.

Mr. WALBRIDGE moved to amend so as to put the resolution on its passage.

Mr. HOLTON: I may forestall that action by stating that a similar proposition, if I rightly understand the resolution, was before the Committee, and they declared, deliberately, that they did not consider it a subject pertinent to this Convention.

Mr. COVINGTON: If that is the impression of the Committee, that will probably be the action of the Convention; but I should like to see it brought to a direct vote. I think it is a very important resolution indeed, and one I should be very glad to see adopted, so far as I am concerned. I am in favor of the motion to amend.

I am very sorry to learn from one of the members of the Committee on Transportation, that a similar proposition was voted down in that Committee; and if we fail now to adopt this resolution in the Convention, that fact, going before the country, will do a great deal towards encouraging this old system of State legislation upon works of general importance and general necessity to the entire country. My friend from St. Louis referred to the power of Congress as relating to the regulation of commerce between the States, but not of the means of commerce between the States. I may be pardoned for saying to this Convention, that that gentleman is now engaged, in behalf of large Western interests, in the promotion of the means of commerce between the Western States, — for the establishment of a successful means of communication between the Ohio and Mississippi rivers; and he is engaged in a most laudable work. I should be sorry, if he, or any Western delegate who wants to see the Western lake and river navigation improved, should vote against a resolution looking to the securing of artificial means of communication in those States which are not supplied with natural means of transportation.

Mr. BRYSON: With the single remark, that I do not wish to vote for it, I will withdraw my motion to refer, and say that I am willing that it should go before Congress, leaving it to them to determine whether they have the constitutional power, and, if they have, whether they should exercise it.

Mr. NAZRO: This is a very important question, and one on which I am not prepared, at this moment, to vote; (Applause;) without expressing any opinion upon it, but in order to facilitate business, as I understand the Committee on Foreign Commerce are ready to report, I will move that the resolution be temporarily laid on the table, until that report has been acted upon.

Mr. MUNN: I would gladly, from feeling, vote for this resolution, were it not that it seems to me that every step we advance, tends to a centralization of the power of the States in Congress; and some point we must reach at which to stop, otherwise you may altogether wipe out State Legislatures, and blot out State boundaries. That is why I shall vote against the resolution.

Mr. CHAMBERLIN, of Cleveland: Mr. HOLTON is mistaken in saying that a resolution similar in character to this, was before our Committee. It may have been before a Sub-Committee, but there was none before the full Committee on Transportation. I believe we have laid it down as a rule, that all communications be referred to the appropriate Committees. I do not say that I would not vote for that resolution, but I want to examine it. It seems to me there is too much stump oratory about it. I don't want a member to come in here, when the members are impatient and anxious for their anticipated visit to the State House, and try to force a thing through the house. I hope it will be referred to a Committee.

Mr. NAZRO: At the present stage, I shall vote against it. If I could have time to look into the subject, very likely I should vote for it. If we express any opinion, I want it to be the deliberate opinion of this Convention, and not something forced upon it. Therefore, I renew my motion to lay it on the table.

Mr. BRUNOT: This resolution is one of the greatest importance. I was about to say, that it was more important to the men of this nation than was the proclamation of emancipation to the slaves of the South. I come from a State where we have been more completely in a state of slavery to a railroad company, and are now, than were those men in the hands of the planters who owned them. I want this Convention to affirm the right of the people to carry their commerce wherever they please, through this broad land. There can be no harm done by the resolution. It is simply referring the matter to Congress, with the expression of our desire for freedom of transportation through the country, and a recommendation to them to get it for us, in some wise way. I hope, sir, the resolution will be adopted without much dissent.

Mr. BRYSON: If the object in referring it to the Committee is to kill it, although I do not like the phraseology, I am decidedly opposed to the reference. Every man who has been engaged in business knows that there are monopolies which are the curse of our country to-day, and that there are States controlled by those monopolies. You cannot go to Washington without paying toll to some particular State. The National Congress has this question before them. I objected to the resolution on account of a certain expression of opinion contained in it; still, if the desired object can be reached in any way by the Congress of the United States, and these accursed monopolies can be broken down, I say, let it be done. I am not ready to stand here and say that any State shall have the power to prevent the people of my section from coming here. This is one country, and we should all have equal privileges in it; and we ought not to be obliged, in passing from one section to another, to show our passports, or pay a tariff to any particular State.

Mr. ATKINSON: It is evident, as we get into the discussion, that this is an important question, and as at present advised, I shall vote against the resolution, unless it goes to a Committee.

Mr. BISSELL, of Toledo: I hope gentlemen will refrain from entering into the discussion of the merits of this question on the motion to lay on the table, or on the motion to refer. If it is laid on the table, or referred, gentlemen can express their opinion upon it when it comes up again. I wish we could come to a vote at once, because there is a Committee ready to report now.

The motion to lay on the table was lost, and the resolution was referred to the Committee on Transportation.

Mr. ATKINSON introduced the following resolution, which was referred to the Committee on Currency and Finance:

*Resolved*, That it is inexpedient to alter the weight of the standard dollar of the United States, as such a course as proposed while being a partial repudiation of our debt would add to the confusion now existing in the minds of our people as to what constitutes a dollar.

Mr. MORGAN, of St. Louis, offered the following resolution, which was adopted:

*Resolved*, That the Boston Board of Trade be and hereby are requested to cause to be published, in pamphlet form, the proceedings of this Convention, and that the Chairman of each delegation before leaving the city, is requested to state the number of copies desired by his Association; the cost of publication to be paid by the different bodies, in proportion to the number of copies subscribed for by them.

Mr. SCHOULER, of the Massachusetts Senate, with a Committee of both branches of the Legislature, entered the hall, and announced that they had come to escort the Convention to the State House. A recess was therefore taken, to enable the Convention to visit the Legislature.

## AFTERNOON SESSION.

---

The Convention, after the reception at the State House, returned to the Board of Trade Hall, and re-assembled at four o'clock, when, on its being called to order, Mr. Tobey submitted the following report from the Committee on

## FOREIGN AND DOMESTIC COMMERCE.

The undersigned, a Committee of the National Commercial Convention, to whom was referred the subject of "the restoration of the foreign commerce of the country from its present greatly depressed condition," beg leave to report, that the limited time of the session of the Convention affords but an imperfect opportunity to present the subject referred to your Committee, with the completeness which its important and comprehensive character demands. Your Committee therefore feel constrained to deal principally with statements, many of which will be found fully substantiated by official documents from the Secretary of the Treasury of the United States.

They first would refer to that branch of his report of 1864, upon the foreign and domestic commerce of the United States, which relates to *transatlantic steam commerce.*

With such statements, together with existing facts as to the present depressed condition of commerce so painfully apparent, your Committee must rely on the Convention in a good degree to supply the irresistible inferences, and to complete the arguments as to measures which should be adopted by Congress for the immediate relief of the foreign and domestic commerce of the United States. In 1838 the British steamer Sirius made an experimental trip from England to New York, which first inaugurated ocean steam commerce between Europe and the United States. She was followed by the Great Western, which ran for several years, say from 1840 to 1846, almost alone, to New York. But transatlantic steamship trade could hardly be regarded as regularly established until it was done by the Cunard line in 1840, from Liverpool, by the way of Halifax, to Boston. A few years prior to the trip of the Sirius, in 1838, the British Government inaugurated the system of subsidies to its steam commerce, by granting large and liberal compensation for the transportation of mails from England to India by the way of Alexandria, to a line of steamers known as the Peninsular and Oriental Steam Navigation Company. For this service, which was fortnightly, your Committee are informed £230,000 sterling per annum was paid. This compensation was subsequently largely increased until it reached £400,000. The contracts having not long since expired, the Government advertised for bids, and £500,000 was *the only bid.* The British Post Office Department made its contracts with this Company, with the proviso that it should submit its accounts to Government quarterly, and if it should appear that the Company had not earned ten per cent. per annum clear of all expenses, the additional £100,000 asked for should be added.

These figures are not obtained from an official document, but are from a source regarded as authentic and reliable. It is, however, well known that England has recently renewed her subsidy to the Cunard line, and that her policy from the first has been to subsidize her ocean steam commerce to almost every part of the world, until she has covered nearly every sea and every route necessary to complete a continuous line around the globe, excepting that from San Francisco to China.

We cannot better illustrate the beneficial results to her commerce and other interests, and the corresponding disadvantage to that of the United States, than by quoting from the official report of the Secretary of the United States already referred to, which is as follows: —

"The steam marine of Great Britain is intimately related to that of the United States, so far as foreign trade is concerned. The increase of foreign shipping of all classes conducting the foreign trade of the United States is almost wholly British, and the successful lines of steamers newly established, as well as those which have at any time taken the place of American lines, are also nearly all British. The statistics of British shipping are, therefore, essential to the proper consideration of the changes in progress directly affecting American shipping.

"The first table which follows shows the tonnage of all nations entering British ports for five years to the close of 1863, the steam tonnage not being reported. The most conspicuous fact apparent in this table is the increase of the aggregate of British tonnage over that of the United States:

SUMMARY OF TONNAGE ENTERING BRITISH PORTS.

| | In 1859. | 1863. |
|---|---|---|
| British, . . . . . . . . . . . . . | 5,388,953 | 7,299,417 |
| All foreign, . . . . . . . . . . . | 3,700,597 | 3,838,529 |
| United States, . . . . . . . . . . | 1,077,948 | 692,337 |

"The increase of British is near 2,000,000 tons, while that of the United States declines 385,611 tons in five years. A still greater decline is apparent when the maximum year, 1861, is compared with 1863, the first giving a total of 1,647,076 tons, and the decline to 1863 being therefore 944,739 tons. This decline is undoubtedly due to the immense number of American vessels sold abroad in 1861, 1862 and 1863, the great majority of which were purchased by the British.

"*Thus the increase of steam vessels, which is wholly foreign, combines with the loss of the magnificent fleet of sailing ships, long the pride of the United States commerce, to expel the United States flag from the chief centres of foreign commerce.*"

Another striking illustration of the effect of steam commerce on export trade may be found in the experience of England, in the establishing a line of steamships from there to Brazil in 1851. In five years from that date the trade with that country increased three hundred per cent. Earl GREY is said to have remarked that swift letters bring back swift orders for manufactured goods. England now exports annually to Brazil thirty-two millions of dollars' worth of its products, against only ten millions imported from there, leaving a balance in favor of England of twenty-three millions. In 1859, exports from the United States to Brazil were six and a quarter millions of dollars, *nearly half of which was in flour*, and our imports from there twenty-two and a half millions of dollars, leaving a balance to be met in our settlement of exchange, and paid for in England, in gold. The products exported from the port of Boston to Brazil formerly amounted to a million of dollars, and it has now fallen to less than two hundred thousand dollars. We cite these facts to show the intimate relations between commerce and the export of the products of the country. Does it not clearly show, that facility of transportation by steam largely stimulates the exports of a country to distant markets? It is this well-devised system of subsidized steam commerce, persistently pursued by England for nearly forty years, which has transferred the great bulk of transportation of valuable merchandise, of specie, first-class passengers, and mails, from American vessels to a foreign flag; *for previous to the war, not a successful line of American steamships was running between the United States and England, and to-day the American flag is not borne across the Atlantic by a single American-built steamship.* Our diplomatic agents and Government despatches must be conveyed under a foreign flag. But while American steam commerce has thus been driven from the Atlantic by our subsidized and otherwise favored rivals, England and France, it is an important and striking fact, that American-built sailing vessels, *without Government aid in any form*, were enabled to compete with foreign sailing vessels in the carrying trade in every part of the world; taking guano from the islands of the Pacific to fertilize the soil of England, and transporting the products of China and of India directly in successful competition with British sailing vessels, into London docks. Indeed, in consequence of the high cost of constructing first-class Indiamen from wood material grown in England proper, American shipbuilders had already sold newly constructed vessels to England prior to the recent war. But the war of the rebellion changed all this. With our sailing commerce nearly chased from the ocean by confederate cruisers, aided by the unfortunate views taken by the British Government as to belligerent and neutral rights, with a depreciated currency, enhanced price of labor, material, and the cost of subsistence, to which has been added taxation on almost every article of material which enters into construction, and also on all contracts connected with shipbuilding, and tax after construction, the cost of building and employing American built vessels is far in excess of that of foreign construction, as will appear more fully in a detailed report made to the Legislature of Maine within a few weeks, to which we especially refer for carefully prepared statistical facts. In proof of the decline of our commerce, we quote from the Official Report of the Special Commissioner of Revenue, for 1866.* "Our commerce upon the high seas, at one time so potent a means of acquiring national wealth, and at the same time of exhibiting to the world a proud indication of our growing strength and spreading influence, has fallen to so low a point that, while in the year 1853 it was fifteen per cent. greater than that of Great Britain, and maintained a close competition with it up to the year 1861, it had fallen in 1864 to less than half as much, and is now, probably, not over a third. Furthermore, that while in 1860 two-thirds of our imports, and more than two-thirds of our exports, were carried in American bottoms, in 1866 nearly three-fourths of our imports, and over three-fifths of our exports, were carried in foreign bottoms. The accompanying tables furnish the data."

We are also furnished with the following statements from a member of the New York delegation, now present:

"At the present time there are in New York only thirty-six to thirty-eight American ships. Aside from those in the California trade, only four or five American vessels. Mr. C. W. FIELD stated recently, in a speech in New York, that there was not then a single American ship loading for a foreign port in New York."

---

* See page 198, to conclusion.

The first-named gentleman, who for many years has been practically engaged in foreign commerce, estimates that previous to the war he has seen in New York from one hundred and forty to one hundred and eighty American vessels at one time, and vessels of all nations, numbering perhaps six or seven hundred. He adds that before the war, seven-eighths of the sailing vessels were under the American flag. We further ask attention to the fact that Maine, in 1859, owned seven hundred and thirty-nine thousand eight hundred and forty tons of shipping; in 1866, two hundred and seventy-four thousand, four hundred and sixty-eight,—a decrease of about sixty per cent.; and what is true in this instance, is also measurably true of other ship-building portions of our country, as official reports will show.

The decline of our commerce is an admitted fact, and must be obvious to all. As to the means by which it shall be restored, different opinions doubtless exist. Your Committee, however, assume that the legislation and policy of England, which, for nearly forty years, has been undeviatingly followed, with great advantage, not only by liberal encouragement to steam commerce, but *by the remission of duties on all articles entering into the construction of her vessels of any class, and still further by allowing her vessels to be supplied with tea, coffee, sugar, and, indeed, all articles required on shipboard, by being taken out of bonded warehouse, duty free, while at the same time exactly the opposite policy has been pursued by the Government of the United States, should furnish us with a clear precedent in this matter.*

The commerce of our lakes and rivers also requires relief. Next to production in vital importance to the natural resources, lies the equally important question of cheap transportation. In proportion as the cost of building and sailing our ocean and inland commerce shall be reduced, shall we be enabled to transport the products of the soil more cheaply,—hence the immediate and direct interest of agriculture in this question. The grain of the West, especially Indian corn, must reach the hungry population of Ireland and of England, as indeed all distant markets, at a very low rate, if it be consumed by them at all. Transported over a line of nearly five thousand miles from the place of production, the cost of transportation must of necessity bear so large a proportion to that of original production, that, if it be not carried at a low rate, the crops will be worth more for fuel, and be burned in the future, as they have been in the past, under certain relative conditions of the market at home and abroad. The question of the restoration of the commerce of the country by

American built vessels, under the American flag, is emphatically, and in the highest sense, *a national one*, for it ever has been an indispensable source of national wealth.

The mercantile marine commerce of the United States has been so intimately allied to and blended with the naval power of our country, that it may be regarded as the indispensable auxiliary of the navy, as the naval history of our country will abundantly show. By our energetic and daring privateers, and by the men in the naval service drawn from our merchantmen, this country contested the assumed supremacy of England on the ocean, and wrested the sceptre from her in the war of 1812. By a similar intimate union and coöperation between the navy and our merchantmen, our coast was blockaded for more than two thousand miles during the rebellion.

We believe it is not too much to assume that the splendid achievement of the Kearsarge, the brilliant victories of FARRAGUT at New Orleans and Mobile, of ROGERS at Savannah, of PORTER at Fort Fisher, and others equally worthy of mention, could not have been accomplished without the hardy sons of the ocean taken from our merchant ships, and previously educated in the merchant service. The tens of thousands of seamen drawn from the New England States to recruit the navy, are in proof of the truth of this position. The admission of foreign-built vessels to American registry, as proposed by a few persons, would be the last blow to prostrate American shipping interests still more; and indirectly, yet effectually, render our navy dependent in part on foreign mechanical industry and material. By such a transfer of industry to the workshops and shipyards of Europe, as must result from the *purchase of foreign-built vessels*, the gold of our treasury must be transferred in payment for them to the same nation which so largely coöperated in the work of *destroying American shipping;* capital and labor hitherto employed here in construction of vessels and steamers must be dispersed, and when it shall be again necessary to extemporize a navy and a fleet of transports, we shall have the privilege of drawing on English workshops, which, under her construction of neutrality, may possibly be closed to us. But the proposition of thus denationalizing American shipping commerce appears so unpatriotic, as well as unwise, that we forbear to expend argument upon it.

As an *economical measure* to the Government, can it be doubted that the mercantile marine, with the men and workshops sustained by private capital, are a cheaper resource to the navy to meet an emergency, than mammoth establishments, and immense naval fleets, adequate to the possible and sudden exigencies of the Government, kept up at great cost to the Treasury? As the people do not believe in large standing armies in time of peace, neither do they wish to be taxed to keep up large naval establishments in time of peace, with little or no commerce to protect. The high position of the United States as a naval power, in comparison with England and France, has been acquired by the coöperation and aid of maritime commerce; it can only be sustained in the future by a similar intimate relation and alliance.

The Honorable Secretary of the Navy, in his able report, acknowledges the important services rendered by our merchant marine in the following language: "The position and influence of a nation among the great commercial and maritime powers of the world are, *to a great extent, dependent on its naval ability*," and adds, "it has contributed much in aiding and bringing to successful issue a series of naval enterprises and achievements wholly without precedent or parallel."

Your Committee forbear to add further important considerations, for want of the necessary time; but they trust, in view of what has already been stated thus imperfectly, that this report will be as unanimously adopted by the Convention as it has been in the Committee, and they earnestly urge the adoption, also, of the following resolution:

*Resolved*, That this Convention respectfully and earnestly urge on the Congress of the United States the enactment of such measures of relief to the foreign and domestic commerce of the United States as shall enable us to compete with the commerce of other nations on the ocean, and thereby permit the promoters of our merchant marine to regain for our country her proud position on the high seas, from which she has been driven by the late war of rebellion.

Mr. Tobey: In submitting this report and resolution, (which I am very much gratified to say were unanimously adopted by the gentlemen who were present, and which I hope will commend themselves to the unanimous approval of the Convention, for it does seem to me that the matter has been placed on such broad, national ground, that no one can dissent,) I beg leave to say a very few words, for which I presume myself alone to be responsible, by no means desiring to commit thereby any other member of the Committee in the slightest degree. Some of my remarks may support the report; others may be a little more definite than the report is, in terms.

In the first place, I disclaim here, in Washington, and everywhere else, the idea of coming forward, in this hour of the financial embarrassment of our Government, to ask it to put its hand into the treasury to protect a special interest, or to have anything to do with what I call class legislation. I have recently said to members of Congress, and I say here, if the relief we ask cannot be obtained consistently with all the other great interests of the nation, and equally for the benefit of the West and the East, the North and the South, I beg that no relief may be granted; for, first and foremost of all, I am prepared, as always, to stand by the best interests of the Government, and of the whole people.

And now, sir, I feel that I should do injustice to this occasion, and to this Convention, if I should fail to recognize the cordial sympathy and accord which we of the East have received upon this question, from the gentlemen of the West. We have a right to expect of Eastern men, who are familiar with commerce, that they will give their aid to this great interest which they have studied, and with which they are well acquainted; but the support of gentlemen from the West must be on national grounds, and not because of any particular acquaintance with the subject. I am happy to be able to state, that I received from the Postmaster-General of the United States,—a Western man as he is, coming from Wisconsin,—the most emphatic assurances of support in views which I had the honor to lay before him; and, more than that, I think I do not violate the confidence of private conversation in repeating what he said to me: "I have tried to impress upon Congress the idea that they had better risk twenty-five millions in the ocean, than not restore the commerce of the United States." That remark has the right ring to it, whether coming from the West, or from anywhere else. I think we have a right to congratulate ourselves that this is the sentiment of very many of our Western friends. Of course they do not all take the same view. It is too much to expect entire unanimity upon such a subject; but when I remember that the blood of the sons of the West and of the East flowed and mingled together, in the conflicts of the late war, I cannot believe that those sons of the West have any less regard for, or interest in, the flag of our country, than the sons of the East, whether it floats from the Alleghanies or beyond them, or in the remotest corners of the globe. I believe that these gentlemen, as they go to distant ports, and see the emblem of our nationality thrown to the breeze, feel their hearts beat as warmly in the sight of that flag, as do those from our Eastern coast; and for that reason I think we have a right to presume that their patriotism will prompt them to encourage Congress to grant such relief, in general terms, as we speak of here, as shall very speedily restore the flag of the United States to its former position upon the ocean. Such a state of things as now exists, has not been known from the foundation of the Government. Not a steamship, to day, carrying our flag across the Atlantic; and only six or eight American ships lying in the port of New York, outside of the coasting trade, and the California trade! And yet we claim to be the peer of France or of England on the ocean! In 1812, England claimed naval supremacy, and we disputed that claim successfully. Now, I would like to inquire if she is not to-day the mistress of the seas, commercially; and I would like to ask my fellow-countrymen if that is not a painful fact? And if that nation is the mistress of the seas commercially, how far is she from being mistress of the seas as a naval power? We have kept our position with England and France as one of the first naval powers in the world, because we have been able to extemporize a few vessels upon our coast, and have defended our firesides and homes by the brilliant exploits of the navy as well as of the army. It seems to me we can well afford to undertake, in this most economical way, to assist and strengthen the navy of the United States by promoting and sustaining the commerce of the United States. (Applause.)

Mr. ATKINSON: At the risk of being considered an otherwise-minded man, I must say that I should wrong myself, if, while I rise to second the resolution, I did not point out that this report is one limited to foreign transportation, rather than a report upon foreign commerce. I have not a dictionary at hand, but I should define "foreign commerce" to mean, the exchange of commodities with other nations, and not simply the transportation of them; and while the latter is a very large and a very important interest, it is a subordinate one, and I cannot but regret that the report is limited to that subordinate portion of the question.

Now, sir, we have assembled here partly for the purpose of asking an abatement of taxation, and other Conventions have been held for the same purpose; but it seems to me that we, as well as others, work round and round, and always avoid the root of the matter. We confine ourselves to the question of the internal taxes, and ask an abatement of them, mainly upon the ground that our manufactures will be ruined, unless the relief is granted; but this position is not tenable, and the reason assigned is not one which can be claimed to give due cause for the request. It is of little consequence to the country whether I am ruined, or you, or you; and Congress has no right to legislate for our especial protection. Neither is it true that heavy taxes will cause any general disaster to manufacturers as a body. It will ruin the weaker or more unskilful portion in any particular branch, but the men with strong backs and large capital will tide over the temporary depression; the business will then become concentrated in the hands of a few, who will add the tax to the cost of their product, and will charge a good round additional profit for the service rendered in collecting it.

The demand for economy should be made in the name of consumers and not of manufacturers, and we should ask Congress to reduce taxation in order that we may increase production and in order that there may be a great consumption from the abundance and cheapness of commodities.

Having thus met the question of internal taxation, then comes the very question which it is evident this Convention means to avoid, if it can—namely, the revision of the tariff. We have passed a resolution which seems to me, (permit me to say,) an absurd and utterly ridiculous one, in which we have declared that we desire Congress to regulate the balance of trade. I am afraid it will make us a laughing-stock. Trade regulates itself; I defy Congress or anybody else to regulate it. The balance of trade will settle itself, whatever laws you pass. The real fact is just here, that we place all the obstacles in the way of foreign commerce that we know how to, and then we dogmatize and seek to find some empirical method to get relief. There will be no relief to the foreign commerce of this country until our legislators undertake a new adjustment of the revenue laws, whether these relate to internal taxation or to the collection of duties; and in such re-adjustment, consider only how they shall get the necessary revenue with the least injury to the productive power of the people, and attempt nothing else. That is the one and only duty that should be urged upon them. We ought not to ask rebate of duties nor drawback for taxes, nor subsidies, nor bounties, but simply to demand that Congress shall let the balance of trade alone and not muddle their brains or any one's else by trying to regulate it; and should so legislate for the collection of revenue as to leave commerce as free as the necessity of the revenue will permit. One has well said, that in matters of trade the word "foreign" has no place, and should be expunged from the commercial dictionary.

So long as the laws of the United States are to be made to foster and protect and rear great iron babies with clay feet, which, the bigger they grow, the more Government pap and artificial support they want, so long may foreign commerce ask to be relieved by this or that empirical method, and so long will it get no relief.

That would have been the ground that I should have taken as the representative of foreign commerce, and it is the ground I would like to have seen taken by this Convention. And I say this as a manufacturer. Not that I advocate the separate adjustment of duties on my particular interests, upon one theory or another. We all stand or fall together. The cost of my manufactures, the cost of all the products of labor is raised because the taxes, whether internal or external, diffuse themselves throughout the community, and raise the general cost of all production. And whatever may be my theory, I am bound, sir, to claim *protection*, in the very most vicious sense of that word, to my particular interest, so long as the general policy of the country is in that direction. So long as there are taxes and duties upon iron, taxes and duties upon fuel, taxes and duties upon power, taxes and duties upon tools, taxes and duties on provisions, taxes on processes instead of results, taxes on the necessities and comforts of the people, we cannot compete with foreign manufacturers, and we must ask duties for protection on cotton cloth and everything else imported from abroad that competes with our manufactures. But let this question be taken up on its broad ground, let the legislation of the country be directed to getting the revenue with the least injury to the productive power of the people, and then we can stand upon a logical and unitary system, and demand its enactment by Congress. Have done with this piecemeal, botched-up, empirical legislation! And, sir, in order that we may have done with it, — before any adjustment of taxes or tariff on foreign commerce, or anything else, let us try to find out, as I have said in connection with another matter, *what a dollar really is.* Before we undertake to adopt an uniform system of measures or weights, let us try to get back to a uniform standard of value. Let us get back to the use of real instead of mock money. The adjustment of measures of bulk and weight and length upon an uniform principle is of no effect and will promote neither justice, truth nor honesty, if the standard of value which dominates all exchanges is false and fluctuating, as our inconvertible paper money is.

Of what consequence is it if your yardstick is made of india rubber, and measures thirty-two inches on a cold day, and on a hot day measures thirty-six inches, if your money fluctuates in the same manner, making all trade gambling or speculation — speculation in the bad sense? Why, sir, until we have an uniform standard of value, which dominates all other measures, all your adjustments of measures of bulk and weights go for nothing. This cheat, this moth, which is picking the pockets of the people, does away with the benefit of your adjustment of weights and measures. What would any gentleman here give to be guaranteed, for the ensuing year, against the risk of loss in his business by reason of the fluctuations in the relation of paper to gold? Does anybody say less than one per cent? I have not found any merchant in Boston who says less than one per cent.; they mostly say five or six. What amount of tax does that indicate? If it is worth one per cent., all will agree that in the long run the one per cent. gets into the cost of production or the exchange of all commodities. All insurance gets into cost; all risks are covered, in the long run, because no business will continue in which all risks are not paid for. Now, sir, the license tax, or tax of one-tenth of one per cent. assessed by the United States Government on sales, was paid last year, on an aggregate of sales of commodities amounting to between eleven and thirteen thousand millions of dollars. One per cent. on that sum represents a tax of from one hundred and ten to one hundred and thirty millions of dollars per annum, imposed upon the people in the exact proportion of their consumption of every article, whether of necessity, comfort or luxury; and therefore taken out of the pockets of the hard-working laborers; for, sir, seven, eight or nine out of every ten in this country are men who receive wages or fixed salaries, and not men who work by means of an accumulated surplus of capital; and presently the instinct of the people, if not their reason, will cause them to rise and overthrow or bottle up, the men who advocate the continued use of this false, counterfeit mock-money which we now are forced by law to use.

I say that it is worth one per cent. to be guaranteed against the risk of loss from the fluctuation in value of our paper money, and that this amounts to a tax upon consumers of one hundred and ten millions of dollars to one hundred and thirty millions of dollars per annum. It may be asked, who gets this sum? and I say, the superfluous middle men who produce nothing, — the stock and gold speculators, — the many shrewd men who know how to take advantage of these fluctuations and who accumulate fortunes for which the lifetime of man would not be long enough, were it not for such fluctuations. Has not the marked feature of the past few years been the numerous instances of enormous accumulation of private fortune, while the wealth of the nation was being depleted? Is not this the era of extravagance, — of vulgar wasteful expenditure? I say, sir, that this false money is the tool by which the labor of the country is forced to contribute to maintain this speculation, this enormous and unhealthy accumulation of wealth in few hands, and this wasteful extravagance, and it is this one per cent. guaranty or tax amounting to over one hundred millions a year, which is the fund thus contributed by the people.

I wish that this Convention may be brought to a fair and square vote, by tellers, upon this question; and had I not expected a minority report from the Committee on Taxation, I should have insisted, this morning, upon a division, and a count by tellers upon that question, with regard to the balance of trade. I wish this Convention could be brought, and I hope it yet may be, to a vote, delegation by delegation, upon the question, "Upon what principles shall the laws for the assessment of revenue be devised?" I am afraid it is too late now; but I should have been unwilling to come into this Convention without taking my stand upon the principles I have indicated, and which I call the broad and national ground.

Mr. TOBEY: I very much regret that any one of my colleagues should manifest even the semblance of a disagreement with the principles now before this body, which are of the most general and patriotic character; and I especially regret that the objections should come from one whom I know has always been ready to do everything necessary for the support of the Government.

Mr. ATKINSON: I did not object to the principles of the report. On the contrary, I seconded the motion to adopt the report.

Mr. TOBEY: So far as Congress is concerned, it seems to me that the report covers the whole ground. The efforts of the manufacturers of the country, including New England, to obtain some relief from Congress for their branch of industry, do not indicate the slightest disposition to relieve commerce in any way; and it must be remembered (and I state it without fear of contradiction) that the effort made last spring for the relief of commerce, was the first effort ever made in the history of this Government in that behalf. That was the first time the owners of the commerce of the country were ever found knocking at the doors of Congress for assistance, except for steam commerce. As the report expressly declares, our ocean commerce, without any aid from the Government, has contended by its enterprise, all the world over, with that of other countries, until the war of the rebellion; and now, after that it has defended our homes and firesides,—but for that, sir, the spindles of my friend [Mr. ATKINSON] would have stood motionless,—I am confident that no man can say one word against relief to the commerce of the country, provided it be given in the right time, and in the right way, by the Congress of the United States, as in the interest of the nation, and not for the protection of commerce alone. I wish to call particular attention to the fact, that while the manufacturing interests, embracing a wide and ample range,—from the cotton and woollen manufacturers, to the manufacturers of cigars and whiskey,—are now in Washington, asking for relief, the representatives of commerce present themselves now, for the first time, and only in consequence of the effects of the rebellion. I feel confident that this intelligent National Convention will support so broad and patriotic a resolution as this; and I trust it will be endorsed unanimously, as it was in Committee; the Committee being constituted of gentlemen from almost every State, twenty-seven in number, and fifteen or seventeen of them being present during our deliberations.

Mr. HICHBORN, of Maine: Mr. Chairman, I have only a single remark to make in support of the resolution. The gentleman from Boston will pardon me for suggesting that I think history would be untrue to herself if she did not record the fact, that after a nation has passed through such a crisis as we have passed through, its laws require readjustment; and I hope that that gentleman, and others, in the room of complaining here of the condition of things, will make up their minds to be thankful that we are no worse off, and that they will memorialize Congress, not only in relation to commerce, but to every other interest, to pursue that course which is just to the interests of the whole country. We cannot possibly satisfy ourselves, or anybody else, simply by complaining.

I understand that this Convention was called very largely from the industrial interests of the country, to come up here and say what we all need in our individual capacities, as well as for the common good of the whole country. If that had not been the case, I cannot think it would have been wise for us to come here. When the gentleman says that other interests besides that of commerce require relief, I have no doubt that it is so; but if he complains that the manufacturing interest is not protected, what shall the man say who is connected with foreign commerce? If two-thirds or three-quarters of the manufacturer's spindles do not revolve, because he has not been helped, it is a source of regret; but our foreign commerce has been wrested from us, and we ask only that Congress will enact such measures as will afford relief. We take it for granted, that the Congress of the United States, when you, coming from every part of the country, shall ask them to give relief, will seek the method themselves, and that they are abundantly competent to do so. We in the shipbuilding interest have accepted the condition of things growing out of the war. We went as boldly for the war as any other class, and suffered, in this specific matter, more than any other interest in the country. But of this alone we do not complain; we only ask that you, in a spirit of generosity, will petition Congress to grant some relief, in their own way, and in accordance with their own views, to a great and suffering branch of national industry.

Mr. Atkinson: I trust I may not be considered as having opposed the report and resolution of the Committee. It seemed to me the last opportunity that I might have to make rather a broad speech, and therefore I took it. I do not wish to oppose, but I second the report and resolution.

Mr. Ropes, of Boston: Mr. President, I will not detain the Convention more than two minutes. I merely wish to state a fact, which the Chairman of the Committee would have stated if it had been in his mind while speaking. A friend on my left has just stated to me, that the postages on letters between this country and Europe amount to two and a half millions a year. That amount, of course, is available either as a remuneration for carrying the mails, or, if you please to call it so, as a subsidy to the mail steamers. I was once a passenger on one of the Cunard steamers, and took occasion to tell the captain that his company was receiving a large subsidy from the British Government. He replied at once, "We are willing to sail our steamers without subsidy, provided we are allowed to charge eightpence (that is, sixteen cents of what should be our coinage,) for every letter carried." On those terms, they would be happy to carry the mails, without receiving one farthing more from the government.

The question was then put, and the report and resolution were adopted unanimously, amid general applause.

Mr. Nazro moved that a copy of the resolution, signed by the officers of the Convention, be sent to every member of Congress.

Mr. Tatham, of Philadelphia: I was going to ask if the report is not sufficiently important to be addressed in the form of a memorial to Congress. I think in that way it would be spread more fully before the country.

Mr. Nazro adopted the suggestion of the gentleman from Philadelphia, and the motion passed in that form.

A communication was read from Mr. RICHARDSON, of the Stonington line, extending an invitation to the members of the Convention to travel by that route to New York.

Mr. CULVER, of Chicago, offered the following resolutions:

*Resolved*, That while we would not abandon the general principle of taxation, we would respectfully suggest to Congress a remission of duties paid on all material of foreign production entering into the construction of steamships and sailing vessels; and a drawback on all material of domestic manufacture used in the building of such ships and vessels equal in amount to what would have been the duties, if said material had been imported; believing that this return, if granted, would enable a crippled industry to place itself in such a position of restored activity as to greatly increase the wealth of the country, and thereby the volume of its revenues.

*Resolved*, That we would recommend that the period of time for which this remission of imposts and of internal duties be guaranteed, be limited to the return of the country to a specie basis, and not more than ten years.

*Resolved*, That in our judgment the internal revenue tax on the gross receipts of steamers, owned by citizens of the United States and sailing under our flag, should be repealed.

Mr. STRANAHAN moved their reference to the Committee on Foreign Commerce.

Mr. HOSEA, of Cincinnati: As a member of that Committee, which has devoted a great deal of labor to this matter, and brought in a report which covers the whole ground, it seems to me it would be most appropriate to lay them on the table.

The resolutions were so disposed of.

An invitation from the Hon. THOMAS RUSSELL, Collector of the Port of Boston, was read, tendering to the Convention the use of a steam-tug, to visit the Navy Yard, and other places of interest in the harbor.

A communication was read from Mr. STEARNS, President of the Old Colony Railroad, tendering to the members of the Convention a free passage home over that line, to New York.

Mr. FRALEY submitted the following report, from the Committee on

## CURRENCY AND FINANCE.

The Committee to whom were referred the subjects of Currency and Finance, beg leave to report the following resolutions, and recommend their adoption by the Convention:

*Resolved*, That as the existing indebtedness of the nation and of individuals, and the exchangeable values of all property have been practically adjusted to the amount of currency now in circulation, there should not at present be any expansion or contraction thereof, but that the legal tender currency should be gradually, but steadily, approximated to the specie standard, by the funding thereof, on and after the first of January, 1869, in amounts not exceeding three millions of dollars per month.

*Resolved*, That the national honor and good faith alike require that the Government should not avail itself of the right to pay off the five-twenty bonds until by a general resumption of specie payments the public debt, as it matures, can be paid in specie or its equivalent.

*Resolved*, That the inequality in the distribution of the national bank currency between the different sections of the country requires some action on the part of Congress.

*Resolved*, That to this end, the following change in the national banking law be recommended to Congress: —

That any persons, proposing to form a new bank, may present to the Comptroller of the Currency in national bank bills, of any banks having a circulation of more than sixty per cent. of the capital of such bank, the amount proposed as capital of the new bank, which the Comptroller shall redeem in greenbacks. Thereupon the Comptroller shall cancel such bills and return them to each bank of issue for redemption, returning to such bank the bonds pledged as security, whenever a sufficient amount of bills shall have been cancelled to liberate one or more bonds. And that, thereupon, the persons presenting such bank bills shall be entitled, upon lodging bonds, and otherwise complying with the provisions of the law, to form a new bank, and receive from the Comptroller an issue of currency not exceeding sixty per cent. of its capital.

*Provided*, That no national bank currency shall be issued to any new bank in any State in which the amount of national bank currency already issued to the banks of such State shall bear a greater proportion to three hundred millions of dollars than the representative population of such State shall bear to the representative population of the country; and,

*Provided, further*, That the aggregate amount of currency issued to the national banks shall in no case exceed three hundred millions of dollars, until such time as the banks shall have resumed specie payments.

*Resolved*, That a system of free national banking can be safely allowed so soon as bank notes are payable and paid, on demand, in coin, and not before.

*Resolved*, That it be recommended to the Congress of the United States to enact a law authorizing contracts to be made in writing, which shall be payable in gold or silver coin, and securing the specific performance of such contracts.

*Resolved*, That the Congress of the United States should by law supersede the usury laws of the several States, and make seven per cent. per annum, the uniform rate of interest, when no contract has been made for any other rate, and authorizing contracts to be made in writing for the use of money at any rate of interest upon which parties, able and willing to contract therefor, may agree.

Mr. FRALEY: I would state, in presenting this report, that it has not been unanimously agreed to by the Committee, but agreed to by a large majority of the Committee as a whole. We have all (I speak for those who have concurred in the report) given up many of the ideas with which we came into the presence of this Convention. Our individual views have been modified by contact with each other, and we have presented a scheme which appears to us to unite, as far as it is possible to unite, the judgment of the Committee upon these several questions. I understand that my friend from Detroit, (Mr. FIELD,) who does not concur in this report, but who was cut off from presenting the views of the minority by a motion that the Committee rise and report to this Convention, will probably present the views entertained by himself and the minority of the Committee; and after he has done so, I propose that the Convention shall proceed to the consideration of the resolutions reported by the Committee; and after hearing what may be urged against them, if it should be your pleasure, I will endeavor to defend the propositions as presented, and ask the concurrence of the Convention in them as a whole. (Applause.)

Mr. BABCOCK, of New York: I think the report a very able one, and I am satisfied to sustain it. I move its acceptance.

Carried.

Mr. FIELD: Dissenting from the views presented by the majority of the Committee, I beg leave to offer the following as a substitute:—

*Resolved*, That with the view to stimulate domestic production, to secure the resumption of specie payments in a healthy and permanent shape, the duties on importations of foreign manufactures should be so adjusted as to keep the balance of trade with foreign nations in favor of the United States.

*Resolved*, That in the present abnormal condition of our trade with other nations, specie payments should not be attempted until the precious metals from our rich mines accumulate so as to make resumption an easy matter, and until labor, the chief source of national wealth, shall restore harmony not only to foreign and domestic trade, but health and stability to the national finances.

*Resolved*, That while this Convention is opposed to any expansion or increase of the public debt, we are in favor of the contraction of compound interest notes, three per cent. certificates, temporary loan and certificates of indebtedness bearing interest, and payable in lawful money, amounting on the first of January to $83,047,409, and the issue of plain greenbacks in lieu thereof, but without increasing the aggregate public indebtedness or circulating medium.

*Resolved*, That the payment of no part of the principal of the public debt should be made in the present unsettled state of affairs, and not until all the States of the Union are in a financial and industrial condition to pay their due share, and then its reduction should be slow, commencing with the payment of a small sum annually, and gradually increasing the amount with the increase of population and wealth of the country.

*Resolved*, That the national banking act should be amended so as to make it a free banking law instead of a monopoly.

Mr. SLOANE moved the adoption of the report of the majority.

Mr. WARD, of Detroit: Before that motion is put, I wish to make one remark. I object to the report, on the ground that it contemplates a considerable reduction of the circulating medium and currency of the country; although, as a whole, I like the report very well. The people of the West are not in a condition, nor are they willing, to have the currency reduced below what it is now; and I think a very large proportion of the members present will agree with me, that the universal sentiment is, that they are not willing to have any further immediate contraction of the currency.

Mr. BUZBY, of Philadelphia: I presume that the Convention is pretty well fatigued with the amount of its labor, and would naturally like to adjourn; but inasmuch as our temporary President has told us that this currency question strikes at the very roots of society, it is proper that we should give some attention to the matter. There is one point on which I wish at this time to speak, and that is in reference to a free banking law, established by the nation. I wish in some way to get this matter in here, because many Western members are very deeply interested in it, with many of us at the East; but in the disposition that is manifested to despatch the whole thing, I do not exactly see clearly my way. If the Chairman of the Committee would accord me the right to present a motion in connection with this subject, of a national free banking law, I think I could get along. I will take it for granted that I have permission, and will offer one accordingly. I offer this resolution as an amendment to the substitute:

*Resolved*, That this Convention recommends to the Congress of the United States the adoption of a free banking law, under whose provisions the circulation of the banks should be based upon national securities; the number of banks, the amount of banking capital, and their distribution throughout the country, to be regulated by the natural law of supply and demand. The details of the system to be similar to those controlling the administration of existing national banks, with such improvements as experience has shown to be advisable.

Mr. President, many of us favor the adoption of a measure of this kind, and desire to have this Convention recommend its adoption by Congress, because this seems to be the only natural, logical, and true basis on which to place the banking system of the country. We believe that the banking business should be as free as any other business; that if banks of issue and circulation be good for one part of the country, they are good for another; that so long as, by the distribution of the existing national banks, the East and the seaboard have the lion's share, it is nothing more than right that Pennsylvania, the Middle States, and the West, should enjoy equal advantages. If there is anything utterly idle in the world upon the subject of finance, it is for any body of men to attempt to prescribe, at any time, the amount of currency that should be used in a country. As well might a man undertake to dictate to me how much money I should use in my business. We are not children. We feel able to be trusted with money, and we ask that we may be. Badly as we might manage it, it is impossible but that it would be managed infinitely worse, if Congress should undertake to manage the matter for us.

If banks and banking are an advantage to the public, the West is as much entitled to their use as the East. In lieu of a free banking law for the whole nation, it has been proposed to remove bank capital and circulation from quarters where they are supposed to be in excess, to others where they are deficient, without disturbing the existing gross amount of either. I do not believe that any portion of the country would cheerfully submit, under any circumstances, to be deprived of capital, and the machinery of circulation, for the benefit of another portion. Let the East keep what it has, and permit the Middle States and the West to supply themselves, by creating banks and circulation under a general law to be passed by Congress. This would leave the whole matter to be regulated thereafter by the natural law of supply and demand.

It is time that the miserable quackery practised by Congress in pretending to state, year by year, what amount of currency is needed by the country, should come to an end, and be left to a broader and wiser solution by the people at large. For this purpose a national free banking law should be enacted.

Only two objections to such a law are urged: First, we are told there will be too many banks; but banks cannot be established without capital. Competition would lessen their profits, and number, as it does, other business. This would be a sufficient restraint. Second, it is said the circulation of paper money would be inordinately increased, by a free banking law. The reply to this assertion is, that you cannot place in the channels of business more circulating medium than they can receive.

Let me illustrate this remark by quoting an article from the *New York Tribune*, to the following effect: "In 1861, Secretary Chase estimated the whole amount of our currency in circulation at four hundred and seventy-seven million dollars. The report of the Comptroller of the Currency for October, 1867, gives the total currency then circulating as four hundred and seventy-one million dollars.

Thus it is seen, that our active circulation does not exceed five hundred million dollars; but this does not prevent gentlemen from asserting that our paper circulation now amounts to one billion five hundred million dollars. They make this huge amount by pressing into service every possible form of our national debt, including bank deposits, etc. The Comptroller of the Currency, however, does not figure as they do.

Let us, then, decide in favor of a free banking law, which will heal all jealousies and disputes between different sections and enable them all to use their energies successfully in promoting the welfare of the entire country. I propose my resolution as a substitute for that part of the majority report which relates to this subject.

Mr. Ropes, of Boston: Is the resolution before the Convention?

The President: No, sir; the question is on the adoption of the substitute. The Chair understood that the gentleman was offering this as an amendment to the substitute; but he just informed the Convention that he would offer it as an amendment to the original report. The question, therefore, is on the adoption of the substitute offered by the gentleman from Detroit.

Mr. Fort, of Oswego: I am not in favor of the substitute offered by the gentleman from Detroit, neither am I wholly in favor of the majority report. We all seem to be in favor of a free banking law. It appears to me that the difficulty in the matter of the currency lies just here,—that we are endeavoring to tell this country just how much currency they want, and how much they don't want; and any one acquainted with the business affairs of our nation, knows that at some seasons of the year, when produce is being moved, we require much more than at others. Let any man establish a bank where he finds a place where the people are willing to use his bank; let him put by public securities for every dollar he issues; and let him, whenever his circulation is presented at his counter, or at his redeeming agent's, redeem it in currency; and then, if the business men of the East do not want our bills when we send them on, let them send them back to us, and make us take care of them; and when we get out too many bills,—more than are required,—we will lock them up in our vaults.

I have been connected with banking institutions in the State of New York. Before this national banking system was in vogue, we had a free banking law, and, before the suspension of specie payments, we were obliged to redeem our bills in coin at our counter, and through our redeeming agents in New York. The result was, when our redeeming agents sent home our bills faster than we cared to use them or redeem them, we locked them up in our vaults; and at some seasons, we had almost our entire circulation locked up; and at other seasons, when the produce was moving, and people wanted money, it was all out. Make your national banking law on the same principle; compel the banks to redeem, not only at their own counter, but at points that shall be designated in the law; then let them put all the bills afloat they can; and when the people do not want them, let them send them home, and the banks will be glad to lock them up.

The question was then taken on the substitute, and it was rejected.

Mr. BUZBY moved that the report of the Committee be considered by sections; but the motion was lost.

Mr. FRALEY: Permit me to say that it is competent for any gentleman to call for the division of any question, before a legislative body, which is susceptible of a division. There are five or six distinct propositions in the report of the Committee; and any gentleman who desires to have the question taken upon each proposition, has a right to call for it, under general parliamentary law. I hope the Convention will proceed to the consideration of the report by sections; that gentlemen who desire to be heard on the several subjects connected with the report, shall be heard; and I would propose, after giving full opportunity for debate upon them, at eleven o'clock to-morrow morning to close the debate, and that then the question shall be finally put.

Mr. BUZBY: I made the motion simply to save time, in order that, having considered this matter of free banking, we might proceed with it. I am obliged to my colleague (Mr. FRALEY) for the suggestion that it is competent for me to call for a division of the question, and I propose that we proceed with the consideration of the question of a free banking law; I move, therefore, that we strike out all after the word "resolve," in the fourth resolution, and substitute the language which I have placed in the hands of the Secretary.

Mr. VERMILYE, of New York: I move the adoption of the first resolution.

Mr. Turpin, of Chicago: I move to erase from the first resolution all after the word "thereof."

Mr. Vermilye: That is just the important part of it; and I hope the gentleman's motion will not prevail.

Mr. Chamberlain, of Albany: I move that the business before the Convention be postponed, that we adjourn until to-morrow morning at ten o'clock, and that in the meantime this report be printed upon slips, for the use of the members. I am not prepared to vote upon it until I can have it before me in that shape.

Mr. Britton: These are very important propositions. It is impossible for the Convention, at present, to understand precisely what is contained in the report. It should be printed, by all means. We have ample time for it. The business of the Convention will be facilitated by now passing over this report, and having it printed, so that each member may, to-morrow morning, understand what it contains. I second the motion.

Mr. Stranahan: I move that we adjourn to to-morrow morning, at ten o'clock, with the understanding that the question shall be taken upon the report of the Committee, as a whole, at twelve o'clock to-morrow.

Mr. Forsyth, of Troy: I hope no such motion will prevail.

Mr. Ropes: I hope so, too.

Mr. Forsyth: I do not see, for my part, why we cannot proceed now with business. I live only two hundred miles from here, and it would make no difference to me if we should adjourn over until Monday morning, so that I might go home, as the members of the New York Legislature do; but there are gentlemen here who cannot stay all the week to dispose of the report of this Committee, and why can we not take a vote upon it now?

Mr. Stranahan: With the leave of the house, I will withdraw my motion, and move that we pass over this business. I understand there are some other matters to be brought before the Convention. My object was simply to enable the members to vote understandingly upon the report.

The motion to postpone and print was carried.

Mr. Stevens, of New York, offered the following resolution, which was adopted:

*Resolved*, That this Convention, in view of the bill now before Congress, proposing a reduction of the value of the American dollar to that of the five franc piece of France, respectfully urge the impropriety of such action, without a limitation which will maintain the integrity of existing contracts.

Mr. NELSON, of Chicago: I call for the report of the Committee to whom was referred the resolution of Mr. WALBRIDGE.

Mr. HOLTON: I suppose I hold in my hand the report to which the gentleman refers. Before reading it, I beg to say, what I think is true of a majority of the Committee, (for there is to be a minority report,) that they deeply sympathized with the gentleman's proposition, in many aspects in which they viewed it; but the more they looked at it, and the longer they looked at it, the more clearly did they come to the conclusion which I shall presently state. I wish, before that, to disabuse the Convention of a wrong impression which they may entertain from a remark that I made, that I thought the Committee had considered the subject matter contained in this resolution. I find that I was under a misapprehension; that the Committee had not considered any of the material points embraced therein, and that they were therefore entirely unprejudiced.

The Committee beg leave to report, as follows:

The Committee to whom was referred the resolution introduced by the Hon. HIRAM WALBRIDGE, having duly considered the same, recommend its indefinite postponement, and ask to be discharged from its further consideration.

The report was accepted.

Mr. BRYSON: In behalf of a minority of the Committee, I present a report in the following resolution, and I move its adoption as a substitute:

*Resolved*, That this Convention do hereby respectfully request the national Congress to exercise such power as is conferred upon it by the Constitution to regulate the commerce between the different States, so that the monopolies of through railroad lines shall not be permitted to prevent the construction of through lines for the general benefit; and that no discrimination shall be made against through travel or commerce.

Mr. WETHERILL: I rise to a point of order in regard to the minority report. A resolution, presented by a gentleman, was referred to the Transportation Committee; the minority report is not a report upon the original resolution, but a separate and distinct resolution, offered in its stead.

The PRESIDENT: The Chair thinks the gentleman's point of order is not well taken.

Mr. BRYSON: Allow me to say, that I read this resolution before the Committee. They considered that it embraced the subjects to which the original resolution related; but as the majority were opposed to passing it, and were in favor of the report, which has been presented by the Chairman, they unanimously consented that this might be offered to the house in order that it might be passed upon here.

Mr. WALBRIDGE: I am willing to accept the resolution as a substitute for the one offered by me, and second its adoption.

Mr. NAZRO: I hope the resolution will not pass. It raises a very serious constitutional question. I think many gentlemen have grave doubts whether Congress has the constitutional right to take the action contemplated by the resolution, and I, as one member of this Convention, am very desirous that we should ask nothing of Congress that is not clearly constitutional; I hope, therefore, that the resolution, in that form, prejudging the matter, and telling Congress that it is constitutional for them to enact such a law, will not pass.

Mr. MUNN: Bear with me one moment. I may be a little heavy, but I will not be long. I am opposed to the resolution, upon the same ground that I stated previously. I do not think myself that it is constitutional, though I am not a constitutional lawyer. It is centralizing power too much in the General Government. If the States of New York and Pennsylvania are willing to sink their sovereignty for the sake of getting rid of New Jersey, the State of Illinois is not willing to do it.

Mr. BRYSON: I ask for two or three minutes to explain. [Calls of "Question," "Question."]

Mr. NELSON: While I would deprecate the centralization of power in Congress equally with my friend, I would as strongly deprecate the revival of the extreme State rights doctrine. We have suffered somewhat, I think, from that source. I think there is quite as much danger of our suffering, as was mentioned this morning, in consequence of some little territory, accidentally stuck in here and there, granting a monopoly to some railroad, and the whole country made to endure it; and inasmuch as this resolution does not pretend to define the constitutional power of Congress, as I understand it, I cannot see where we are laying down any constitutional law at all. We simply state, as the judgment of this Convention, that these monopolies, interfering with our freight and travel; all over the country, are a nuisance. That is all we want to do, and I believe it is the duty of the Convention to do that much.

Mr. BLAKELY, of St. Paul: The measure under consideration at this time, as I understand it, is the minority report of the Committee. In the halls of Congress, a gentleman who makes a report, whether minority or majority, has the right to close the debate upon the matter under consideration. The gentleman from St. Louis has read his report, but has not advanced a single argument in favor of it; neither has any other gentleman been allowed to speak in favor of it, although two or three gentlemen have addressed us against it. I claim, that under the rules of Congress, the gentleman who made the report is clearly entitled to be heard in answer to the objections which have been made, and I ask that he be heard the usual length of time.

On motion of Mr. FRAZAR, of Cincinnati, leave was granted to Mr. BRYSON to speak ten minutes.

Mr. COVINGTON, of Cincinnati: I wish only to occupy the time of the Convention a very few minutes. I cannot for the life of me understand why this Convention, which has to-day recommended the building of ship-canals from the lakes to the St. Lawrence, leading out to the Atlantic, on that route, and connecting the lakes with the Mississippi River by way of the Illinois River over a route where the water is so low, for six months of the year, that it is not possible to navigate those streams, — I say, I cannot understand why this Convention, which has expressed itself in favor of such measures, should object to this resolution, which has for its object the securing of the right to go from one section of the country to another.

Now, gentlemen, I may not, and probably do not, understand this question; but I want to say this, — there seems to be a glaring inconsistency in this matter. The gentleman from Chicago (Mr. MUNN) has raised a question about the right of the Government to interfere. Now, I am not very old, but I am old enough to remember when the Government built a national road extending from Baltimore to St. Louis; and the rights of the States were not then thought to have been infringed. HENRY CLAY was the projector of that enterprise; and just outside the City of Wheeling stands the monument to that great man which the people of the West have erected in honor of the part he took in carrying forward that great national work.

Then the gentleman speaks of the centralization of power in the General Government. I want him to recollect that there is a great centralizing power in the railroads. Railroad monopolies are more to be feared than the centralization of power in the Congress of the United States. (Applause.) Gentlemen, the people of this country send the members of Congress to Washington, and they can exert an influence upon their representatives. We in Ohio can tell our representatives how to vote on this question; you, gentlemen from St. Louis, and you, gentlemen from Minnesota, can do the same thing; but when the State of New Jersey undertakes to prevent us from travelling across her territory unless we pay tribute, who of us has authority to say a single word?

I do hope that this Convention will not hastily throw this subject on one side. Give it a careful consideration. It is an important matter, and ought to have the attention of the Convention. I do not want to dictate to Congress what they shall do. If they think it unconstitutional, let them so decide; but do not let us decide for them. I understand the resolution to be merely a recommendation, and there certainly can be no objection to our sending this out, as we sent out the other propositions in reference to internal improvements.

Mr. Holton: I dislike to occupy one moment of the time, but I wish to say that the Committee, in considering this matter, found that our whole seventy thousand miles of railroad in this country is the creature of the States; that it is you in Massachusetts, you in Ohio, you in Pennsylvania, you in Wisconsin, you in Illinois, who have originated these railroads from point to point, and from centre to centre, and that under the benign and fostering care of your own State Legislatures, they have gone on with gigantic momentum, with immense power, beyond anything that has been known before in the history of any country, to their present point,—unfinished, immature, but still the great agents of the nation's prosperity. It is proposed by this resolution to interfere, in a great measure, with the legislation that has begotten these great enterprises. It must be borne in mind that there is a natural disposition in every community, to take sides against a local corporation; and the Committee found, that the further they went into the subject, the greater did it spread out before them, and that they could not, without more reflection than could be given to the subject here, make an affirmative report, taking this matter out of the hands of the States and carrying it up to Congress, seeing that to concentrate the question there would be to call the whole lobby of the country there upon it. That was our view. Not that every gentleman did not feel aggrieved and indignant at the course which New Jersey has pursued for fifteen or twenty years, but upon the whole, it was the judgment of the majority of the Committee, (some of whom were at first ready to support the resolution) that we could not act upon it now — that it ought to be considered perhaps five years longer. It was proposed at one stage of our deliberations to turn it over to the National Chamber of Commerce, but we found we had no right to communicate with that body. But the question was whether there could be time for reflection; and we felt, (with no disrespect to the learned and able gentleman from New York or any gentleman who supports his resolution) that we could not deal with so grave a question, in the unfinished, incomplete and inchoate position in which it stands.

Mr. Blakely: I regard this question as of immense importance. I see, looking from St. Paul towards New York, the Hudson River, Harlem and New York Central Railroads consolidated; and the attempt was made to take in also the Lake Shore road, and I do not know but it may be done, for I believe some of the directors of the Central belong to the Lake Shore, and it looks to me as if there was even now, without the authority of legislation, without the consent of the States, a consolidation forming of immense lines of railroad reaching from the seaboard almost to our locality. When that is done, the people of the West will be called upon to pay a little more transportation money than they do now. I understand that these combinations in the West are affecting us already. My friend who has just taken his seat, lives at one end of a railroad, and I live at the other end of the same road; and I know that with us it is a strife which shall own the State — whether or not the Milwaukie and St. Paul Railroad shall own the State, or the Chicago and Northwestern Railroad. That is the position in which we find ourselves; and if the time shall ever come when the Milwaukie and St. Paul or the Chicago and Northwestern shall get control of the State, God help Minnesota!

Mr. Bryson: In reply to the gentleman who spoke in behalf of the interests of the monopolists, I have this to say, that there is no proposition in this report which looks to affecting any railroad that has been established. There is nothing more in the language than simply this, that any railroad already established shall not control the States, so that no other good road, which would be beneficial to the different States, shall be built. It merely says that you shall not first build a line through a State, and then say to the people of every other State, "You shall pass over this line." Furthermore, I wish to state, that it does not interfere with the railroads in their internal workings in the States. But suppose we are situated on the other side of the Mississippi. Take, for instance, Missouri. She has commerce; she has to travel with goods to New York, Philadelphia and Boston. Now, if the State of Illinois can say, "We will sustain a monopoly, and, as other States have done, we will impose a tax upon through travel, and will discriminate against it;" unless there is power in the United States to say that this shall not be done, and that freedom shall be given to every State in the Union, then Missouri must pay just what Illinois pleases. If she can impose one cent in this way, she can impose a million dollars. It is the question of right.

But I wish to call your attention to the fact, that we do not propose to enact the law; we simply carry the question up to the constitutional lawyers of the Supreme Court, to the United States in its National Congress, and say, "Gentlemen, consider this subject. Is it right, is it fit, that one State should be permitted to bar the privileges and rights of through commerce?" We only say "through commerce;" there is nothing about local commerce or local State interests. If the right be conceded, where is our National Government? Then Illinois could say, if the armies of the United States were to be fed in the West, "We will stop those provisions by taxing them a million dollars on every hundred pounds." Then Kentucky was right in saying, "Troops shall not pass through our territory to conquer the South." If that was not right, is it right to impose a tariff upon through commerce and travel. All we ask is this, that no State shall be allowed to impose restrictions upon or in any way to cripple the commercial interests of other States beyond them.

With these few remarks, I leave it to the Convention to decide whether we should ask the attention of Congress to this subject, involving, as it does, such vast interests. That is all we propose to do. We only ask Congress to consider the question whether one State may in any way restrict the through commerce of another State. I think, sir, that this Convention will certainly vote for my proposition, for it is for the interest of the whole country that the produce of the West shall find the cheapest markets in the nation. If there are more lines, the greater will be the competition; and if you say Congress is to make laws for the general benefit, why not permit capital to be used for the benefit of the Western States, which have the produce to sell, and of the Eastern States, which want that produce at the cheapest rates? We do not decide upon the constitutionality of such an enactment; we simply call the attention of Congress to the subject, and I am certain that the constitutional lawyers will take cognizance of that fact when they come to consider it.

Mr. WALBRIDGE: I ask the unanimous consent of the Convention to a modification of my original resolution, which I think will relieve the Convention, and accomplish the object, and meet the concurrence of the majority as well as of the minority of the Committee.

The modification I propose is as follows:

*Resolved*, That this Convention considers it important to the general interests of the people of the whole United States, that the National Government shall now promptly exercise whatever constitutional right is exclusively vested in it to regulate the means of trade and commerce between the American people in all sections of the country, as it has always done in reference to trade and commerce between them and foreign nations, and that, holding these opinions, this Convention hereby recognizes the propriety of congressional action in nationalizing the railway system in the way that it has lately nationalized the telegraph system, by authorizing companies to extend their lines all over the United States, wherever and whenever the public interests may require.

I trust that this resolution will have the unanimous sanction of this intelligent body. I think the Convention will make a mistake if they fail to pass it. We have lately crystallized this nation. We have said that these States are component parts of one great Federal Union. If we refuse to pass this resolution, we are going back to that condition of affairs which recognized State rights. I thought, when we took three hundred thousand men and laid them in their narrow graves, — when we mortgaged indefinitely the resources of this Republic to level that standard of State rights,—we had buried it so deep that it would never more spring up forever. (Loud applause.) I had fondly imagined that the sacrifices we have made, had demonstrated that this was to be an united, harmonious, and homogeneous people; and that that flag, under which we had triumphed from the Atlantic seaboard to the golden shores of the Pacific, was to float over one people. I find that I have been mistaken; that this idea of State rights still lingers in the breasts of some. I ask for no special privileges; I ask for no land; I ask for no subsidy. I only ask that freedom shall exist; that if the capitalists of Boston or New York desire to build a road alongside of the railroad of my friend, the able and accomplished President of the line from Pittsburgh to Fort Wayne and Chicago, Congress may authorize them to do it, and that there shall be open and free competition. The Congress of the United States, in this era, is not the Congress of the eras that have preceded it. This is a liberal Congress. In response to the sentiments of the American people, they have recently passed a law that any three, four, five, six or seven gentlemen are competent to construct a telegraphic line, wherever and whenever they please. I know not how many lines there are between this city and the great metropolis of the nation; but if our respected President and Secretary here desire to build another, they have the right to do it; and the law provides, that if they run over the territories of the United States, they may use the land of the United States for its construction. We desire, that when the nation is rising to a higher plane, a loftier elevation,—when the business men of the country are coming forward to develop the resources of the nation and restore it to its pristine glory, they may have liberty to construct lines of communication wherever they please, unobstructed by the action of any State. We ask no subsidy, I repeat; we ask no money; we only desire that we may respond to the wants of this great people, and construct our lines wherever the public interests may demand; and we ask the government to give us this liberty. This is all. If you desire that I shall not reflect upon State legislation, I strip the resolution of its verbiage, and bring it down to the naked question, "Shall the Congress of the United States suffer means of communication to be established between the different States of the Union, wherever capital is willing to make the investment, in response to the demands of the business interests of the country?"

One word in conclusion. No sordid personal motive animates me in the consideration of this or any other public question. For twenty-five years I have been in the habit of speaking to my countrymen upon public men, and concerning public measures; and in all that time, I challenge any voice to say that the suspicion of personal interest has ever been on the garments of him who has the honor to address you.

Mr. FRALEY: I object to Mr. WALBRIDGE's proposition, and prefer the resolution of the minority.

The question was then put, and Mr. BRYSON's resolution was substituted for the majority report, and adopted.

The Convention then adjourned, to meet on Saturday, at ten o'clock in the forenoon.

# FOURTH DAY.

SATURDAY, FEBRUARY 8, 1868.

---

THE Convention was called to order at a quarter past ten o'clock, by the President, and prayer was offered by the Rev. ROB'T LAIRD COLLIER, of Chicago. The reading of the Journal was dispensed with.

Mr. BRUNOT offered the following resolution:

*Resolved*, That after the vote shall have been taken upon the report of the Committee on Currency and Finance, no new business shall be introduced into the Convention, unless by unanimous consent.

Mr. BRUNOT: The object of this is to prevent what we should all regret, that the business which has made progress so satisfactorily should be marred by any hasty action upon new subjects, and especially after many of the members may have left.

The resolution was unanimously adopted.

Mr. FRALEY: If there be no reports of Committees to come in, I move that we now proceed to the consideration of the report of the Committee on Currency and Finance; and I would say, that my view upon it is, to give, for such reasonable period as the Convention may seem disposed to allow, the freest scope for the introduction of amendments to the report; that each gentleman who has an amendment to offer shall offer it, and state his views in regard to it, and that then it shall be informally laid upon the table; and when the debate is closed, we will proceed to take the question upon each amendment, unless the Convention shall otherwise order. My object is to give to every gentleman a full and free opportunity to present his views upon this interesting question, in the same way that the fullest expression was allowed in the Committee from which this report came.

Mr. ROPES, of Boston: Mr. President, I rise to move the adoption of the first resolution; and I do it with the greatest satisfaction, because I believe that the series of resolutions which the Committee have agreed upon, furnishes a broad basis of general principles on which we can for the most part stand together. I do not pretend to say that they express all my own views, or all the truth. No resolutions could express the whole truth on such a subject. Some of us would go much farther, and many would not go so far, but on the whole we can all accept them. Nothing has been more gratifying and satisfactory in this Convention, than the fact that merchants and men of business, from all parts of the country, East, West, North, and in part the South, are able to agree on some general principles which they alike recognize, and are willing to adopt. I am happy to see gentlemen from Chicago and Detroit take the broad ground that we have but one true and honest standard of value, and that is the gold coin of the United States; and that no permanent departure from that standard is to be recognized or tolerated. I rejoice to see that our Western friends have no desire to make capital out of irredeemable paper; and they may be assured that we at the East have no wish for a monopoly of currency or banking. Quoting in part the language employed yesterday upon this floor, I would affirm that of all the quackery with which our financial system has been cursed, there is none so absurd, so mischievous, so ridiculous as to suppose that the wealth of a country can be increased by issues of irredeemable paper. There is but one standard of value available, and that is specie; when that is reëstablished, we can safely have free banking, *and not before.* Our Western friends are welcome to issue as much currency as they please, provided *they will redeem it in coin.* Until that can be done, *not another dollar of paper should be issued.* By all means let us have, as General BUTLER proposes, a thousand millions of paper, but with this condition which General BUTLER does *not* propose, that every dollar of it be redeemable in coin.

It has been suggested in the minority report, that new greenbacks should be issued to take the place of compound interest notes withdrawn from circulation. But, sir, when those compound interest notes were issued, it was well understood that it was done as the last resort of an utterly exhausted treasury, and in the expectation that they would not permanently serve as currency, but would gradually be gathered up, and withdrawn from circulation as investments, until their maturity. But I am sorry to say the banks gathered up these notes, and locked them up in their vaults, both as investments and as reserves of "lawful money," thus evading the law, and released their greenbacks to go all over the country, and produce an enormous inflation; and then, when we came to the banks to draw our money, they had nothing but compound interest notes to give us; and this scarcity of their own creating caused the pressure for money so persistently, but falsely charged upon the Secretary of the Treasury. We do not want currency, we want capital; and above all, we want a sound measure of value. We want to come to this as wisely, as gradually, as prudently as possible, but we never shall have peace or safety till we get to it.

Mr. NAZRO: I have an amendment which I desire to offer to the Convention.

Mr. TURPIN, of Chicago: I rise to a point of order. My point of order is this: yesterday afternoon I moved to strike out of the first resolution all after the word "thereof." That question is first in order this morning. The Convention postponed action, and agreed to take it up this morning.

Mr. FRALEY: The gentleman can move his amendment immediately after Mr. NAZRO.

Mr. NAZRO: The amendment I propose is in the form of an additional resolution:

*Resolved,* That the bonds of the United States already issued were exempted by law from taxation; and that having thus been issued, it would be a violation of the law of contracts to impose a tax upon them now, as well as a breach of faith on the part of the Government.

Mr. TURPIN: I again move to strike out all of the first resolution after the word "thereof."

The ten minutes' rule of this Convention, wisely adopted, will of course prevent any extended discussion; but I wish to state one or two facts, which I think may be of use.

We think, in the West, that we are scarcely yet ready for a contraction of the currency. I wish to state, especially to gentlemen on the Eastern seaboard, that at the commencement of the war of the rebellion, the entire banking capital of Illinois, some forty millions of money, was wiped out at once, as if by fire. The West has great resources, but it requires some time to develop them; and we are anxious to gain a little more time in this matter of the currency.

The want of a circulating medium in the Western country is not only destructive to our own interests, but I think I can show, by the statement of a single fact, is also injurious to the people of the East. The exorbitant interest we are required to pay not only in discounts, but in commissions on acceptances, must be added to the cost of the articles we produce. That is a law of trade; and while we suffer from the want of curreney, we have to add to the cost of it, the interests and discounts which we pay in the West, and this finally comes out of those who consume what we produce and sell.

Mr. DORE, of Chicago: It would be far more pleasant for us of the West to agree with you of the East touching this matter, if we deemed it expedient to do so. We realize, as well as anybody who resides in the East possibly can, that our currency is below par; that is to say, it is virtually diseased; but, as with the human body diseased, so with the currency, nature, or, if not nature, the condition of things to be, if not now existing, should, in the main, be relied upon for a cure. The extent of this disease is measured exactly by the depreciation of the currency. If everybody in the country sincerely believed that the Government would fulfil its obligations, the disparity between the price of gold and the value of the currency would not exist. The depreciation of the currency, therefore, measures precisely the want of confidence on the part of the community that the Government will fulfil its obligations. First and foremost, then, what we want is confidence, and we cannot have confidence without stability. The constant apprehension that the volume of the currency will be materially increased or diminished, has seriously retarded legitimate business enterprises in every part of the country. The question naturally arises, Whence this lack of confidence? The reply is too evident: the greatly-increased expenditures of the Government, and the failure of the Government to collect the revenue. The people of the country are not yet able to quite understand why it was necessary to expend more than two hundred per cent. to pay the expenses of the Government in 1867, over what it cost to do this in 1861. The people do not believe that it is necessary to expend thirty or forty millions,—and certainly not forty-seven millions,—upon the navy. Why, sir, if it were put to the vote, the people of this country, in my judgment, would vote that it would be far better that three-fourths of the navy should be burned, than continue such an annual expense. The nation is by no means so easily frightened as to deem it requisite to keep up such a show of marine power. Moreover, sir, I contend that the people are not able to understand why it should be necessary to spend eighty-three millions of money upon the army, or anything like that; certainly not more than one-half. Why, sir, who wants to go to war with us? or with whom do we want to go to war? (Applause.) A Government founded like ours, upon the intelligence and the affections of the people, numbers its standing army, as has been proved, only by the number of its male citizens capable of bearing arms. (Applause.)

I say, then, let these expenses be reduced, and every other governmental expense that can be. Sir, let it be borne in mind that the great disturbing element of this nation is now no more, and that the interests of every section of the country are so far identical as to be promoted only by measures of peace. Ceasing to fear one another, we by no means need fear anybody else. (Applause.) Let it be borne in mind — forever borne in mind — that every dollar of money unnecessarily expended, either upon the army or the navy, is unproductively expended, and therefore utterly destroyed. (Applause.) And, further, that this nation can well depart from the custom of the old world in spending its vital energies upon means of defence — standing armies and great navies.

Let these things be done, and then let Congress so modify the law, if it needs modification, that it will be utterly impossible for those who defraud the Government, purposely, to escape the penitentiary. (Applause.) I undertake to say, that so long as the stealings of a week can purchase immunity from punishment for the frauds of a month, the collection of the revenue can never be honestly made.

We of the West are of opinion, that prior to the war, we never had currency enough to transact our business. There was too much extemporized paper, altogether. We used to receive drafts in our legitimate business — "A. pay B." — "B. pay C." — "C. pay D." until there was no more room to write upon the paper. We did not know, when it got down to Boston or New York, whether it would be paid or not.

I wish to say, furthermore, that I think there is one great desideratum to be borne in mind. If I am rightly informed, we had not, at the commencement of the war, anything like the amount of currency, *per capita*, which they had in foreign countries — not quite half, I think. The argument would be that we should have much more. Why? Because, on account of the extent of the country, a great deal of time is expended in transit in order to enable money to perform its legitimate function of exchange. Moreover, it is not to be forgotten that the tendency of gold itself is constantly to depreciate. There are those present who are much better acquainted with this matter than I am. I apprehend there are many present who are fully conversant with the history of gold as a medium of exchange, and know that from time to time in the world's history, its actual value has been determined by the amount of wheat it would buy. Taking that as the standard, how much wheat will a gold dollar buy to-day, compared with what it would buy ten years ago? Prior to 1849, the whole coinage of the United States was less than two hundred millions. During the eighteen years, since 1849, our coinage has not been less than a thousand millions. And it should be borne in mind, that this great production of gold has not been confined to us, by any manner of means. All over the world, there have been extraordinary efforts put forth for the production of gold. Sir, Yankee ingenuity is continually on the stretch to devise new machines to extract the gold from the mines of the country and in every other country. Now, then, what I apprehend is this, that since we are getting out the gold literally by the ton instead of by the ounce, as in years gone by, the time is not distant when we shall be able to pay a large portion of our Government debt, and not feel it very much.

Here is one very particular point to which I wish to call the attention of the Convention. Supposing we have, to-day, twenty-five per cent. more currency than we want. I think it is estimated that the entire population of this country and the business of the country will be duplicated in twenty years. How many years would it take us to get down to the absolute quantity, simply by the natural increase of the population and business of the country? Just five years.

Sir, for the reasons I have assigned, I do not want the volume of currency reduced.

Mr. BUZBY: Heartily sympathizing with the amendment which has been submitted by the gentleman from Chicago, (Mr. TURPIN,) I desire to state a fact which I happen to have in my possession, which seems to tell in favor of this despised paper money, which is so much decried, although it was this same paper money which was our salvation during the war. The price of gold, in May, 1865, was one hundred and thirty-seven and a half, and the amount of legal tenders in circulation was seven hundred and fifty-two millions. On the first of November, 1867, the actual circulation was reduced to five hundred millions, and the price of gold was over one hundred and forty. That is, with an actual decrease in the circulation of two hundred and fifty-two millions, there was an actual increase of three per cent. in the price of gold. Now, this fact proves that gold has been demonetized, and is an article of merchandise, and that we are not to depreciate our paper money by continually quoting the premium on gold. Does any man doubt that the currency of this country, based as it is upon a property of sixteen thousand millions of dollars, is practically as much a representative of value as gold can be?

I merely rose to support the amendment, and to say that this paper money is not the despicable article gentlemen would try to make it appear, and that it would be for our interest to use it, instead of making war upon it, and thus crippling the commercial energies of the country.

Mr. Wood, of Philadelphia: It makes very little difference what we call our circulating medium,—whether we call it gold, silver, or paper, if it contains a certain value. The gentleman said that gold is demonetized; the same as other metals are. It makes no difference whether we call them money or merchandise, if they pass from hand to hand bearing a certain value. Gentlemen forget that a gold dollar represents a certain amount of actual labor. It takes a certain number of days work, a certain amount of pork, to represent a gold dollar, and it represents the same value all over the country so long as the supply remains the same. If we increase the supply of gold, of course a gold dollar represents a less amount of labor than before; it takes a less amount of pork, and a less amount of bread and butter to produce it.

The gentleman from Chicago remarked that the gold premium was the measure of the distrust which the people of the United States felt in the Government's paying its indebtedness. I think he is a little wrong in that. I think it is not so much the measure of distrust in this country as the measure of distrust which is felt abroad. The people of Europe would gladly invest in our securities if they felt absolute certainty that our bonds would be paid in full. They would gladly invest in them at six per cent. rather than invest their money at two or three per cent., as they have for the last year; just as the people of the Eastern States would gladly invest in the securities of the West, if they felt perfectly assured they would be paid.

Something has been said with reference to economy. If we reduce the expenses of the Government so as to lessen taxation, we shall have specie payments in a short time. But economy may degenerate into parsimony, which is a bad thing. We tried the experiment of parsimony before the war, and were almost ruined. We tried manning our forts with two or three men, and we know what it cost us. I suppose our whole debt would have been saved if we had had three companies of United States troops at Charleston and three at Savannah, instead of a handful of men to take care of those forts.

It is said that currency is scarce in the West, and that Western men need money, while in the East, at present, we have actually a surplus; money is not producing the legal rate of interest in the Eastern States; but we may question if this disparity would not be the same if the circulating currency were doubled, and whether the business of the country would not draw that money into the Eastern States. Suppose we doubled the amount of currency in circulation, would not the same business circumstances draw it into the Eastern cities, and thus the disproportion be just the same? So, if we diminish it three millions a month, why would the disparity be any greater? Why should we be taking it from the business of the West rather than the business of the East?

Mr. TAYLOR, of Cincinnati: I propose the following amendment to the first resolution: Strike out all after the word "thereof," and insert "but the policy of contraction should be kept steadily in view, and be resumed at the earliest moment when the condition of the country will warrant it."

Let me say, at the outset, that although I come from the West I am thoroughly in accord with the sentiment of the East on the finance question, as expressed by the gentleman from Boston, (Mr. ROPES,) and am inflexibly opposed to any expansion of the currency in any form, and I would stay until Christmas, if necessary, to vote against expansion. (Applause.) I congratulate the Committee on the general result of their labor. They have evidently carefully, patiently and wisely considered the important subjects referred to them, and, as a whole, I can cordially endorse their report; but I am puzzled to comprehend why they have fixed upon the first of January, 1869, as the earliest period when the contraction of the currency could be safely resumed and when it must be resumed. I am in favor of contraction now, when money is easy at the great commercial and financial centres, or at the earliest possible moment when it can be safely resumed, and am for continued contraction until specie payment is brought about. I think the Committee has erred in naming any definite and arbitrary day for the resumption of contraction, and I would ask if they had a prophet among them who could foresee what would be the corn, wheat and cotton crops of 1868; as upon these mainly will hinge our ability to pursue contraction of the currency at the time specified. We may be less able to contract then than now. This objectionable clause in the first resolution leads me to suspect that possibly the Committee have been in consultation with the brilliant financial Senator from Vermont, (Mr. MORRILL,) who has introduced a bill into the Senate fixing upon a day for the resumption of specie payments by the Government, and in order to fortify the Treasury for resumption has provided by a clause in his bill for the monthly sale of the gold in the Treasury, leaving only a sufficient balance to meet the ordinary current expenses of the Government;

or perhaps they have been advising with the distinguished Secretary of the Treasury, who, in a well-known speech, made about two years ago, proclaimed that he had taken out a sort of patent to bring about specie payments, but who has not yet achieved the promised and desired result. It seems to me that it is not possible, in the present condition of the currency, to arbitrarily fix upon any specific day for the resumption of contraction or for specie payments. I am opposed to expansion because I look upon an irredeemable paper currency as one of the greatest curses ever inflicted upon a country, and I believe it will be found that the present depressed condition of our shipping interest is owing more to our depreciated currency and to our barbarous tariff than to any other cause. (Applause.) I do not agree with those who think the price of gold, or rather the value of our bonds abroad, (because these mainly govern the premium on gold,) is influenced in any large degree by the amount of currency in circulation. It is not the large volume of currency that keeps our bonds so much below par. It is a lack of confidence on the part of foreign capitalists that keeps them down to about seventy-two, and this lack of confidence grows out of our profligate expenditures, our decreasing revenue, and our unsettled condition; and we cannot reasonably expect to see our bonds appreciate in value until we practice economy and have a redundant revenue. Until recently we have been alarmingly profligate in our national expenditures, and our revenue has fallen off so greatly that doubts have been expressed as to our ability to pay the interest on the debt and meet the necessary expenses of the Government. When we present an opposite spectacle to foreign capitalists by the exhibition of strict economy in our expenditures and by the steady yearly extinguishment of our debt by a surplus revenue, they will have confidence in our bonds and these will quickly appreciate to par and command a premium. I regard all the various funding schemes introduced into Congress, looking to the borrowing of money at four to five per cent., and to the sale of the bonds at par, while our six per cent. bonds are selling at about seventy-two, as simply "jackassical," (if I may use the word;) there ought not to be any talk about new loans and new bonds until by the practice of the most rigid economy and by the steady reduction of our debt, the five-twenties have appreciated to par. When this result is achieved and not until then should we talk about a new loan. When it is achieved we can readily borrow money at four to five per cent. interest, and pay off the five-twenties, and thus largely reduce the national burden. I do not concur with those who think taxation should be reduced to the point where the revenue would barely meet the necessary expenses of the Government and the interest on the debt, leaving to the next generation its payment. On the contrary, I think it would be wise policy to continue to tax ourselves sharply, certainly enough to yield a surplus revenue, to be applied to the payment of the debt. I differ also from those who take a desponding view of the situation, and represent the country as nearly or quite bankrupt, and as groaning under oppressive and intolerable taxation. The condition of the country is not so bad as this. Taxes have increased and are not altogether properly adjusted. Some branches of business are greatly depressed by this and other causes, and all have felt in some measure the natural and inevitable shrinkage always following the withdrawal of paper money, which always creates false values; but the general condition of the country is not nearly so bad as it is represented to be by those small politicians and stump orators, who rarely pay any taxes themselves, but who go about the country and to serve their own base and interested ends, fill it with their dismal howlings. I should like to see more economy, a more general determination to pay the debt, and less grumbling and howling about taxes. The resources of the country are enormous and are increasing; and we have but to use these judiciously and to insist upon economy in our legislators, and we shall soon triumphantly emerge from our present financial difficulties. I hope the resolution reported by the Committee recommending Congress to legalize contracts in coin will be adopted by the Convention and by Congress; as I believe this would materially aid in hastening the return to specie payments, and is certainly a move in the right direction; I hope also that the Convention, however its members may differ in opinion on minor matters, will be an unit in maintaining the national faith and honor. (Applause.)

Mr. WETHERILL: I feel that I am called upon to reply to the remarks of the gentleman who last spoke, because it seems to me his expressions were rather harsh. I think he said that we had suffered long enough from a "barbarous tariff." I think I can prove to him, conclusively, that unless we have a proper tariff, we never can resume specie payments, (Applause); but that is not the subject under discussion. I also take exception to his remark, that because we cannot tell what sort of a crop we are to have next year, therefore we should make no calculation upon a crop at all. It seems to me that the shrewdest merchant is the one who is able to see an inch further into the future than his neighbor. The merchant who cannot see beyond his own store door, I will guarantee, in this good City of Boston, will be sure to end in bankruptcy. We must make calculations on the future. If we want to know what our crops will be for the next five years, it is reasonable to take the average of the crops of the past five years. We must act upon experience, and without it we shall be very much at a loss.

Now, what will be the effect of the amendment proposed by the gentleman from Chicago? Virtually, nothing. This Convention, called together with so much trouble and difficulty, to give expression to our views and feelings in such a way that they shall be known and felt throughout the country, will simply say, "Gentlemen at Washington, you have done perfectly right, you have already met the emergency and stopped contraction; you have finished your work, and you may as well go home, so far as the currency question is concerned." Now, when I look around me and see the amount of intelligence assembled here from every quarter of the country, representing the vast industrial interests of the country, I am sure we ought to do more than this. I am sure that the people of my State would not be satisfied to have the Philadelphia delegates say that nothing more could be done here than simply to endorse Congress. We are here, practical business men, as I understand it, to tell Congress what, in our opinion, will be for the best interests of this country—what we believe to be right and proper; and let us fairly, dispassionately and coolly, with business-like judgment, discuss these questions.

Now, in regard to expansion and contraction. It does seem to me, when we look at this question in its length and breadth, that we are led to this conclusion, that just as early as possible, just as soon as we can, we should resume specie payments. (Applause.) And let me tell gentlemen here, from my own experience, that this resumption of specie payments is not the great bugbear that many of us think it is. All we want is confidence to enable us to resume specie payments. I can tell gentlemen, that in 1857, when we resumed, I knew of a bank in Philadelphia that, fearful, perhaps, of a terrible run upon it, secured in its vaults seven-eighths of its circulation in gold and silver. What was the consequence? They paid out on the first day forty dollars, and took in two thousand. The truth is, no man wants to carry a gold dollar in his pocket if he can carry a bank note that represents the gold dollar.

What, then, does Mr. McCulloch want us to do? He wants us to withdraw fifty millions of legal tenders a year. For what purpose? He honestly and fairly believes, that if that can be done without detriment to the business interests of the country, in three years we can resume specie payments. And how? In three years, he will withdraw one hundred and fifty millions of the three hundred millions of legal tenders, and the balance will be held by the banks, and when we resume, they will hold these as a reserve, as gold, because they will be the same as gold.

Every business man knows that he must make his return to the Government; and on that return, Mr. McCulloch levies his tax. He could not support the Government an hour without the agricultural and manufacturing interests of this land. Knowing this, will he crush the men who support him? I doubt it. When, two years ago, he was troubled, and the business community trembled, what did he do? He did what Congress asked him to do then; and for three months past there has been no contraction. And what is the consequence? Why, I know a man in Philadelphia who refused to accept a loan of two hundred thousand dollars, at four per cent.— he could not use it. Do you say, in the face of such a fact, that there is not plenty of currency now? And if, with this abundance of currency, the business of the country is still depressed, I ask this Convention to inquire if there is not another reason for the trouble. We have plenty of currency at the present time; I think there is no man on this floor who will not say so: and yet our business communities are in a depressed condition. We must get at the secret of it, and perhaps the secret is not the contraction of the currency.

Mr. Buzby: I rise simply to say that I do not consider the remarks of the preceding speaker a correct representation of the sentiment of the business community of Philadelphia.

Mr. Field: The first resolution of the report under consideration contains a proposition that the legal tender currency be contracted after the first of January, 1869, at the rate of $3,000,000 per month. Mr. Turpin, of Chicago, has moved that this proposition be stricken out, and in rising to support the motion I will briefly present my views on this important subject.

It is assumed that contraction of the greenbacks will secure resumption. And the discussions thus far do not appear to be pertinent to the question before the Convention. Gentlemen have expressed their views in favor of gold and silver as the true standard of value. They deplore the existing state of affairs, and express with great earnestness a desire for speedy resumption. I beg to remind gentlemen that that is not the question before the Convention. There can be no difference of opinion as to the importance and advantage of resumption.

The question is, can we have specie payments by *coercion* and by an act of Congress fixing the day of resumption? And will contraction or destruction of the greenbacks *force upon us* the gold and silver to supply the demands of our foreign creditors, and the requirements of our people for currency?

I fail to see on what law of political economy the Committee rely to support this singular proposition, and it appears to me that the Pope's bull may be equally effective in the regulation and movement of the comets. The Secretary of the Treasury has been travelling on the road called contraction at a rapid pace for over two years. And with what results? And what does the experience in contraction teach?

A careful examination must convince any intelligent man that instead of leading us one step nearer resumption it in reality conducts us further from it and postpones that prosperity, or that industrial and financial condition favorable to resumption. Let us for one moment inquire what contraction has accomplished for the finances of the nation, and its effect during the past two years on the industry and business of the country.

### CIRCULATION COMPARED.

On the first of September, 1865, the circulating medium consisted in part as follows:—

| | |
|---|---|
| United States notes, | $433,160,569 |
| Fractional currency, | 26,344,742 |
| National bank notes, | 300,000,000 |
| Compound interest legal tender, | 217,024,160 |
| Temporary loan certificates, ten per cent., | 107,148,713 |
| Certificates of indebtedness, | 85,093,000 |
| Treasury five per cent. legal tenders, | 32,536,901 |
| Treasury notes, legal tenders, past due and not presented, | 1,503,020 |
| State bank notes, | 78,867,575 |
| Total, | $1,281,678,680 |

On the first of November, 1867, the amount of currency in circulation, of the description above mentioned, was as follows:—

| | |
|---|---|
| United States notes and fractional currency, | $388,405,565 |
| National bank notes, | 300,000,000 |
| Compound interest notes and three per cent. certificates, | 78,165,170 |
| State bank notes, | 4,000,000 |
| Treasury notes, | 878,503 |
| Temporary loan, ten per cent., | 2,474,625 |
| Certificates of indebtedness, | 30,000 |
| Total, | $773,953,863 |

Total contraction in two years and four months, $507,724,817, being a reduction of forty per cent.

Has this unparalleled *contraction* either reduced the price of gold or enhanced the value of national securities yet outstanding? And has it promoted the prosperity of the country? You know, Mr. President, it has not; on the contrary, its effect, together with excessive internal revenue taxation, has been to paralyse trade, suspend our industries and throw labor out of employment. We find that notwithstanding this unparalleled contraction — exceeding more than double in this brief period the total reduction of the issues of the banks of England from 1814 to 1823, a period of eight years, — that the price of gold to-day is higher than it was when this suicidal scheme was inaugurated. This is an instructive lesson on the policy of contraction, and it is unnecessary to go further to show that it is not the remedy for existing evils.

It is quite remarkable that neither Mr. McCulloch nor any other of the numerous doctors on finance have attempted to explain in what miraculous way *contraction* is to *produce gold and silver* to supply all our wants.

We know there is no demand for gold among ourselves save for imports, neither is it hoarded here. It is demanded from abroad and this demand is in excess of our supply, and, as with every other commodity, scarcity enhances the price. It is not as has been asserted here a want of confidence in the minds of our people in the ability of our Government to pay all her obligations in good faith, for I challenge any man to find an *American* who has hoarded the precious metals or who has had any doubt or apprehension as to the integrity and stability of this great nation.

The price of gold in the market is controlled by foreign exchange, and the price of foreign exchange is controlled by the balance of trade. The statistics show that our foreign trade is in an abnormal condition, and it will continue unhealthy so long as we continue to import goods of foreign manufacture exceeding the amount of our exports, and so long as we continue to be the debtor nation. Water does not more naturally seek a level than does gold flow from one nation to another for payment of balances created by an unequal exchange of commodities, and nothing can be more certain than the fact that there can be no permanent resumption of specie payments in the United States until the balances between them and foreign countries shall be made easy, and until provision shall be made for returning bonds at unpropitious times.

The importations from foreign countries (including the usual estimate for undervaluations and smuggling) have in the last eight years exceeded the amounts of our exports in gold valuation, including $517,000,000 in specie, leaving the balance against the United States $951,429,186.

The balance against this country, in the fiscal year 1866, was in gold value $143,520,000, and for the fiscal year 1867, $136,000,000. In addition to this large trade indebtedness, it must be borne in mind that at least $1,000,000,000 of our National, State, Municipal and Railway securities are held abroad, and for which provision and calculation must be made.

This, briefly, is our condition in trade and indebtedness with foreign countries, and it does not present a very bright picture. Our domestic affairs are not as yet settled and in a satisfactory shape. The withdrawal of at least two millions of men, North and South, from productive employments — taken very largely from the farm and plantation — together with the destruction of $5,000,000,000 of property during four years of rebellion, has had a disturbing and demoralizing effect on the industry and productive forces of the country. Short crops have also increased the embarrassments under which the people suffer, raising the price of breadstuffs not only beyond the reach of many of our fellow-citizens, but leaving no large surplus for exportation.

Considering our condition at home and our indebtedness abroad, Mr. President, it seems to me that any recommendation to Congress to fix the day of resumption would be unwise in this Convention.

I believe the true remedy for existing evils and the only agency we can with certainty rely upon to bridge over the vacuum in our production and wealth occasioned by the war, is the labor of our hands and *increased production.* When our labor shall again fully resume the old places — when the pleasant sounds of industry shall make glad every village and glen — and when the field, the mine and the factory shall fill our empty ships, it will restore harmony to foreign and domestic trade, and give health and stability to the national finances. With peace and prosperity in our country and by the aid of two crops of cotton, we shall within two or three years so far settle the balance due to Europe that gold will flow back to us as it did before the war, and then as all demand will cease and the supply be large, specie payments will come as the dew falls, doing good to all but injury to none.

It is logical to say that if our labor could be in full exercise and furnish a surplus of commodities other than gold for exportation in amount exceeding our imports, and our debts paid, the balance of trade would bring back gold. It has done this heretofore. Then with the increasing supply from California a demand for gold will cease, and it will fall below national or bank credit, because our good Government and good laws make good credit in a normal condition of things better than gold.

Labor increased our national wealth in the last decade from $7,135,780,228 to $16,159,616,068. The same ratio of increase will, within a short time, not only overcome the waste of the late war, but the balance in foreign trade now unhappily setting so heavily against us. Wise legislation that shall protect well our industrial and commercial interests and give stability to all governmental affairs, will greatly increase the power of labor in our midst, and which when relieved of excessive taxation will soon make us the most prosperous and independent nation on the earth.

The highest estimate of the amount of coin in the United States is $200,000,000, including $100,000,000 in the National Treasury, and the production of California does not exceed $50,000,000 per annum. Now, sir, the amount exported to Europe, in 1866, was $86,044,071; in 1867, $60,975,186. The shipments in the month of January last, were $8,000,000.

These facts indicate not only the course of trade, but from what quarter the demand comes for our precious metals, exceeding annually in amount the supply from our rich mines.

If the exhaustive process is not checked by the wholesome restraints of law, it will be an easy matter for the advocates of resumption by coercive measures to calculate how long before the first of January, 1869, we shall be in a financial condition to transact business on a "*specie basis.*"

In the fiscal year 1867, we imported the following goods which should have been produced in our own country, from our own materials and by our own hands:

| | |
|---|---|
| Wool and woollen manufactures, | $51,341,754 |
| Wood and manufactures, | 7,004,857 |
| Lead " | 2,841,391 |
| Iron and steel " | 25,360,861 |
| Hemp " | 3,045,126 |
| Glass " | 3,958,063 |
| Flax " | 19,534,425 |
| Cotton " | 23,737,528 |
| Clothing " | 7,985,434 |
| Books and pamphlets, | 1,314,650 |
| Other manufactures, | 5,573,053 |
| Total, | $151,697,142 |

For such manufactures, Europe is now gleaning from this country all the gold we produce, and taking a mortgage on us in the shape of bonds for all that we have not the ability to pay. It is in this way that we *invigorate* the labor of Europe instead of fostering our own industry by protective measures.

For the reasons stated, Mr. President, I am opposed to the resolution of the Committee and in favor of the amendment offered by Mr. TURPIN, of Chicago. We must wait for labor to harmonize affairs and adjust values to a condition of national health and prosperity.

What we require now, in my judgment, to promote that industrial and financial condition which we must reach in order to secure as speedily as possible a resumption of specie payments in a healthy and permanent shape, is the relief of our industry from the burdens of excessive internal revenue taxation, and also such an adjustment of the duties on importations of foreign manufactures as to keep the balance of trade with other nations in favor of the United States.

I should be willing to urge on Congress the importance of immediate legislation on these questions, with the view to *restrain* the importation of manufactures, which we have the ability to produce at home, and which compete with our labor and disturb our finance. I take the ground that our good currency cannot delay or postpone resumption, on the contrary its destruction, in my judgment, would impede our approach to resumption, for the high rate of interest which money commands all over the country, particularly at the West, is the most satisfactory proof that the circulating-medium is not excessive.

If the public debt be funded by the issue of bonds on long time and bearing interest, and if greenbacks are made convertible to the bonds of the Government at par, and at any national bank, our currency, with such facilities to absorb unemployed capital, cannot become redundant.

Mr. STEVENS, of New York, submitted the following as an amendment to the first resolution reported by the Committee:

Strike out all after the word "Resolved," and insert as follows:— That this Convention, utterly rejecting the false modern theories that there is any other true measure of value than those precious metals which the usage of nations from earliest ages has declared to be money (namely, gold and silver); and believing trade and commerce must languish so long as this measure of value which is its life-blood, is vitiated or corrupt; firmly hold that the first and greatest need of the country is to restore specie to the currency.

*Resolved,* That in the judgment of this Convention there is no other way of restoring specie to the currency than by a contraction of the paper issues, and the making of a place in circulation for the entry of gold and silver — a process which should be carefully graduated over a long period of time so as not unjustly to distress any branch of industry or commerce, while specie payment should only be required by law when the power of the country to maintain such payment shall have been clearly shown by a continued practical resumption.

Mr. STEVENS: As one of the Finance Committee who have submitted the report to the Convention, I feel it my duty to say that the whole of the report is by no means satisfactory to me, and that the statements of the clause now under discussion are most objectionable. I believe neither in any one of the premises of that resolution nor in the conclusions depending thereon.

It is said in the resolution that the values of the country have been adjusted to the present amount of currency. I do not believe that the values are harmoniously or fairly adjusted to the satisfaction of any general branch of industry, whether commercial, agricultural or manufacturing. An examination of the list of prices would show very great irregularities in values.

Was the commercial community of Boston satisfied, when its last steamship was withdrawn, or the merchant of New York, when but a few days since, he looked over the Shipping List of New York and found there no ship loading for an European port under the American flag? Did Mr. Senator SPRAGUE express any very great contentment on the part of the manufacturing class in his late speech? Are the agricultural interest satisfied when the prices of wool are so fallen that we hear that in the Western country the poor sheep are not cared for for their fleece, but are slaughtered daily for their skins?

If this shows a "practical adjustment" of values, it is of a kind which seems to satisfy none of the great interests of the country. And yet it is because of this so claimed adjustment, that the Committee asks the Convention to give out to the world that it desires "neither expansion nor contraction" at the present time, but proposes a rest until the first of January, 1869.

If this be proposed for political reasons, well and good. Say nothing on the subject, but do not base the conclusion on false premises. If there were ever a time when contraction should be going on, it is now when money is worth but three per cent. in the New York market. I believe that the time to contract is when money is cheap and to stop contraction when it is dear. I do not believe it is generally known that Mr. McCulloch has reduced the currency from one thousand millions, as it stood on the thirty-first of August, 1865, including all those parts of the debt which performed the functions of money, to seven hundred millions, by the first of November, 1867. The Secretary was imprudent in contracting during the fall, when the West needed all the currency it could obtain to move the crops. If he had governed himself by the state of the money market instead of an arbitrary policy, he would not have been stripped of his powers. As it is, "he has killed the goose which laid his golden eggs." But there is still another fault in Mr. McCulloch. He alarmed the country by the announcement that he intended to resume specie payment by the first of July, 1868. Now, every one in the country, whether financier or not, feels instinctively that specie payment means ante-war prices, and dreads a reduction in value which will fall wholly on his shoulders. On the other hand, the naming of a *distant* day, would be a fair notice to every one to prepare for such a reduction.

Again, the resolution of the Committee recommends the arbitrary reduction of three millions per month, after the first of January, 1869. The gentlemen might find that it would be a more severe strain to contract the currency at that rate next year than it had been at any period yet. As the currency of the country approaches its natural limit, contraction will be severely felt.

I am of opinion that the withdrawal of one hundred millions more of currency, thereby reducing the same to five hundred and fifty millions, would be followed by the appearance of gold, and that the currency would thereafter be strengthened without contraction, gold flowing into it as fast as paper should be withdrawn.

Holding these views, and dissenting from every part of the resolution, I offer the amendment thereto, which I have read.

Mr. Davis, of Toledo: I rise simply to propose a resolution. The general feeling seems to be, that we are to strive to get back to specie payments as soon as possible, and we want the first step towards it. I therefore introduce this resolution as the first leading step:—

*Resolved*, That this Convention recommend to Congress to provide by law that from this date no national bank shall be allowed to sell any part of the gold received from Government as interest upon the bonds pledged for its circulation, until such time as the entire amount of the reserve required by law to be kept by the bank shall be made up of coin.

I introduce this resolution as an additional one. I would say that such a law would be entirely against my interest, individually; but there must be some point at which to begin, and the banks of the West, I am quite sure, will be satisfied to reserve this coin, and take their legal tenders and put them into circulation as a reserve.

Mr. ALEXANDER, of St. Louis: I have a resolution which I want to offer as an addition to the report:—

*Resolved,* That the Secretary of the Treasury should be directed by Congress to receive legal tender notes in lieu of gold for duties to such an extent as his experience has taught him can safely be done, instead of selling surplus of gold.

Mr. BUZBY: I rise to a point of order. Previous to the adjournment last evening, I called, as I had a right to call, for a division of the question on the adoption of the report, and that it be taken up by sections, *seriatim.* We are now considering the first resolution, and my point of order is, that by the rules of Congress, under which we are acting, after an amendment to an amendment has been made, no other amendment can be considered, and that you cannot receive a substitute for the whole when you are considering one section of the report.

The PRESIDENT: The Chair frankly admits that we are proceeding somewhat informally. It was proposed to permit the widest discussion, in order to obtain the views of gentlemen from different sections of the country; also, that the Chairman of the Committee on Currency and Finance should review the propositions, and that they should then be taken up and voted upon. This is what the Chair understood to be the wish of the Convention. Now, if it is the pleasure of the Convention to change the mode of considering this question, they can do so.

Mr. WARD, of Boston: I would merely suggest, that if gentlemen who have resolutions to offer would offer them when the resolutions to which they are pertinent are under consideration, we can go on in the manner we have adopted. If my friend from Missouri will withdraw his resolution, and introduce it at the proper time, we can go on.

Mr. ALEXANDER: I believe it is the proper time right here. We are talking about getting back to specie payments. Now, I apprehend one great reason why we are not having specie payments is because the Government requires for one particular thing a kind of currency that it pays out only for another particular thing. To illustrate. We will suppose that the Secretary of the Treasury, during a certain period of time, collects, say thirty millions of gold. He has three millions more than he wants, and he goes into the market to sell it. Suppose he should say he will take ten per cent. of legal tenders in lieu of gold; that if you have a hundred dollars to pay, you may pay ninety dollars in gold, and ten in legal tenders, and so on. He has had experience enough, in the calculation of the gold revenue, to tell about how much gold he will get. He wants a certain amount each year to pay interest, and, as I understand, he has in the treasury vaults, at this time, about a hundred millions. It occurs to me, that if he will tell the people that for this thing for which he requires gold he is ready to take legal tenders, he may run the machine for a year on the gold he has now, and at the end of the year, he would have a very considerable amount of legal tenders, paid for duties, and I think the premium on gold would be considerably reduced from what it is now. That is my idea. Gold is now only performing one duty,— or two, you may say; but one only which our Government makes it perform,— namely, it is paying duties. Every day, some body has to pay duties on the importation of foreign goods. He must go into the market with the legal tenders and buy gold for that purpose. That makes gold a commodity, and one class of speculators will operate for the purpose of raising the price, just as much as they can, and another class to depress it; and just so long as it is in that shape, just so long will gold be kept as an article to speculate in. Now, if the Secretary of the Treasury could run the machine for about a year, on his capital,— that is, pay the gold interest, it seems to me that these people who are speculating in gold would find their load too heavy to carry, and that the premium would be reduced very materially.

I have thought this matter over a good deal, and I cannot see where lie the objections to it. There may be some; but I do not see why the Secretary of the Treasury should be made by the laws to collect gold from the people to sell it back to the people, to pay their duties with. I think the people can do it better in another way. If he would simply take the amount absolutely necessary, I think it would be better.

A Delegate from Cincinnati moved that the propositions be taken up according to the rules of Congress.

Mr. BRYSON: I rise to a point of order. As we have decided to be governed by the rules of Congress, I rise to state what I know is the actual course of proceedings in such a case as this in Congress.

When any gentleman, a member of a Committee, reports for that Committee to the House, that gentleman is fully empowered to state to the House that he will permit all the amendments to his entire report to be laid before Congress, to be considered at once, and when he calls the previous question, he will select from those amendments the propositions which he will accept, (I have seen fifteen or twenty before the House at once); and after that, all other amendments have to be brought in by special vote.

Mr. HERRICK, of New York: Experience has proven that the commercial centres are almost synonymous with the money centres. It seems that the advocates of expansion ——

Mr. FRALEY: I rise to a point of order. This proposition is now before the Convention, under an order which was unanimously agreed to, according to the practice of the House of Representatives of the United States. That order cannot be departed from unless you postpone the consideration of this subject, for the purpose of taking up the motion made by my friend from Cincinnati. I wish gentlemen to submit their amendments; I wish to have an opportunity of hearing them, and I wish to make a speech upon this whole question; but if the order that is proposed by my friend from Cincinnati be observed, it might become my duty to trespass upon the Convention six times instead of once. I hope the gentlemen who have already had an opportunity of presenting their amendments will consent that other gentlemen may submit their amendments also, and state the reasons upon which they urge their adoption; and I assure gentlemen, that being disposed to allow the utmost freedom of debate, I shall not suddenly spring any question upon them until the Convention is disposed to receive it. We might, by not hearing all that members desire to say upon these questions, find ourselves embarrassed at the close of the discussion, by conflicting amendments that might be adopted by the course now proposed, and be obliged to go over our whole work again, when we can simplify it by taking up each resolution, to be offered, and by having them all before us, and knowing what they are.

Mr. CASS, of Pittsburgh: As I understand the views of the Chairman, I have embodied them in writing.

*Resolved*, That the Convention will now receive and debate all propositions to amend the report of the Committee on Finance; and after all such propositions are presented, the Chairman of the Committee shall close the debate, whereupon the Convention shall proceed to consider the several resolutions of the Committee, and amendments *seriatim*, without further debate.

A Delegate inquired if a vote upon the propositions of the Committee cut off all amendments and substitutes.

The PRESIDENT: There is to be no debate after the Chairman of the Committee closes, and the propositions have been presented and debated. There has not been a speech here to-day which has not touched every resolution presented by the Committee.

Mr. BUCKLEY, of Detroit: If I understand the position of the Convention, I think we are entirely out of order. In the first place, the Convention voted to adopt the rules of the House of Representatives. A resolution was adopted yesterday, that the resolutions should be taken up separately. The resolution before the Convention, if I understand it, is the first resolution in the report; but the different amendments which have been presented to the Convention this morning, by the several gentlemen representing the different portions of the country, have had reference, not only to the first resolution, but to every resolution contained in this report. My own views are (I may be wrong,) that the first duty of this Convention is to entertain the first resolution. If there is an amendment offered to that resolution, it should be entertained by the Convention; if an amendment to that amendment is proposed, that also should be admitted; and there amendments should stop, until the amendment to the amendment is disposed of. It seems to me that is the only way we can ever get through the report.

The PRESIDENT: I will state briefly that when the gentleman from Philadelphia made the suggestion, I proposed to put it to the Convention as a motion, in order to ascertain their sense upon it; but by unanimous consent, it seemed to be adopted and acquiesced in. Perhaps in that particular I failed to get an authorized expression of the sense of the Convention. It was assumed by the Chair that the proposition was acquiesced in, and a wide range has been allowed. Now, the question is upon the resolution offered by the gentleman from Pittsburgh.

Mr. CASS said he would add to the resolution, "and that the vote be taken at one o'clock." (Calls of "Question.")

A Delegate from Cincinnati stated that many of the delegates would have to leave at twelve o'clock; and if the resolution passed, they would be precluded from voting upon the report.

A Delegate from Chicago: I move that the words, "and that the vote be taken at one o'clock," be stricken out. We did not come here to go home, at all events, on Saturday night. The gentleman from Cincinnati said he had made arrangements to stay here until Christmas, if necessary; and I suppose a majority of the Chicago delegates are ready to stay as long as he will, in order to come to some sensible conclusion on this most important matter.

The clause fixing the time for taking the vote was stricken out, and the resolution was then adopted.

Mr. HERRICK: Experience, as I before remarked, has proven that the commercial centres are almost synonymous with the money centres. It seems generally understood that the advocates of the legal tender currency are found in the West. While we acknowledge the genius and enterprise and activity of the West, and while we expect to reach a specie basis only by taking the wealth from the fertile fields of the West, yet sir, we think that possibly we at the East may understand this question a little. It seems to me that the gentlemen at the West misunderstand this matter, and labor under the impression that legal tender money or paper money will stand in the place of accumulated wealth. The commercial centres of the seaboard have, from their longer existence, piled up this wealth; and until our Western country is older, and until the people there have accumulated capital, no panacea will be found in the greenback currency. Two dollars a bushel for wheat is no better for the farmer or the agricultural interest than one dollar and fifty cents in gold, and by maintaining this legal tender system, the more paper we have the more we shall want. It was claimed by the able speaker from Chicago, that in five years the natural production of gold would harden up this greenback currency into real money. Five years will also accumulate wealth from the earth to replace the wealth destroyed in the rebellion; and I advocate the measure as it stands, because I believe that by taking five years, (as it is only proposed to do,) the productions of the earth and the hardening up of this currency by the accumulation of gold will produce the same results; and therefore, let us submit to the minimum contraction of three millions per month.

Mr. BLAKELY: It is my impression that the whole country is looking to this Convention with the expectation that it will propose some plan by which we shall reach, at some time, specie payment. Congress has been debating the question for the last three years, and our greenbacks are worth less than seventy cents on the dollar. Notwithstanding we reckon our currency in dollars and cents, still, when we come to coin, which we have already learned is the basis of values, we know that a paper dollar is worth less than seventy cents. Until the day comes when we can provide ourselves with means to meet that currency in gold, we shall never make any progress. We are going round in a circle. The idea of having an irredeemable currency, as some gentlemen claim, of fifteen hundred millions, with which to do the business of the country, is simply a farce. Six hundred millions was sufficient before the war. There are now two hundred and ninety-seven millions of national bank currency and three hundred and ninety-one millions of legal tenders; and the deposits and general circulation of the country amount to almost a fabulous sum. With a view, however, to reach, as I hope we may, some time when we may say, "we are preparing to resume specie payments," I support the resolution offered by the gentleman from Toledo. The amount of coin that will go into the banks on that proposition will be twenty millions a year. The amount of reserves held by the banks under the law is about one hundred and fifty millions; consequently, every twenty millions that goes into the banks in place of the legal tenders now held, releases twenty millions of legal tenders; and we shall approximate at least so far towards the resumption of specie payments on the part of the banks. Three years time would place in the hands of the banks sixty millions of dollars in coin. This would look like proceeding towards a resumption of specie payments; that grand confidence, to which the gentleman has referred, would be restored to the people; and the only question then would be, when will the Government itself commence to redeem its circulation? We should have sixty millions of coin and ninety millions of greenbacks in the hands of the banks; and when the Government should proceed to redeem its own circulation, the banks would have available for their purposes, one hundred and fifty millions of dollars to sustain themselves in the resumption.

I would like to have that resolution come in, in place of that portion of the resolution which requires the Secretary of the Treasury to withdraw three millions a month.

Mr. Buzby: I now propose to call up before the Convention the motion that was postponed yesterday afternoon in regard to a free banking law.

The gentleman from Boston, I believe, who opened the discussion this morning, was pleased to direct some remarks towards my argument of yesterday. Now, I have some figures here which I think bear directly upon this point, and somewhat touch the position of New England in this matter; and they suffice to show that he should be content with the present distribution of the currency, while the other portions of the United States may be directly the reverse. I read from a printed statement which I cut out of a paper a month or two ago, wishing to preserve it for use thereafter.

The writer says that before the war, with a banking capital of eighty-five millions, the New England States had a circulation of thirty-four millions. To day, with one hundred and forty-five millions of capital, they have one hundred and three millions in circulation. That is, they have a little more than trebled, in the short space of seven years. Thus well provided at home, they find themselves ready to dispense with treasury notes. The writer goes on to add, that of the five hundred millions of legal tenders in actual use in the country, New England has more than a fourth, leaving the balance for the use of the rest of our immense domain.

Is it surprising that New England should be entirely satisfied with this position of affairs? Is it at all surprising that the rest of the country should be very much dissatisfied?

It was suggested in the Committee that we should scale down some of these banks in the East; but I submit that is an impracticable proposition, which could not be realized, and that an infinitely easier way will be to pass a free banking law. This will satisfy the mind of the West, and they are not so poor but that they have capital in the shape of five-twenties, with which they could secure the circulation, and have the advantage of the national currency for the transaction of their vast business, as well as this section of the country. Why should this Convention refrain from expressing an opinion in favor of granting to the West the power to transact its own business, not only for its own benefit, but for the benefit of the whole country?

Mr. ENDICOTT, of Boston: It seems to me, Mr. President, that the resolutions reported by the Committee meet perfectly the wishes of the gentleman from Philadelphia, and of those other gentlemen, who have advocated a free banking law. For myself, I can truly say that I abhor monopolies, and will advocate a free banking law the moment that the banks are able to maintain specie payments. The true policy, in my opinion, is for Government to require the banks to be always prepared to meet any probable demand upon them, even in a moment of panic, by keeping a larger reserve of specie than has hitherto been required. The public grants to the banks certain valuable privileges. In return, it has a right to demand at all times, *security*. The banks must be prepared to meet their liabilities, not only when not called upon, but when they are called upon, that is in the time of a commercial crisis. It is sometimes said that the specie reserve is so much idle capital. The office of the specie in bank is, like the ballast in a ship, to keep the monetary system steady. The ship may get on very well and perhaps sail faster, in good weather and a smooth sea, with little ballast. But she cannot live in a heavy storm, and may be thrown on her beam ends. This has usually been the case with the banks of this country. In easy times, they go on with full sail and little ballast, and when the inevitable revulsion comes, they are not prepared for it, and have no alternative but a general failure, i. e., a suspension of specie payments. Compel each bank to have in its vault a reserve equal to twenty-five per cent. of its immediate liabilities, circulation and deposits, and you have then placed them in position to relieve, rather than aggravate, a financial crisis.

As to the present unequal distribution of bank circulation, I can very well appreciate the sensitiveness of our Western friends upon that point, and I claim that the resolutions of the Committee completely meet their wishes. The resolutions propose to allow new banks to be formed at the West, reducing the circulation of the Eastern banks in the same proportion. The only real difference will be that the Western banks will have the profit of the circulation. The currency will flow off as now, without regard to the place of issue, to the centres of capital. For whatever the West has to give in exchange for money, there is now plenty of currency at command. The creation of new banks will not give the West any new capital; that must come as the product of labor applied to the teeming soil, or as attracted from older communities by tempting rates of interest or profit. So far as I know Eastern sentiment, there will be no objection to giving the West a larger share of bank circulation, if it can be done without increasing the volume of irredeemable paper, already greatly in excess. It has been urged in this Convention that there is no such excess, but I claim that the fact that paper is not at par with gold is conclusive proof to the contrary. My friend from Chicago, (Mr. Dore,) contends that this is owing to want of confidence in the Government paper. I cannot agree to this. Very few persons question the ability of this Government to fulfil its engagements, and the indignation which our Western friends express when accused of any leaning toward repudiation is a sure guarantee that the disposition to pay will not be wanting. Greenbacks are worth but seventy cents on the dollar in gold. Will any gentleman say that the probability of payment is less than three out of four? No, the depreciation is caused by non-convertibility and redundancy. When the paper currency is at once convertible into specie, the circulation will adjust itself to the wants of the country. When more is needed, it will be loaned from the banks, or if the banks are not able to discount, exchange on Europe will fall below the specie shipping point, and we shall supply our wants from the current of gold constantly passing from California, through New York to London. This is just as much at our command as the grain sent from Chicago through New York, to Liverpool. We shall as surely supply our needs of gold as of flour, shipping only the excess. When there is too much circulation, the excess of paper goes back to the banks for redemption, and the gold thus obtained goes abroad, until the equilibrium is restored. With specie payments suspended, and the paper circulation not convertible, there is no outlet for the excess. Foreign nations will not take our greenbacks, and prices must rise sufficiently to employ the redundant supply. Or to speak more correctly, the value of the paper dollar must fall in proportion. The *value* of commodities is not enhanced, only the nominal *price*. If all kinds of property were equally and instantly affected, no great harm would result, excepting between debtor and creditor. But they are not equally affected. Some kinds of merchandise will rise quickly, and out of just proportion, others slowly and in too small proportion. The result is a complete unsettling of values, uncertainty of all engagements for the future, an unwillingness to rely upon patient industry and slow gains, speculation and finally bankruptcy and ruin. The effect is precisely as if the community should adopt as the standard measure of length an india rubber yardstick, sometimes measuring thirty-six, and as often but eighteen inches. We have been, for the past few years, measuring our values by dollars, worth from forty to seventy cents, thus making an apparent, but not real, increase of wealth.

No greater curse can befall a business community than the adoption, as the measure of values, of an inconvertible and fluctuating paper currency. The evidences of its demoralizing power are to be seen on every hand; let us lend our voices to bring the country back, as soon as possible, to a sound and honest condition of the currency.

With the permission of the Convention, I will show the present active circulations of the country, as compared with 1860:—

JANUARY 1, 1860.

| | |
|---|---|
| Bank circulation, | $207,102,477 |
| Bank deposits, | 253,802,129 |
| Specie in bank, | 83,594,537 |
| Specie in Treasury, | 6,695,225 |
| Specie in private hands, | 100,000,000 |
| *Amount carried forward,* | $651,194,368 |

| | | |
|---|---|---|
| *Amount brought forward,* . . . . . . . . | | $651,194,368 |
| Deduct reserves: | | |
| Specie in bank, . . . . . . . . . | $83,594,537 | |
| Bank notes on hand, . . . . . . . . | 25,502,567 | |
| | | 109,097,104 |
| Active circulation, January 1, 1860, . . . . . . | | $542,097,264 |

OCTOBER 1, 1867.

| | | |
|---|---|---|
| Greenbacks and fractional currency, . . . . . . . | | $391,029,557 |
| Compound interest notes, . . . . . . . . . . | | 78,839,580 |
| Bank circulation, . . . . . . . . . . . . | | 297,896,984 |
| Private deposits in bank, . . . . . . . . . . | | 537,922,575 |
| United States deposits in bank, . . . . . . . . . | | 27,715,580 |
| Specie in banks and United States Treasury, . . . . . | | 113,551,774 |
| Specie in private hands, . . . . . . . . . . . | | 100,000,000 |
| | | $1,546,956,050 |
| Deduct: | | |
| Specie in bank, . . . . . . . . . . | $10,253,115 | |
| Specie in private hands, . . . . . . . . | 100,000,000 | |
| Bank bills in bank, . . . . . . . . | 12,174,313 | |
| Legal tenders in bank, . . . . . . . . | 100,550,849 | |
| Compound interest notes, (all,) . . . . . | 78,839,580 | |
| | | 301,817,857 |
| Active circulation, October 1, 1867, . . . . . . | | $1,245,138,193 |

Increase from 1860, 130 per cent.

Increase, omitting bank deposits in both years, 146 per cent. The deposits should be included, as they are available as currency (by means of checks) in making the exchanges of commerce. Omitting them, the excess of currency becomes greater.

What is the probable increased requirement of the country? The increased population is about twenty per cent. The increased disbursements and receipts of the Government (say seven hundred millions) are in proportion to the sales of merchandise which last year paid tax (excluding stocks and gold) about six per cent. Allow twenty-nine per cent. for imaginary needs, and we have still an excess of seventy-five per cent. beyond the proper wants of the country, and which must be employed. Prices ought then to stand on the average about seventy-five per cent. higher than in 1860. In confirmation, I will refer to a table of prices, recently published in *Hunt's Merchants' Magazine*, showing the prices, from 1860 to 1868, of all the leading articles of merchandise. The average advance from January 1st, 1861 to January 1st, 1868, is about seventy-six per cent.

(Mr. WARD, of Boston, suggested that more currency was required than formerly, as sales were more generally made for cash.)

In reply to the question of my friend from Boston, I will say that I do not hold to the doctrine that cash sales require more currency than sales made upon credit. The proper office of money seems to be *payment*, and I fail to see why any more money is required to pay a debt just incurred, than would be required to pay the same debt at maturity of a six months' credit. Settlement by note does not *pay* a debt. It merely makes a postponed payment negotiable, and in this way may give employment to more rather than less currency. It may be sold and resold, requiring money for payment at every transfer of ownership.

The gentleman from Detroit, (Mr. FIELD,) has endeavored to show that contraction will not bring us back to specie payments, and cites, in proof, that gold is dearer to-day than it was in 1865, notwithstanding the contraction of the currency that has taken place in the meantime. He will find, if he examines the quotations for gold during the last few years, that the prices of merchandise have shown the depreciation of the paper currency much more correctly than have the quotations for gold. Other important considerations affect the price of this commodity. At the close of the war, the mass of the people looked in confident expectation for an early resumption of specie payments, and this opinion of course depressed the quotation. At that time and since, we have exported large amounts of our securities, supplying the market with exchange on London, and having a powerful effect in reducing the price of gold. So that it may be safely asserted that since the close of the war, gold has been relatively cheaper than commodities. The table of prices, to which I have already referred, shows the following average prices of fifty-six leading articles of merchandise:—

| January 1, 1861. | 1862. | 1863. | 1864. | 1865. | 1866. | 1867. | 1868. |
|---|---|---|---|---|---|---|---|
| 100 | 113 | 142 | 197 | 297 | 233 | 203 | 176 |

These averages conform with remarkable exactness to the prices which the various changes in the volume of the currency at those different periods might be expected to give. They show further that we have gone through with more than half the inevitable shrinkage in prices which must attend the transition to specie payments. Shall we, by further expansion, lose all that we have gained? Is it not rather the part of wisdom to keep on in the path of contraction, involving some farther shrinkage of nominal values, if you will, some real loss of property; but the sure and, as I believe, the only road to mercantile prosperity, as it is to national honor.

Mr. McCHESNEY, of Chicago: I rise to support the resolution of Mr. BUZBY. I agreed that the report of the Committee should be made to the house, reserving to myself the right to vote against some of the resolutions, and to support some amendments. I accepted the report at the time, because it proposed to make a redistribution of the currency, but it would give us, at the West, a very small proportion after all.

According to the present distribution of national bank currency, these New England States, with a population of 3,185,783, have a circulation of $103,300,639. Add to the New England States, New York, New Jersey and Pennsylvania, and the population amounts to about 10,500,000, with a circulation of $220,483,911. Take the nine States of the Mississippi valley — Ohio, Indiana, Illinois, Michigan, Iowa, Wisconsin, Missouri, Kentucky and Tennessee, with a population of 11,049,296,— something over half a million more than the first named,— and they have but $54,566,015 of the circulation. Now, it is proposed to scale down the old banks, in order that we shall have our proportion of the circulation in the Western States. Looking over the statement here, I find that the report of the Comptroller of the Currency in November, 1867, was, that there were 1,639 banks, with a capital of $424,394,861, having a circulation of $299,103,996. Scaling that down to sixty per cent., it takes from their circulation $44,467,880.

This is not the first time that some of us have been advertised that all the wealth and all the brains were in the Atlantic cities; it has been published often enough in the papers; but we may perhaps understand what we want in the West, as well as gentlemen on the seaboard. We claim that the domestic commerce may be worthy of some consideration, as well as the foreign commerce. We find that these gentlemen on the seaboard base all their calculations on gold, to bring them on a par with foreign countries, leaving us in the West to take care of ourselves. Perhaps we can do that, after a time. We have done it pretty well, so far. I have been asked several times, since I have been here, whether the West was going to repudiate the bonds, and adopt Mr. BUTLER's proposition. I think you will find, when you come to a vote on the second resolution contained in this report, that the people of the West are loyal to their pecuniary obligations as they were proven to be loyal to their political obligations. (Applause.) We demand,—we do not ask it as a favor,—we demand a fair distribution of the national currency, and if we can get a free banking law, we will take that; but we think that, with the growth of the country, we can get back to specie payments, the greenbacks will be withdrawn, and your national banks will have but very little basis. Five years will leave them only one hundred and eighty millions of greenbacks for a reserve; the balance must be paid up in gold. Now, we find that from 1860 to 1868, the population of the City of Chicago increased from 109,263 to 220,000, and that the assessed value of the real estate and property increased in the same period from $37,053,512 to $192,249,644; and during that time, the City of Chicago paid to the Federal Government, in taxes, $24,628,392. The annual tax paid by the City of Chicago to the Federal Government was just about the amount of the banking capital we have there, under this national banking law.

In regard to the statement of the gentleman from Boston as to the currency. He counts the deposits as so much available currency.

Mr. ENDICOTT: The argument is all the stronger if the deposits are left out.

Mr. MCCHESNEY: I have not gone into that calculation. I merely want to say, I remember that at the time of the suspensions in 1857, it was found that the Safety Fund banks had large deposits, but representing, on the other side, protested paper. So you might make any amount of available currency according to that; but it would only represent worthless paper.

Mr. MUNN: Some of our people are in a hurry; I am not; but to bring the thing to a point, I move to strike out the last resolution. I do it because our banking capital is now restricted by the Government of the United States. I do not propose that it shall assume to itself all the powers that were exercised by the Colonies even before they were independent of the English Government. The usury laws have always been under the control of the several States. Other gentlemen think we had better let it remain so for the present. I should be in favor, if this passed, of a free banking law; then I think we of the West could regulate the price of interest. That is all I have to say.

Mr. ATKINSON, of Boston: The main question before this Convention for discussion appears to be the enactment of a free banking law. It is quite evident that the Convention will only tolerate a discussion of the currency question from the specie stand-point, and this, Mr. Chairman, is to me one of the most gratifying results of the holding of the Convention. I confess, sir, that I dreaded this discussion, and that I feared the result, until it had become evident that the *true West* was here represented. It has been said, sir, and has been believed in the East, that the West is practically an unit in favor of the continued use of inconvertible paper money, and of what is called payment of bonds in greenbacks. On my return from an extended tour in the West last autumn, I denied this, and affirmed that the solid, substantial men of the West were right, and that we needed only to give them time and they would make their influence felt. But, sir, I knew the inflationists and the repudiators to be active, unscrupulous and aggressive; and I feared lest they should pack some of the delegations, and thus cause this Convention to misrepresent the business community as much as the political knaves who advocate disguised repudiation under the name of payment of bonds in greenbacks, now misrepresent or mislead their constituents.

But, sir, my fears were groundless; the true and honest purpose of the business community to get back to specie payment is by none more truly represented than by the Western men here present, who are from sections that have been the most distrusted; and therefore the main point of discussion is only upon the question of free banking, and upon that I propose the following resolution:

*Resolved*, That this Convention advocates the immediate passage of a free national banking law, with suitable provision for the redemption of notes issued by national banks; *provided*, that for every additional note issued to or by any new bank, a legal tender note of equal amount shall be withdrawn.

This, Mr. Chairman, would be one, and a very effective step toward specie payment. What the West and South need, if they need anything, is more real capital invested in banking, not more paper promises, which may bring capital to the holder sometime or other when the nation chooses to pay them, but which for the present are mere evidences of debt.. Capital can only be the actual existing surplus result of past labor put into form for use; as such it has substantial value; as such it is constructive; as such it is evidence of wealth and is a real possession to its owner; and a bank bill convertible into specie on demand is evidence of the title of the holder to such capital in existence and held by the bank or held by the promisors of the notes discounted by such bank. But the paper promise of the Government is evidence of destruction, not construction; of labor and wealth consumed in the war; it is only a mortgage upon the labor of the future, and represents no capital in existence.

Increase the quantity of these paper promises in circulation either directly or by an additional issue of bank notes redeemable in them, and you have not added a single dollar to the real capital of the country. You may have added certain instruments by which the distribution of the true wealth of the country may be altered and rendered inequitable, but you have added no productive force to the community.

What the West needs is more actual, real capital, invested in the business of banking. Now, sir, if a free banking law is enacted upon the plan proposed, with the provision that for every new bank note issued a greenback shall be cancelled, you are taking a positive and effective step toward making every national bank note redeemable in specie, that is in real capital of which real or specie money is one form.

There is doubtless a large amount of real capital in the West and South—or capital that would go there, to be used in banking, except for the limitation of the law. Suppose it should prove in the next two or three years that there were two hundred million dollars thus waiting opportunity, and that such sum should be subscribed to new banks. Such capital would then be mainly invested in Government bonds; the Government would then have it available for the purpose of buying up one hundred and fifty million dollars of its legal tender demand notes, it would so do, and issue to such new banks seventy-five per cent. of their capital in new notes, say one hundred and fifty million dollars. The volume of the currency would then be the same, but the amount of lawful money would be so much less. The new banks would be obliged to keep a reserve of lawful money, which should not be less than twenty-five per cent., and this would take fifty million dollars more legal tenders out of circulation.

When one hundred and fifty million dollars of legal tender notes had thus been actually funded, the day would not be far distant when the Government could propose to pay the remainder in gold.

Now let us look at the effect of this operation upon existing banks. They as well as the new ones must keep a reserve of lawful money, and as the legal tender notes were being absorbed or funded by the establishment of the new banks, all the banks must begin to retain the gold paid them and to make it a part of their reserve. This they must do under the operation of natural law,—for self-protection,—to avoid bankruptcy,—and presently you might find the banks not only retaining gold but buying it, thus creating a demand; that demand would induce the supply, and all other commodities would adjust themselves gradually to gold prices.

It might prove that by such establishment of new banks in the South and West, some old banks now in existence in the East would become superfluous, and such result would be natural and right. When the currency is made absolutely redeemable in specie, the aggregate amount required will regulate itself; but our present forced circulation of irredeemable paper cannot be regulated or defined; neither is it self-regulating; the prices of commodities must adjust themselves to the arbitrary and unchanging volume of currency, not, as under a natural system, the volume of currency to the uses for which currency is wanted.

An arbitrary or fixed amount of inconvertible currency will always be least wanted when there is the most to be had, and most wanted when there is least; it will be very plenty between crops, and very scarce when crops are moving; therefore we can never have enough, and shall always have too much, until it is withdrawn. It is a thief, and will steal from labor an unfair share of its earnings, until its promise can be performed, and a real dollar can be had on demand. Its advocates are more dangerous enemies to the country, than were the rebels of the South.

Having given this hasty statement of the grounds on which I would advocate a free banking law, I will now say a few words in support of the resolves presented by the Committee; and I cannot forbear a reference to a letter of my own, which was printed a few weeks since in the *New York Evening Post.* I believe nearly every point made in the report of the Committee is substantially made in this letter; in it, I made the following propositions:

1st. To legalize gold contracts at once.

2nd. The immediate enactment of a free banking law; all new banks to be organized on a specie basis, and free from the mischievous and absurd trammels of usury laws.

3rd. The absolute sale of four million dollars a week of ten-forty bonds, or the like; such sales to begin July 1, 1868; payment to be made in greenbacks, to be cancelled.

4th. An enactment that on and after January 1, 1870, gold coin shall be the only legal tender.

I advocate the first proposition upon the following grounds: It is alleged that business is now conducted upon a cash system, and this is technically true; but yet credit is essential to all the movements of society. The farmer who plants a field of wheat, credits or trusts some one to reimburse him in the future; the manufacturer who lays the foundation of a mill, the storekeeper who lays in a stock of goods, all trust or grant a credit to the future. The ordinary transactions of society, such as the raising of a crop, the stocking of a store, and the moving of a crop from the farm to the market, take from three to six months. The ordinary mercantile credits, when granted, also fall within six months. Now the return to specie payment cannot be easy to men who enter into an obligation to pay money when legal tender notes are worth seventy-five cents on a dollar, and who are obliged to pay in real dollars at one hundred cents, yet such a change must take effect; the curse of fluctuating money is an injury to the whole people, and cannot be tolerated in order that a few debtors may be saved from loss. But we are bound to give them fair warning. Having suspended contraction for the present, we must give the opportunity to those who choose to incur a liability, or to lay the foundations of large mills or other works, to do so upon a gold basis, and thus avoid the danger of fluctuation. Then, by giving warning that after six months we shall again begin to fund the demand or legal tender notes, we shut the mouths of those who choose to incur a debt payable in legal tenders. They could not, after such warning, allege that we had no right to interfere with a given volume of currency, to which business had adjusted itself.

As to the country growing up to the existing volume of currency, I do not believe in it. The bank note circulation of Great Britain was less in 1865 than in 1845, because the railroad and telegraph system had so facilitated the exchange of merchandise, as to cause each bank note to perform its function oftener. But we shall never know how much currency is needed until we have free banking on a specie basis; then the volume of currency will regulate itself.

It will thus appear that I had practically come to the same conclusions as are presented in the report of the majority of the Committee, including free banking, only upon a specie basis. I therefore second the resolutions as a whole.

The amendment I have offered is not my own; it was suggested by a friend who is not a member of the Convention; and as it appears to me to have great merit, and to offer, perhaps, a more speedy method of reaching specie payment, I have offered it.

Mr. Holton: I was hoping not to have felt called upon to say a word on this great and important question, but I am constrained to make one remark on behalf of the West, upon which so much responsibility is laid at this juncture. I do not for a moment sympathize with the idea that is put forth here by some, that the West is any less concerned in the question of getting back to rock-bottom, than is Boston or Philadelphia. (Applause.) Wisconsin is in earnest in her efforts for the payment of her debts, and in carrying forward the great question, not only of the regulation of internal commerce, but of external also. I put the question to a Boston gentleman last night, "Why are your ships rotting at your wharves? It is," I said, "because we are away from the rock-bottom on which the nations of the earth transact business." (Applause.) When we can get back to rock-bottom, we shall again have free commercial intercourse with the world. We stand forty millions against nine hundred millions, and we cannot afford to live apart and alone. I should deplore any proposition here that should not have the effect, among other things, to cause me to notify my wife that she must cut the ribbons from her bonnet, and my daughters that they must come down to plainer dresses, and myself, too, that I must reduce my expenses, in order that this country may again participate in the commerce of the globe; and also, that I personally may know, by this standard,—the best mankind has ever fixed,—what is the value of my real and personal estate.

Mr. COLE, of St. Louis: I am very glad the honorable gentleman from Milwaukie has expressed himself as he has on this important question. I wish to offer a resolution; it will not be new to many gentlemen present, but I would like to hear their views upon it:

*Resolved*, That this Convention respectfully request the Congress of the United States to authorize a loan, to be negotiated in Europe, of two hundred millions of dollars, at not less than par, and at a rate of interest not exceeding six per cent., with the distinct agreement that the proceeds of said loan shall be used exclusively for specie resumption.

I believe that we can resume, and that resumption is the only panacea for the evils under which we are laboring. I do not believe that one-half of this amount would be required. The fact that such a loan had been authorized would unloose millions of dollars now hoarded up in old stockings and bags, and hid away in the banks, which would immediately go into the circulation of the country. The West is for resumption; without it, the West cannot live; nor can we live as a nation.

Mr. GANO, of Cincinnati: I ask for a temporary suspension of the business before the Convention, in order that I may introduce certain resolutions, upon which I desire action before any of the delegates, who may be obliged shortly to take their departure from the city, shall leave the hall. I beg to move as follows:

WHEREAS, The Boston Board of Trade, with a regard for the prosperity of the commercial interests of the nation, only excelled by its munificent hospitality, and with a sense of courteous propriety toward its kindred associations that may well serve to incite us all to foster a spirit of mutual forbearance, of kindly interest, and of generous emulation; has taken the lead in efforts to produce such action at the hands of the several bodies represented in this Convention, as will elevate them in their relations to one another, and to all industrial interests; therefore,

*Resolved*, That the most cordial thanks of this Convention are due, and are hereby tendered to the Boston Board of Trade, for its efforts to further the objects which have brought us together, and especially for its assiduously polite attentions, bestowed with unremitting zeal upon us all, both as individuals and as representatives. Its members shall always be welcome to the best our hearts and hearths can tender.

*Resolved*, That even though no positive or direct advantage should result from our deliberations and discussions, yet, nevertheless, we realize that the inspiration drawn from the patriotic and enterprising spirit pervading the atmosphere of the Old Bay State, will serve as an invigorating tonic, exciting in us a more jealous concern for what is right, and refreshing us for new achievements in commerce, in science and in art.

*Resolved*, That the members of the Boston Board of Trade have drawn so largely on our gratitude, that our reserves are well nigh exhausted; and that we must consequently go into bankruptcy on the social obligations which we acknowledge to be due to the citizens of Boston, to their municipal authorities, and to themselves individually. Boston can divide the assets remaining, and we mortgage ourselves for the balance, swearing here and now never to repudiate the debt.

*Resolved*, That our thanks are hereby tendered to the officers of the Convention for their prompt, constant and courteous attention to its deliberations, and for their able administration of its business.

*Resolved*, That our thanks are especially due to Mr. HAMILTON A. HILL, for his arduous labors in behalf of the purposes of the Convention, as well in the preliminary work of bringing it about, as in aiding to make effective its deliberations.

*Resolved*, That our acknowledgments are gratefully tendered to the various transportation companies that have so kindly tendered to the members of the Convention the courtesies of their lines.

The resolutions were unanimously adopted, and three hearty cheers were given for Boston and for Massachusetts.

Mr. NAZRO, President of the Boston Board of Trade, in response to the resolutions, said:

MR. PRESIDENT, AND GENTLEMEN OF THE CONVENTION:

I did not suppose that a vote of the nature that has just been taken would be proposed, and come up at this particular moment, but you will pardon me for detaining you to reply briefly to the flattering compliment just paid us. We have been together four days, during all which time there has been manifested, from the representatives of all parts of the land, a deep interest in the action of this Convention. When I have taken you by the hand, gentlemen, I have found the warmest grasp of friendship, and, as has been said before, "though we met as strangers we shall part as friends." I have felt and appreciated the language of the poet, that

> " Parting is such sweet sorrow,
> That I could say good night until it be to-morrow."

We cannot say *good night*, gentlemen, for we go to our respective homes probably never to meet again. Gentlemen, we are soon to separate officially. You take with you our respect and affection; and I trust that when you shall have left us, you will entertain kindly feelings toward us, and that you will not feel it in vain that you have paid us this visit. We shall not probably meet together again in this world; but let us remember,—let me say, not only gentlemen, but dear friends,—that there is a country where there will be no parting. And before leaving for your distant homes, permit me to commend you to the protection of Almighty God; that He will guard, protect, and keep you through all your lives; and that when the closing scene shall come, He will receive you into His blessed kingdom, through the intercessions of our glorious Redeemer. Gentlemen, I take of you an affectionate farewell.

The consideration of the report of the Finance Committee was then resumed.

Mr. CASS, of Pittsburgh: It is not my purpose to debate the propositions presented here by the Committee. I propose to leave that to the Chairman, who is able to defend the report. I wish only to make an appeal to the Convention to support the report as it has been presented here. Unfortunately, and against my judgment, I was put upon that Committee. We have been in session, as you know, two whole days; and we have presented here a report which, in its entire length and breadth, I presume at first had the approbation of hardly any of the thirty members, except, perhaps, the Chairman, and I am not certain that it had his. We had, therefore, each one, to make a concession; and the debate shows that we might go on here piling amendment upon amendment until we waste the report all away. I hope that amendments will not be made so as to emasculate the report; but that we shall adopt it as it stands. I ask, therefore, that you will forbear, and that you will take the report, as I and the other members of the Committee took it, namely, as the very best thing we could bring to you under all the circumstances.

Mr. WARD, of Boston: I understand the first resolution of the report to be before the Convention. I wish to say a word or two in regard to it. In the first place, it appears to me that the resolution itself contains an error. It states that property values have already adapted themselves to the amount of currency. Let us look at this. About a year ago, a law was passed by Congress, providing for the contraction of the currency, — the very thing contemplated by this resolution. At that time, if I recollect rightly, gold was at one hundred and twenty-seven. Immediately, under the operation of that act, gold commenced to rise, and went up as high as one hundred and sixty-seven, there being a contraction, in the meantime, of one hundred and thirty millions. That is one point for the Convention to look at before acting upon this proposition. Here, under the operation of this very plan now proposed to be repeated, gold went from one hundred and twenty-seven to one hundred and sixty-seven, and in the meantime, there were a hundred and twenty or a hundred and thirty million of dollars withdrawn. That is the simple fact. I make no comment upon it, for I have not time.

Mr. TOBEY: I wish to suggest to my friend, — whose views I appreciate, and I know this Convention will appreciate, — one simple consideration. It is quite evident that the document we are discussing is as expansive as the currency itself, and that we can never end the debate unless we bring ourselves to some limit. There has been no subject before us so important as this subject of the currency; and, for one, I should be glad to spend three days in the discussion, so instructive and so interesting. I have forborne, myself, to present any views, — holding some as I do very definitely, of more or less value, perhaps not much, — preferring to listen to others. I hope that some measure will be suggested by the Chairman of the Committee by which we can speedily come to a vote upon the main subject. It should not be forgotten, that there has been a full discussion in Committee, and that with the differences we have, we shall never reach a better platform, on the whole, (though from some of the views we may dissent,) than the report of the Committee itself.

Mr. FRALEY: I believe amendments have been offered to every proposition submitted by the Committee, but if there are any others to be suggested, I am willing to postpone what I have to say for ten minutes, to enable such propositions to be introduced. At the end of the ten minutes, I would like to bring this debate to a close. (Loud calls of "Go on," "Go on.")

Mr. President, I approach what I have to say upon this subject with a great deal of diffidence. Almost all the points involved in this report have been presented for your consideration and have been discussed. Many of the arguments that I would have made myself in favor of this report have already been made, and all that has been urged against it I have heard before, in the Committee of conference, in principle if not absolute language. All that I have heard in favor of this report has strengthened my own convictions that it approaches as near to the deliberate judgment of this Convention upon these several questions as it is at the present moment possible to arrive at.

The necessity for some declaration of this sort on the part of such a Convention as this, must, I think, be apparent to every one. As I had the honor to say at the opening of this Convention that the currency question was that which entered into every man's business, into every man's household, and into all the relations of life; so I say again, I believe that the currency of the country should at all times be redeemable in specie. (Applause.) I believe there are occasions sometimes arising from commercial convulsions when it becomes absolutely necessary for the good of the whole country that specie payments should be temporarily suspended. I believe there are other occasions, in the exigencies of war, when from public necessity they must be suspended. And I believe that after the cessation of the causes which have produced such results, specie payments should be resumed at the earliest practical moment when that result can be accomplished without shocking public or private credit, or overturning all the relations of industry. (Applause.)

We have had, Mr. President, three great wars, leading to suspensions of specie payments, from public necessity. And the chapter of history presents to us what occurred upon the termination of each of these three great wars, — the first, the war of the revolution, the second the war of 1812, and the third, the lamentable war among ourselves. Specie payments, suspended during the war of the revolution, were only resumed by the almost wholesale repudiation of the public debt of the United States. The wisdom and the sagacity of ALEXANDER HAMILTON extricated a small portion of that debt from repudiation; and that small portion of the debt, so extricated from repudiation, was faithfully, fully paid by the people of the United States in gold or silver, or their equivalents. The war of 1812 brought about another suspension of specie payments, and at the close of that war specie payments were resumed by universal bankruptcy of the people. Those who recall the fearful times that were passed through from 1816 up to 1824, will realize with peculiar force the fact to which I have alluded — that it was a country of almost universal bankruptcy. And now, Mr. President, we have had a more stupendous suspension of specie payments than has ever occurred before in our history, and the great problem that we have to solve is this: how shall we bring about a resumption of specie payments without national dishonor or individual bankruptcy? And I think the world has grown sufficiently in intelligence upon these subjects to decide that as reasonable men, as business men, as patriotic men, we can bring about a resumption of specie payments without either national dishonor or individual bankruptcy. (Applause.)

Now, Mr. President, the Committee propose to bring about this desirable result by such a gradual and sensible process, commencing upon a definite day, giving sufficient notice to everybody, that it may be almost as silently secured, and as healthfully prospered, as the dews which fall upon our land from Heaven. We ask that there shall be no shock given anywhere. We ask that we shall have sufficient time to prepare ourselves for the process of resumption; and that when it has once been begun, it shall be so gradual that it will not affect those relations upon which the circulation of money in the community depends, nor shock any of the great interests of the country.

I believe, Mr. President, and gentlemen of the Convention, that the passing of the propositions which the Committee have had the honor to submit to you will immediately have a beneficial effect upon the premium (as it is termed) on gold, and upon the foreign exchanges of the country, by inspiring confidence in our determination to approach this question in such a way that it shall be settled without, as I said before, any shock to any interest. It has been said upon this floor that it is not the resumption of specie payments that we want so much as the general confidence of the community in the Government of this country holding faith to its obligations, and the sustaining of the Government, in holding that faith, by the people of the United States. I believe that a majority of the people of the United States are in favor of holding the faith of the United States inviolate. (Applause.) I believe that there is not a man, in whose bosom there is the spirit and feeling of American citizenship, who, if this question were presented to him fairly and squarely, would venture to say that he would repudiate this debt.

I think I have said enough to convince you, gentlemen, that while we may not all agree upon all the details of this first resolution, we will agree so substantially upon them that we can come together and unite in the passage of this first resolution without any amendment. And therefore I decline to accept any of the amendments that have been offered to that proposition. (Applause.)

In regard to the second proposition, that our national honor and good faith alike require that we should abstain from enforcing the right which some insist upon, but which I utterly deny, the Committee have spoken cautiously and carefully — that there should be no attempt on the part of the Government of the United States to redeem any part of the five-twenty bonds, until their arrival at maturity at a period of twenty years from their date, or until by the resumption of specie payments they can be paid in coin. And I believe upon this point I shall have the unanimous support of this Convention. (Applause.)

In regard to the third and fourth propositions, which look to a redistribution of the circulating notes of the national banks, I believe that if the gentlemen of this Convention will carefully consider them in all their details, and carefully digest all the propositions that they contain — as carefully as I have done myself — they will find in them a fair and honorable and just solution of this question. And I here take occasion to say that I am not entitled to any credit for originating these propositions, but that they have come open-handedly and cheerfully, as we have received everything in this city, from the generous hearts of the people of Boston. (Cheers.) They are entitled to the credit of them; and I say to my friends from the West that I believe they are calculated to satisfy all their wants, until we can arrive at that other stage of our journey which is presented in the next proposition, which is that in regard to the free national banks. I believe, Mr. President, that every member of the Convention, without any exception, is in favor of abolishing any monopoly in banking.

(Applause.) And so believing, the only thing that remains is to determine when free banking can be safely and successfully established in the United States. I have always been in favor of a free banking law, from my first entrance into active business life. I have never seen any occasion to change that opinion, but on the contrary it has strengthened with my strength and my conviction has increased with my age; and I say here to-day that for a great manufacturing, commercial and agricultural community, free banking upon proper principles is as essential to their welfare as the circulation of the blood is to the human body. It can only, in my judgment, gentlemen, be safely and successfully established when every note issued by a free bank shall be redeemable at its counter or at some place in some great commercial centre appointed for its redemption, in gold or silver coin. And with these remarks I shall dismiss that part of the proposition, and say that as Chairman of the Committee I decline any of the amendments proposed to that section.

The next resolution is one requesting Congress to enact a law which shall authorize the making of contracts payable in gold and silver coin, and securing a specific performance of those contracts. I think with my friend from Boston, (Mr. Tobey,) that this will be one of the most successful steps for bringing us practically to specie payments, and bringing us to such specie payments by a route that will not disturb the volume of paper currency by any process that some gentlemen on this floor have expressed their fears of. If contracts be made payable in gold or silver, the person making those contracts takes the risk of the prices as compared with the currency of the day, being higher than it was when he made his contract, and he hopes for the benefit of its being lower. It only affects the commodity with which he is about to deal in making a purchase; but as that is his own individual affair, the currency itself will have nothing to do with the question, but it will be simply a settlement of the matter between himself and his debtor. We have in Philadelphia, resting upon the honor of the men who make these contracts, most extensive transactions in coffees and sugars and products of the tropics; and I have never yet heard, although such contracts are at present unprotected by law, any one case in which they have been violated. And this speaks volumes for the commercial honor of our country. We have had in our courts in Pennsylvania, and I suppose there have been elsewhere, contracts, contemplating by their letter, payment in gold and silver coin of the United States, and in some courts and in some places the specific performance of these contracts has been refused; while in others, where the contracts rested not upon the descriptive dollar, but upon a given number of pennyweights and grains of silver or gold, they have been enforced as contracts payable in commodities; and accordingly those who have had the wisdom to make such contracts in ancient times, have been benefited by them under modern legal decisions. Now if we have a law of the United States upon this subject, they can be enforced everywhere; and I believe, as I said at the outset of my remarks upon this particular proposition, that it will be a wise thing for this Convention to adopt this proposition; that it will be beneficial in its operation in putting us upon the right road to the resumption of specie payments, and steadily keeping us there. And upon that point I shall not say any more.

The remaining point is that in regard to the usury laws. This is a subject which has been so thoroughly ventilated in this Commonwealth, and which has been so carefully considered in ancient times by LOCKE, and in more modern times by BENTHAM, and indeed by all the accepted writers upon political economy, that I almost hesitate to say a word to a Convention of business men upon a subject which addresses itself so familiarly to their common sense. By successive stages almost every commercial community have been endeavoring to rid themselves of an usury law. We begin by raising the rate of interest, permitting contracts to be made at a higher rate than that which prevailed before; and finally, we all land by coming to perfect freedom. Such, I believe, has been the history of this question in every commercial country that has acted upon it in an intelligent way. We all recollect the successive stages that prevailed in England, by trying the experiment gradually, first upon one species of contracts and then upon another, exempting some contracts from the operation of the law, and granting it to others, and finally, after a most thorough investigation of the whole subject by a Committee of the House of Commons, the law was made general in its application. The report of this Committee has been, by the Philadelphia Board of Trade, laid before the commercial bodies of the nation, and they have sent it to the Congress of the United States, and it has been favorably considered by the Committee on Commerce of the United States. We ask that usury laws shall be abolished everywhere within the United States, and that, where no contract specifically to the contrary exists, seven per cent. shall be the uniform rate for money. I think that I need not press this point upon your attention, and I therefore decline to accept the amendment which has been offered by one of my friends, to strike out that proposition.

There remains for me, gentlemen, but a brief duty to perform. I accept the resolution offered by Mr. NAZRO. I accept also the amendment in the shape of a distinct resolution, which was offered by the gentleman from Toledo (Mr. DAVIS,) in regard to the holding of coin by the banks.

The amendments were here read.

I will say one word upon the propositions which I have thus accepted. Upon the first one I hold that after a contract or a bargain has been made, it should be specifically provided that no man able and willing to contract, who has made a contract, should try to get away from that bargain by any device, or by any exercise of power. It is the principle upon which we men of business conduct our operations. It should be the principle of Government also. In regard to the other proposition, that the banks should be prohibited from selling their coin, we owe that substantially, also, to our friends from Boston. When it was presented in the Committee, I feared that the public would not understand it; that they would regard it as an attempt to hoard the specie of the country. But I think that, if it be endorsed by such a body as this, they will speedily come to understand it, and that, when they come to understand that for every dollar the banks place in their vaults in coin, under this process, they have a dollar of currency to liberate for it, they will be satisfied that it is not a hoarding of specie. It tends, also, to the desirable result of strengthening all the banks in a reserve that is universally acknowledged as the ultimate standard for the redemption of currency.

I have now said all, gentlemen, specifically, upon these propositions, that I proposed to say. I have for a tolerably long life been engaged with business men, and in various branches of the business of this country. I can scarcely expect ever to see such another Convention together as this. I recognize among its members many whom I had the pleasure of meeting two years ago at Detroit; and I have found in them, in their individual discussions with me, upon the problems that you have committed to my charge, such a disposition to be frank and open in their objections to what has been proposed by the Committee, and to be so wise in their suggestions as to what we ought to do, that I tender to them my grateful thanks for the aid and assistance they have given me in coming to conclusions satisfactory to myself. And I have had from gentlemen with whom no such acquaintanceship existed before, and whose acquaintanceship and friendship I hope I have made by meeting them here now, the same frank, open and generous disposition to submit to my judgment their views upon these very vital and important questions that we are now about to settle by our votes. In the whole course of my life,—and I say it without affectation,—I have never seen together a body of gentlemen in whom I would place a more perfect reliance, upon all the questions that are embraced in the report of this Committee; and I trust that there may be such an unanimity in the adoption of this report, amended as I propose it shall be amended, by my acceptance of the two propositions to which I have referred, that it will go forth to the people of the United States clothed with such an endorsement as will secure its adoption; and that it will work for the healing of the nation, and for our restoration to that condition of things that so happily existed before the late civil war broke out. We have here from a large portion of the country, its commercial representatives. I hope that, under the blessing of Almighty God, before another National Commercial Convention is assembled, all our separated brethren will be brought under the common flag (applause,) and be there to greet us. And I believe, gentlemen, what you have already passed upon,—passed upon, as I understand, with great unanimity,—will be as beneficial to them as I believe it will be beneficial to us; and if you will crown your gifts to the country by the adoption of these resolutions, I believe that this Commercial Convention will have settled all the agitated questions of the day in a manner that will reflect honor upon us, and be a means of prosperity to our country. (Continued applause.)

Mr. President, I now move that the question be taken upon each of the propositions, as I have accepted them, without further debate. After acting upon them as I have suggested, if any of the amendments should be pressed, of course the question will be taken upon them; but I feel almost inclined to ask gentlemen to adopt the report as I have presented it, with the amendments accepted by me. I now move the previous question.

The call for the previous question was sustained. The adoption of the report, with the amendments accepted by the Chairman, was then moved, and it was carried, with but few dissenting voices, amid great applause. The resolutions adopted are as follows:

*Resolved*, That as the existing indebtedness of the nation and of individuals, and the exchangeable values of all property have been practically adjusted to the amount of currency now in circulation, there should not at present be any expansion or contraction thereof, but that the legal tender currency should be gradually, but steadily, approximated to the specie standard, by the funding thereof, on and after the first of January, 1869, in amounts not exceeding three millions of dollars per month.

*Resolved*, That the national honor and good faith alike require that the Government should not avail itself of the right to pay off the five-twenty bonds until by a general resumption of specie payments, the public debt, as it matures, can be paid in specie or its equivalent.

*Resolved*, That the inequality in the distribution of the national bank currency between the different sections of the country, requires some action on the part of Congress.

*Resolved*, That, to this end, the following change in the national banking law be recommended to Congress:

That any persons, proposing to form a new bank, may present to the Comptroller of the Currency in national bank bills, of any banks having a circulation of more than sixty per cent. of the capital of such bank, the amount proposed as capital of the new bank, which the Comptroller shall redeem in greenbacks. Thereupon the Comptroller shall cancel such bills and return them to each bank of issue for redemption, returning to such bank the bonds pledged as security, whenever a sufficient amount of bills shall have been cancelled to liberate one or more bonds. And that, thereupon, the persons presenting such bank bills shall be entitled, upon lodging bonds, and otherwise complying with the provisions of the law, to form a new bank, and receive from the Comptroller an issue of currency not exceeding sixty per cent. of its capital,

*Provided*, That no national bank currency shall be issued to any new bank in any State in which the amount of national bank currency already issued to the banks of such State shall bear a greater proportion to three hundred millions of dollars than the representative population of such State shall bear to the representative population of the country; and,

*Provided, further*, That the aggregate amount of currency issued to the national banks shall in no case exceed three hundred millions of dollars, until such time as the banks shall have resumed specie payments.

*Resolved*, That a system of free national banking can be safely allowed so soon as bank notes are payable and paid, on demand, in coin, and not before.

*Resolved*, That it be recommended to the Congress of the United States to enact a law authorizing contracts to be made in writing, which shall be payable in gold or silver coin, and securing the specific performance of such contracts.

*Resolved,* That the Congress of the United States should by law supersede the usury laws of the several States, and make seven per cent. per annum, the uniform rate of interest, when no contract has been made for any other rate, and authorizing contracts to be made in writing for the use of money at any rate of interest upon which parties, able and willing to contract therefor, may agree.

*Resolved,* That the bonds of the United States already issued, were exempted by law from taxation, and that having thus been issued, it would be a violation of the law of contracts to impose a tax upon them now, as well as a breach of faith on the part of the Government.

*Resolved,* That this Convention recommend to Congress to provide by law, that from this date no national bank shall be allowed to sell any part of the gold received from the Government as interest upon the bonds pledged for its circulation, until such time as the entire amount of the reserve required by law to be kept by the banks shall be made up of coin.

Mr. NAZRO: I have but one word to say, and it is one to which I know you will respond. Allow me to offer the following:

*Resolved,* That the thanks of the Convention be and they are hereby presented to the Hon. E. W. Fox, for the able, dignified and impartial manner in which he has performed the duties of President of the Convention.

Mr. MERRICK, of Philadelphia, put the motion, and it was carried unanimously.

Mr. BRUNOT: I desire to meet one point which was made in the address of the Chairman of the Finance Committee, by the following resolution:

*Resolved,* That this Convention reäffirm unanimously our adherence to the principles of national honor and good faith, as indicated in the second resolution of the report just adopted.

The resolution was adopted unanimously.

Mr. COVINGTON, of Cincinnati: It will be remembered that yesterday, the Committee on Transportation offered a resolution in relation to the Hoosac Tunnel, which the Committee and the Convention understood as being complimentary to the City of Boston and to the State of Massachusetts, and it was supposed that it would be adopted unanimously; but after the remarks made at the time of its presentation, the Convention, in the same spirit, voted to strike it out of the report. I think that, in our desire. to be complimentary to this city and to the State, we have made a slight mistake; and I propose to remedy it by offering a resolution which I hold in my hand, and which I think will not give offence to a solitary man in this grand old Commonwealth. I desire to say, in behalf of my delegation and of myself, (although I have not consulted with my colleagues upon the subject,) and I believe I may say, in behalf of the Convention, also, that the hospitalities we have received here deserve such an acknowledgment.

You will remember, that at the banquet at the Music Hall, the Governor referred to certain exports of the State of Massachusetts,—ice and granite. As a Western man, and as one who feels for the West, I beg to say, that neither granite *nor* ice, nor granite *and* ice, are all of Massachusetts. She has a heart, which is both genial and generous. (Loud applause.) I ask the unanimous adoption of the following resolution:

*Resolved*, That the policy of Massachusetts with respect to the means of transportation within her borders, initiated early by her aid to the Western Railroad, and continued by her more recent grants to the Hoosac Tunnel and Boston, Hartford and Erie lines, challenges our admiration as broad, liberal and sagacious.

Mr. HOLTON: I second that resolution, as Chairman of the Committee on Transportation; their views will be carried out by its passage.

The resolution was adopted.

On motion of Mr. WALBRIDGE, it was

*Voted*, That the Officers of the Convention be authorized to memorialize Congress upon the various questions embraced in its proceedings.

That the Convention adjourn *sine die*, after the closing address of the President.

The PRESIDENT: Gentlemen of the Convention: The hour of our separation as a deliberative body of business men is now at hand; but the associations which will cluster around the deliberation of the momentous questions which you have had under consideration, may be of lasting benefit. You have been engaged in the discharge of a voluntary and a patriotic duty, and although not intrusted with the power of making laws, you have been charged with the higher mission of moulding by just and wise resolves a policy, and of creating and consolidating an intelligent public opinion upon questions vital to the material prosperity of our whole country; and I cannot find it in my heart to allow this occasion to pass without congratulating each member of the Convention upon the auspicious manner in which your labors were begun, upon the practical wisdom with which they have been marked, and upon the advancement made toward the solution of the all-important business questions of the hour.

You have advanced a broad stride in the science of commerce by laying firmly the foundations of a policy destined to unite and represent the material interests of the nation in a Business Congress, to be known as the National Board of Trade.

The policy foreshadowed in the call of the Boston Board of Trade has been most wisely adopted by this Convention as a necessary adjunct to the protection and advancement of those industrial pursuits which constitute the true elements of our prosperity as a people, and are the safest anchorage of security in war as well as the proudest evidences of aggrandizement in peace.

Our work should not cease with our deliberations here, but I conceive it to be the duty and the interest of every one to labor unceasingly in the sphere of his business influence to carry on to practical and triumphant results the line of policy here matured and adopted. The work to be done and the labor to be performed is made attractive and pleasing by the new associations begotten in our intercourse here, and which may hereafter be formed by the business men of the various sections of the Union; associations which we may fondly trust will ripen into enlarged views and bind us together in lasting friendship.

Let each member pledge to this Convention, to his associates and to himself, that he will labor to sustain and dignify agricultural pursuits, to maintain and enlarge our manufacturing interests, and to develop and extend our commerce over river, lake and sea, until our white sails shadowing every wave, shall be at once our wealth and our defence; and let us, too, with one voice, demand national aid for the completion of at least two great continental railways from ocean to ocean, thereby creating competition, which will cheapen transportation.

In pushing on in blended harmony these exalted interests we shall present to the world the spectacle, that in peace or war, we are indeed a nation. Thus we may make evident to mankind and urge to their final acceptance and belief, the fact that we have solved the problem; that we have achieved the high destinies to which we are called; and that America, great in art, in agriculture, in commerce and in arms, shall be forevermore prosperous in peace and victorious in war.

In conclusion, gentlemen, I am charged by the unanimous voice of the delegations representing the Union Merchants' Exchange, the Board of Trade, and I may with confidence add the entire people of St. Louis, to extend to you their hospitalities, with the request that their city be selected as the place of your next assembling as a Convention.

My personal thanks are due and I hereby tender them to each member of this body, to the officers of the Boston Board of Trade, and to the several gentlemen of the various committees of arrangements, representing every branch of the government and every class of the people of this most hospitable of cities, for the generous support I have on all sides received while discharging the duties of the office you have done me the honor to confer upon me.

Wishing each of you a safe return to your homes, and earnestly desiring that prosperity may ever attend upon you, I have to announce that this Convention is now adjourned.

Mr. HILL, of Boston, one of the Secretaries of the Convention, was loudly called for, and said —

GENTLEMEN, — I beg to return you my sincere thanks for the compliment you have paid me.

On motion of Mr. NAZRO, leave was given to the Boston Board of Trade to append the names of the officers of the Convention to the memorial to be sent by them to Congress.

Mr. WALBRIDGE called for three rousing cheers for the Boston Board of Trade, and for the City of Boston, and they were heartily given. Cheers were also given for the West, and for the Middle States; and the Convention was dissolved.

# APPENDIX.

# BANQUET AT THE MUSIC HALL.

---

On Thursday evening, the sixth of February, the members of the Convention, by invitation of the municipal authorities of the City of Boston,* attended a banquet given in their honor, at the Music Hall. The Hall was decorated with flags, evergreens and flowers, and appropriate mottoes were suspended in front of the galleries. At the centre of the upper gallery, facing the organ, an arch was placed, composed of national banners, and having in its centre the arms of the City of Boston. Inscribed on the arch were the words —

NATIONAL COMMERCIAL CONVENTION.

WELCOME.

The galleries were filled with ladies in evening costume.

About six hundred tickets were issued, and the guests assembled, at half-past five, in Bumstead Hall, where an hour was spent in conversation, after which, the company proceeded to the large Hall, where they were greeted with music from Gilmore's full Band, stationed in the balcony.

Dr. Shurtleff, the Mayor of Boston, presided, and occupied the central seat on the platform. At the same table were seated the Governor of the Commonwealth, the President of the Senate, the Speaker of the House, the President and Vice-Presidents of the Convention, the President of the Boston Board of Trade, and other gentlemen.

The company having taken their places at the tables, His Honor the Mayor, said —

Gentlemen of the City Council: — In your name, and on your behalf, I cordially welcome these your guests to the hospitalities of the city; and I know that I fully represent your sentiments, when

---

* The Committee of Arrangements of the City Council, consisted of Messrs. George W. Messinger, Samuel C. Cobb, and Joseph F. Paul, of the Board of Aldermen, and Messrs. Charles H. Allen, Charles R. Train, Francis A. Osborn, George P. Denny, William M. Flanders, and Horace H. White, of the Common Council.

I assure them that it is with feelings of the deepest interest in the objects that have brought to this our city so many gentlemen as are here present this evening, from so great distances, over so many miles of weary travel, and in such an inclement season of the year, that the citizens of Boston, through you, their municipal authorities, extend to them their courtesies and friendly greetings.

Gentlemen of the Convention: — We are all heartily glad to have you with us on this occasion.

The Divine blessing was invoked by the Rev. GEORGE W. BLAGDEN, D. D., at the conclusion of which, the company were invited to be seated and to pay their respects to the good things which had been provided for their refreshment.

After the lapse of about two hours, the party was called to order, and the Mayor spoke as follows:—

GENTLEMEN: The occasion which has called us to the festal board this evening is one that, it is hoped, will result in the mutual benefit of us all. We are here together, assembled in sociality, from all parts of our common country, to testify our interest in those institutions which have for their primary objects the encouragement and extension of trade; and, surely, nothing should awaken within us a stronger sentiment than that which can arouse the dormant energies of a great nation, and bind into one firm bond of union the great commercial cities of the land.

Our beloved country is just recovering from one of the greatest shocks with which it has ever pleased the heavenly providence to visit any portion of mankind; and the resources which have been developed, and the energies that have been displayed in our days of suffering, have demonstrated to ourselves, as well as to all the nations of the earth, the true value that can be deduced from the cultivation of the liberal arts by men, unshackled and untrammeled by any adverse power, and guided and controlled by none other than that which can unite together the good, the great, the talented and the brave, in one common cause for right and humanity. Fortunately we have emerged from this greatest of struggles without the loss of national credit; and we stand this day with a faith unbroken, and a hope of future prosperity undying.

To those gentlemen who are with us for the first time it may be necessary to state that Boston has from time immemorial been noted for its peculiar idiosyncracies; and that it has been known the world over, from its earliest days to the present time, as the place of notions.

But we trust, gentlemen, that during your short stay with us now, you will find these peculiarities to be of such a character as to interest you in becoming more intimately acquainted with them, and also with our people. For I assure you, whatever you may have heard or read to the contrary, that none of the famous blue laws, imported from our mother land by a neighboring colony, ever gained any supremacy over our respectable progenitors, or ever had any influence here. Our ancestors came to this country to enjoy their liberties unmolested and uncontrolled; and you may be certain that if our statute books have been stained with foolish and oppressive whims, these are fast disappearing from our records; forever, it is hoped, to be wiped even from our memories.

From the first settlement of our town — and we date back more than two and a third centuries, with a good claim of being the oldest maritime place of this country — our people have ever been given to the industrial arts, and have been noted for their commercial enterprise. Long before the other great cities of our Union were started into substantial existence, the small peninsula of Boston was eminently distinguished for its trade and widely extended navigation. As early as the year 1631, the then Governor of the colony had built the first Anglo-American vessel and launched it upon the waters of our neighboring Mystic; and the gallant little "Blessing of the Bay" had proudly sailed from our island studded harbor, the pride of New England, and the fair rival of transatlantic craft. Two hundred years ago scarcely a bay could be entered where could not be found our fishermen; and never a seacoast without seeing our snows, our pinks, our schooners, or our pinnaces. Our forefathers were as well acquainted with all the seas and the pathless oceans as now are the sturdy seafaring men of our population of nearly a quarter of a million of souls.

Years before our trimountain hills and everflowing springs of living water had given their hospitality to our fathers, the pilgrim puritans of the Plymouth colony had established fisheries at the mouth of our harbor, availing themselves of our excellent fishing-grounds. But, I must not, gentlemen, carry you back so far as to make you think that we are a people of a past generation. I have been led to make these remarks simply to let you know that you are not among persons who look upon your calling as that of strangers; but that you are with those who naturally feel with you a deep interest in the business relations of the different sections of our country; and from whom you may expect a hearty coöperation in all practicable efforts that may be needful for promoting the special objects of your present Convention.

It is not for me to relate to you what our peculiar advantages are for commercial and trading purposes, nor what our enterprising merchants, manufacturers and mechanics, with the assistance of our wealthy capitalists, propose for increasing our accommodations and facilities for business. These matters are more properly subjects for your own meetings, during your hours of consultation and deliberation. Now, it is far more appropriate for me to draw you from the staid and sober thoughts which have bound you so closely at your business gatherings; and to win you, for a short time, to the pleasures of social intercourse with some of our Boston people. I cannot, even if I would, and if time should permit, specially entertain you with any words of my own; but I have in you, and in some of your friends who so gladly welcome you here this evening, a sufficiency of that versatility of talent that can beguile you from your every day cares, and, I hope, by adding information to pleasantry, make our social hour one of instruction and benefit.

MR. CHARLES H. ALLEN, President of the Common Council, was introduced as the toast-master of the evening.

Mr. ALLEN announced, as the first regular toast,—
*The President of the United States.*

The band played "Hail to the Chief," and the Hon. THOMAS RUSSELL, Collector of the Port of Boston, was called upon to respond,

Judge RUSSELL: Mr. Mayor, and Fellow-Citizens: If the President of the United States were here, I am sure that he would feel new pride in his position as head of the nation which is represented to-night by so much of business energy, and dignity, and talent, and wealth, and success, as are represented by the Convention who are present as guests of the City of Boston. I am glad that they have come back here to New England. They have come back, I say. They went to the West to build broader, and fairer, and richer New Englands than we have here at home, but they have come back to find that there are enough of us to keep the old homestead in repair, to keep a little fire burning on the old hearthstone, and to give a cordial welcome to our friends from the lakes, the rivers and the sea, from the West and the Northwest, and, thank Heaven, we may add, from the South also, as they come home to us. (Loud applause.)

Mr. Mayor, they have heard all sorts of stories about Boston, but you took them out yesterday on the Brighton road, and you showed them one thing, at least, that Boston was not a "one horse town."

(Laughter.) They tell me that when they went around there they thought they saw what they heard of some years ago,—" New England left out in the cold." (Laughter and applause.) Ah, you and I never feared that. If New England were false to the traditions of the fathers,—if she forgot the principles of her ancestors,—she might be "left out in the cold;" but never, never while the fire of faith burns in her heart, and the warm blood of loyalty boils in all her veins. (Loud and prolonged applause.)

You come home when you come to New England, and with all our hearts, and with all our love, we bid you welcome to the metropolis of New England. (Applause.) And now I do not mean to say one other word except just this: You call upon me to respond for the President of the United States. When the President of the United States speaks, there are a great many things that he has not time to say. You must take all those things for granted. (Loud laughter and applause.)

Second regular toast,—

*The Commonwealth of Massachusetts:* Always ready to extend a cordial greeting to the representatives of the industry and enterprise of the other States, and afford aid and encouragement to whatever serves to enlarge and bind together the national interests.

Three cheers were given for the "old Commonwealth of Massachusetts," the band playing, "Should Auld Acquaintance Be Forgot."

The MAYOR: I am happy to announce that Governor BULLOCK is here (applause,) but perhaps you may not be happy to hear me say that he is quite unwell. I have, therefore, taken him under my professional care, and have prescribed a short speech; but I rather think that if he will show himself, and say a few words, you will be satisfied we have a *live* Governor.

The GOVERNOR: Mr. Mayor, you have done me an act of genuine kindness in taking me under your professional, rather than your political and official orders; but I trust, sir, that no other gentleman present will find any preference in that direction. I will trespass, however, upon the weakness to which you have alluded, sufficiently to thank you, and those who are associated with you in the government of the City of Boston, for this opportunity to partake of your hospitality, in the presence of this company of guests, who represent many cities and many States, and who are here to promote the prosperity and the general welfare of the whole country. (Cheers.)

I will not abuse this courtesy, on my account as well as yours, by much speaking; but, sir, I will avail myself of the privilege of the official relation which you have invited me to impersonate, sufficiently to extend in behalf of the Commonwealth a warm greeting from the heart to these our friends who are visiting us from abroad. (Cheers.) From whatsoever State they come, and from whichsoever side of the mountain ranges which have been ineffectual,—and ever shall be ineffectual,—to divide us; whether from the capital city of the father of waters, or the emporium of the lakes so fitly representing the majesty of the forces of commerce and the mechanic arts, or from the queen City of Ohio, the Boston of the West, (applause,) or from the commercial metropolis nearer to us, which already casts every city of this continent, and which will eventually cast every city on the globe, into the shade (continued cheers) — whencesoever they come, in behalf of the whole people of Massachusetts, I cordially extend to them, one and all, the open and the warm hand of a New England greeting. (Great enthusiasm.)

Gentlemen, you are visiting us at a season when of our two proverbial staples of export, the one is quite obscured by the other,—the ice being a little too much for the granite. (Laughter and cheers.) But let me tell you, that neither the snow nor the ice can either chill or obscure the activity, the elasticity, the exhilaration of the intense and warm-hearted Commonwealth which greets you to-night, as fellow citizens and brothers, in the cause of industry, which is the cause of all. (Loud cheers, and shouts of "Bravo.") We have sometimes been called a little provincial; but I believe that in the modern vocabulary, provincialism is only another word for individuality; and if we are to apologize for our individuality, that enforces the necessity of apologizing, also, for our history, which, as citizen and magistrate, I say, God forbid. (Applause.) I feel quite sure, gentlemen, from what passes before me, that a very large portion of your number bear in your cheeks the blood of New England (voice—"That is so";) and it follows as a matter of course that a plurality of your number are by some kind of descent, either lineal or lateral or marital, kith and kin of this Commonwealth of Massachusetts. I doubt if there be a president of a Board of Trade from Portland to San Francisco who is not either a third or a fourth cousin of the President of the Board of Trade of Boston. And I ought here to remark, that I regard that as the highest office in this country. (Applause.) Mr. WEBSTER used to tell a story of a prominent citizen of this city who was in the habit of saying that, in his opinion, Massachusetts ought to give laws to the whole country;

that Boston ought to give laws to Massachusetts; and that for his own part, he would be entirely content to govern Boston. (Laughter and applause.) The hero of that story I understand to be the President of the Board of Trade of Boston. (Cheers.)

Gentlemen, I wish you success in the deliberations of your Convention. I notice by the newspapers, that you have laid out considerable work. I trust it may keep you here many days; and during that period, I commend you to the hospitality of His Honor the Mayor, and the authorities of this excellent city. ("Bravo," and cheers.) After which, gentlemen, I wish you a safe and happy return to your homes. (Prolonged applause.)

The third regular toast was then read,—

*The National Commercial Convention:* A working congress of business men, in which measures may be discussed by those who are most nearly interested in benefiting alike the legislation and the business of the country.

The MAYOR: Gentlemen, I will now introduce to you Mr. E. W. Fox, of St. Louis, the President of the National Commercial Convention, now met in council in the City of Boston.

Mr. FOX: Mr. Mayor: In calling upon me to respond to the toast in honor of the Convention, you have imposed at once a difficult and a pleasing task; difficult, because I can scarce find words to express the appreciation of the generous hospitality of the people of Boston, felt in common by each and every member of the Convention. (Applause.) The frosts of your New England winter may chill the body, but the merry jingle of your sleighing bells have welcomed us in chimes of beautiful symphony, while your wives and daughters have greeted us with smiles from balcony and portal, and the princely munificence of your social cheer warms and gladdens our hearts. (Applause and laughter.)

Nor alone in social intercourse have you become endeared to us, but the far-sighted commercial enterprise of your business men has resulted in a Convention, destined, I believe, to exert an influence of permanent good in uniting and linking together those agricultural, manufacturing, and commercial interests, which underlie our prosperity as a nation, and are the safest and surest guaranties of national permanence and peace. (Renewed applause.) I mention agriculture first, because, upon the producing element all other business and industrial interests depend. The West and the South produce, their rich fields yielding their wealth of cotton, grain and tobacco, while the Eastern and Middle States manufacture and export; and thus bound together, each dependent on the other, the various industries lead on to national wealth and aggrandizement, with a rapidity without a parallel anywhere in history. To modify, to change and assimilate our commerce, to meet the exigencies of a new order of things, growing out of the present financial condition of the country, and to urge our national Congress to such legislation as shall best promote all the interests of our foreign and internal trade and navigation, and to such action as shall give a healthful tone to our currency,—these are the duties of the Convention now in council in your city. If the deliberations of that Convention are commensurate in wisdom to the importance of the subjects under discussion, a great and a lasting good may be attained.

It is meet and proper that such a Convention, with such aims and purposes in view, should be held in the solid City of Boston, because solid and practical results are designed to be accomplished. We have come to you from all parts of the country, representing diversified and varied branches of trade, and you have given us each the warm hand of honest welcome. We are not insensible to your kindness, and we shall ever cherish a fond and abiding recollection of our reception and entertainment by you.

In conclusion, Mr. Mayor, allow me to catch the glorious sentiments that surround this hall, so beautifully entwined with the flag of our country, and invoke with them the blessings of Heaven — Plenty, Union, Liberty and Peace — upon the good people of Boston and of the Commonwealth of Massachusetts. (Loud and continued applause.)

The fourth regular toast was as follows,—

*The City of New York:* The commercial metropolis—the whole country rejoices in her prosperity as an element of our national greatness.

The MAYOR:—Gentlemen, you will now listen to the Hon. HIRAM WALBRIDGE, of New York:—

Mr. WALBRIDGE: Mr. Mayor and Gentlemen: As I stand in this "Modern Athens," in this majestic temple, and witness this Corinthian order and these Ionic columns, I am insensibly borne back through the sea of human endeavor over three thousand years, when the men of that early Athens were wont to assemble, in the presence of fair women, to commemorate some illustrious victory of war. We are met to commemorate that other sentiment which proclaims that "peace hath its victories no less renowned than those of war." From the "Father of Waters," and from the great metropolis of this country, we have come to New England, and we say that New England must remain a part of the United States, and that if any attempt shall ever be made to sever that connection by foreign or domestic foe, it can only be done when that foe shall have trodden over our graves.

In behalf of the City of New York, and on the part of those whom I have the honor to represent, I thank you for this compliment. New York has no jealousy of Boston; New York has no jealousy of any city of this continent. You can inaugurate no great enterprise that does not benefit that great city which I have the honor here in part to represent. New York is national in her sentiments, is national in her associations; and New York intends that this Union shall be restored, the Southern States returned, and the Federal flag again float in triumph over an united, a consolidated and a homogeneous people. (Great applause.)

It is proper and becoming that we are here. Boston, always practical, realizes her interest in opening means of communication between the East and the West, because in the next census the seat of empire is to lie beyond the Mississippi, and these maritime provinces of the East are to be sustained by the industry of the producing classes of the West. These assemblies of Boards of Trade are then of great significance; and I have the pleasure of stating that the Convention has determined that there shall be organized a National Board of Trade; and the origin of that association is due to the City of Boston. (Applause.) Gentlemen of the City of Boston, much as you are delighted to see us here, we are infinitely more gratified to be here; and whenever you extend the invitation, we will all come again. (Prolonged applause.)

The fifth regular toast was announced,—

*The Commercial Cities of the Great West:* They are no less centres of the inland trade and commerce of half the continent than they are important sources of influence on the civil and political destinies of its people.

The MAYOR:—Gentlemen, it is now my happiness to introduce to you Mr. E. W. BLATCHFORD, of Chicago:—

Mr. BLATCHFORD: Permit me, Mr. Mayor, in behalf of my colleagues and myself, to acknowledge the compliment paid our Western cities in the graceful sentiment to which your Committee has requested me to respond. And yet these compliments are paid, not to what has been *already* accomplished, so much as to what will be brought out in the future, as the result of the principles and the efforts which you are so kind as to recognize in the present. They are the traits in the boy, through which may be discovered the character and estimated the power of his manhood. And as this evening's gathering, while forming a beautiful accompaniment to the objects of the Convention, differs from it in its occupations, so let my brief remarks, for which the duties of the day have permitted but the slightest preparation, carry you into another subject than grain, and provisions, and metals, and the multifarious points relating to their production, manufacture, distribution and consumption. And indeed, sir, these representatives of the Western cities would do but meagre justice to our citizens, and to their constant and self-sacrificing labors, did they not call your attention to some of the efforts that are being made in the cause of charity and philanthropy — efforts which, in the results already attained, indicate the possibilites of the future.

In speaking of these efforts for the moment, permit me to use as my reminder the institutions which grace your own city, and which your unwearied attention has permitted us to observe. And upon nothing does the mind rest more gratefully than upon those munificent provisions you have made for the alleviation of human suffering in your hospitals. I am thus reminded that the earliest object that greets the eye as you approach St. Louis—and within a few months it will be the prominent object on the lake as you enter the harbor of Chicago—are buildings similarly consecrated. Your Eye and Ear Infirmary—the perfection of whose appliances and the skill of whose treatment are known to us—reminds of the institutions devoted to the same noble charity in more than one of our Western cities. Your common school system, with its varied beneficent methods—the result of years of faithful study and experience by those now gone to their reward—is the system through which we are endeavoring to secure the results to which you have more nearly attained. Intimately connected with this are our public libraries and reading-rooms —our Young Men's Associations—and, what deserves a fuller mention, did time permit, our Academies of Science and Museums of Natural History, through which have already been given to the world facts and names not unworthy of our years and observation.

Thus, Mr. Mayor, are we responding to the example of our sister cities of the East. The same Christian charity that here would raise the fallen, heal the deaf, enlighten the blind, minister to the suffering, relieve the poor, educate the ignorant, is present there— all-embracing, energetic, persevering. When you read the reports of the movements of fabulous quantities of wheat, and corn, and oats, and provisions, and iron, and lead, and wool, bear in mind that all this holds an intimate relation to a "work of faith and labor of love," whose results cannot be estimated by dollars and cents, as the duration of its influence cannot be reckoned by earthly days, or months, or years. Remember there are many throughout the width and breadth of our Western borders, who, apprehending the true value of this material prosperity, deeply feel the responsibilities it imposes, and would endeavor to direct and use it in a manner demanded by the solemn teachings of the past—by the pressing claims of the present, by the mighty possibilities of the future.

Mr. Mayor, already have these remarks exceeded the time that should limit them, and yet, sir, I should do injustice to the occasion did I fail to recognize the lesson which these facts and this hour forcibly teach us—the unity of thought, the unity of purpose, the unity of action binding together the East and the West. Thus have we been bound in the past—thus are we united at the present—thus, sir, will we be united in that solemn future to whose history we are alike contributing. The past five years have not rolled away without teaching us this truth. When April, 1861, revealed the long-conceived plans of conspiracy against our Government, the two objective points that prominently attracted attention and aroused our fears were our nation's capital and the great river of the West. The Bay State rushed to Washington—Chicago to Cairo; and with united voice ascended the shout of salvation. And when the battle was fought, and the victory had been won, and Illinois—as longed the Spartan mother—received back her son upon a shield, your lamentations ascended with ours, your tears flowed with ours, as sorrowfully we gathered about *all that could die* of our beloved LINCOLN.

The MAYOR: You have heard from Chicago, you will now listen to Cincinnati. I introduce to you Mr. A. T. GOSHORN, of that city.

Mr. GOSHORN: Mr. Mayor and Gentlemen: I have just been unceremoniously seized on to respond for one of the great cities of the Ohio Valley. The President of our Chamber of Commerce is present, but being a modest man and a bachelor, he has called on me, a younger bachelor, to speak, in the presence of these ladies, for the Queen of the West.

We came from a city where wine is abundant and native to the soil, and we rejoice to find the fruits of our industry spread so bountifully before us this evening. When we left our homes, we supplied ourselves with something to counteract the effects of the water, but we are pleased to find that the Legislature of this Commonwealth has, on our account, suppressed the Prohibitory Law for the time being. (Laughter.)

Our city, a few years since, was in the far West, but to-day it is in the centre of the nation. By the thrift and energy of its citizens, it has had a substantial growth in wealth and population, and is now one of the great centres of business in the wonderful West.

With the continued growth of the West and Northwest, and a return of quiet and prosperity to the South, we shall hope to see the cities of the Ohio Valley the great centres of trade, and among the wealthiest and most populous of the nation. I trust that the assemblage, in this city, of so many experienced business men, is the beginning of an united effort that will elevate and strengthen the commercial interests of the country, and result in individual and national prosperity.

We are pleased to recognize, in this occasion, the good will that the "solid men of Boston" bear to the men of the West, who are developing and increasing the commercial interests of the country. By this cordial greeting, and by the presence of the ladies, who have always been first and foremost in the hospitalities of this community, we feel assured, that whatever may result to the politicians, the tradesmen of the nation have a common interest, and cannot be separated.

When our Boston hosts come to the hill-tops and prairies of the West, although we cannot expect to present them with such a magnificent banquet as this, they will find warm hearts, open houses, and a bountiful supply of the good cheer that grows on the banks of the Ohio.

The MAYOR: I have now to introduce to you a representative of Detroit, the city in which the first general Commercial Convention was held. You will listen to Mr. G. F. BAGLEY, one of the Vice-Presidents of the Convention.

Mr. BAGLEY: Mr. Mayor and Gentlemen of the City Council of Boston, representing the municipality of the Athens of America, the commercial centre of one of the oldest States in the Union; in behalf of the City of Detroit, which I have the honor of representing in part at this festive board, I thank you for the kind hospitality which you have extended to the City of Detroit, in common with other cities, East, West, North and South. As you, sir, have alluded to Detroit as having called the first National Commercial Convention ever held in this country, I shall be pardoned if I speak in reference to that subject. Detroit feels pride to-day in participating in this second Commercial Convention, as she sees the legitimate fruits of the seed planted by her some two years ago. (Applause.) Detroit is gratified to see that the important interests of the Southern States of this great Union are represented in this Convention. (Applause.) And I trust that in the discussions of this Convention all local interests, from every section of this country, will be laid aside, and that one grand object will be held up before us, that the financial integrity of this great Republic must and shall be maintained. (Great applause.)

Gentlemen, in discussing the various subjects brought before you, the question of transportation, I think, is one of the most important, and demands your most serious consideration. For as we multiply the facilities of transportation and travel between the different sections of this extended country, we increase the attainability of the necessaries of life, increase the national wealth, and cement an union of American interests, that will be as enduring as the granite of that New England, under whose auspices this Convention has been convened at this time. (Applause.) I thank you, sir, for the courtesy you have shown me.

The MAYOR: Gentlemen, I will now introduce to you Mr. NATHAN COLE, of St. Louis.

Mr. COLE: Mr. Mayor and Gentlemen; I thank you from my heart for the kind toast to my native city, to our delegation, and to the centre of the world, if we are not the "hub of the universe." Our young men are brave, and our old men are warriors; but I confess that the former, by the batteries of those sparkling eyes, were *sleighed* down yesterday, while our old men, alas! to-night are *slewed.* (Laughter and applause.)

Mr. Mayor, there is no West now. The electric nerve has annihilated space, and we stand the central jewel on a string of pearls from the Golden Gate to Sandy Hook. We have other pearls besides. The noble city of Pittsburgh, whose energies have been consecrated to the best interests of the laboring artisans and mechanics of our land. And Cincinnati, the Queen City of the West, the great *porkopolis*, whose founders raised their hands and swore that they would not rest until the last hog had squealed. (Applause.) Nor would I forget Chicago—the glorious jewel hanging pendant upon this string of pearls, her feet laved by the glorious lake, mirroring her beautiful form, dispensing each day her stores of grain to the markets of New York, Liverpool, London, Paris, and the world.

In conclusion, Mr. Mayor, let me say, that soon the iron horse, when the last rail of the Great Pacific Railroad shall have been laid, will shake the dew from his mane on the Sierra Nevada, and, crossing the plains of our country, not many suns will be bathed in the

29

golden Pacific, ere it come thundering into your own depots, announcing, in tones not to be misunderstood, the words of your great statesman, "Liberty and Union, now and forever, one and inseparable." (Loud applause.)

Mr. ALLEN: I now come back to the sea-shore, but shall again return to the West. I come to Philadelphia, and give you—

"*The Pen Mightier than the Sword.*" The Keystone State served the nation with the sword of MEADE and the pen of STANTON. (Applause.)

Gentlemen, you will listen to Mr. J. P. WETHERILL, of Philadelphia.

Mr. WETHERILL: I rejoice to-night, in the name of Philadelphia and of Pennsylvania, to extend to you, Mr. Mayor, and to the authorities of the City of Boston, the full meed of praise for the magnificent ovation of this evening. While I listened to the eloquent address of the gentleman from New York, I was reminded of the admirable address of the President of the Board of Trade, when he said,—"New York will pat the City of Boston, her little sister city, on the head;" and I think to-night New York has done it gloriously. But sir, I am forced to take exception to the balance of his remarks in regard to New York, because, if I recollect aright, the President of the Board of Trade said, also, that New York would "whistle in the dark." And surely, gentlemen, to-night, New York has whistled in the brilliant light of this glorious entertainment. (Applause.) And it gave me pleasure to listen to the eloquent remarks of other gentlemen, coming from the North and from the great and mighty West, for I felt assured that hereafter we shall form such a nation, that we can indeed and in truth say of the National Convention of the Boards of Trade, "*E Pluribus Unum*" —"Now and forever, one and inseparable." (Applause.) The President of the Boston Board of Trade also said that inasmuch as Boston intended to consolidate, it would, in time, take in New York. (Laughter.) I would recommend, sir, that inasmuch as Philadelphia, "the city of brotherly love," is only a hundred miles distant from New York, the City of Boston shall extend to our own city. (Laughter and applause.) While upon this question, allow me to say for Philadelphia, that not only is she the "city of brotherly love," but she has also a vast amount of sisterly affection. (Laughter.) And I think it fitting, in this connection, to extend to the ladies of the City of Boston our warmest congratulations and our hearty thanks. (Loud applause.)

The MAYOR: I now propose to let you hear from the mouth of the Mississippi—New Orleans—which is represented here by Mr. M. A. BRYSON.

Mr. BRYSON: I suppose it is perfectly proper, since the mouth of the Mississippi is interested in the commerce of this great nation, that she should have a voice in the deliberations of this Convention; and as we as a nation have not yet consented that New Orleans, or any part of the great South, should be out of this nation, it has been thought proper by the authorities here to-night, that, as there are no delegates present from the City of New Orleans, I should be called upon as representing, in part, the commercial interests of that city and of the Mississippi in general, at Washington, to speak in behalf of the mouth of the Mississippi. Allow me to say, Mr. Mayor, in behalf of those interests, that their voice is not, as it has been in the few years just past, the voice of wailing which has been echoing until even up to within a few months past, but that the energies of the South, the incubus and burden which have been weighing upon them having been lifted from her shoulders, are now being developed. The New England energy which permeated her veins is bursting its bonds, and there is coming from that great fountain of health and strength the power that shall infuse new life and activity into the commercial channels of our land. (Applause.)

In years that are past, we have scarcely heard of the commerce of the South. It has been bound in iron chains. I have said to my friends there in New Orleans, in looking at these interests: "Gentlemen, unless you leave these old channels, these old avenues, and rouse yourselves in behalf of your own interests, we from the Northwest and others from the North will pour in a wave of enterprise that will free your abundant resources, and bring forth a power that will help bear the national burdens, and lift this great weight of national debt, immense as it is, from the shoulders of the nation." (Applause.) And let me say, gentlemen, in their behalf, that the City of New Orleans has said to me, "We will stand by you in your efforts for the promotion of the general commerce of the nation. We are a part of you; rebellion is gone forever; (loud applause;) we could not raise a corporal's guard on it now. We will stand by you, and shoulder to shoulder, this nation shall show to the world its power and its resources."

I feel when I look at the gray-haired men around me, that it is not my place to speak in behalf of the great Mississippi; but the day is coming when she will be heard; when from her vast plains and valleys and slopes there shall pour forth a wealth that shall gladden many lands; when upon her bosom she will bear to the Gulf and out into the ocean, to feed New England and to feed the world, the products of that great valley, whose resources have laid so long undeveloped. It has been chained in the past; it has been bound in bands of mud and rock, and it has been even stopped by armed bands; but the armed bands are swept away, and the other obstacles shall be swept away; and along that great "Father of Waters," in the grandest valley of the world, shall be seen a country rich in every production, and teeming with the wealth of nations. (Loud applause.)

I thank you, Mr. Mayor, for the honor you have done me, and I know that New Orleans, who has authorized and requested me, though coming from St. Louis, to represent her at Washington, will not go back on anything I have said here to-night. I can pledge her for that, and she will shake hands with you in the great enterprises in which we are here engaged; and I am happy to believe that the bond between the distant sections of the far North and the far South shall be drawn closer together, and the citizens of Boston shall yet shake hands in perfect congruity and unanimity with the citizens of New Orleans, and they shall stand as brothers in every effort for the prosperity and glory of our common country. (Applause.)

Mr. ALLEN: Gentlemen, we will now go still further,—

*The Pacific Coast*—As far as the West is from the East, so far from our hearts is any sentiment, except that of Love and Union with our Western sisters.

To this sentiment, a response will be made by Mr. ALFRED DEWITT, of San Francisco.

Mr. DEWITT: I believe this is the first occasion on which the representatives of the far East and the far West have convened together. I do not consider our friends in Minnesota the far West. We call that State, in California, one of the Middle States. We call that the far West where the men paddle their canoes on the streams leading to the Pacific Ocean.

Our people are at this time about retiring to their homes, to enjoy the society of their families and friends. I know from experience that the memories of our Eastern homes enter largely into the conversations of our homes in that far distant State. The heights of the Sierra Nevada cannot shut out the recollections of our boyhood homes, nor can they stand as monuments of any forgetfulness on our part. They have been already pierced by the Great Central Pacific

Railroad, whose iron bands are now uniting the far East with the far West.

This, I suppose, is a meeting more for conviviality than for sober statistics, and I will merely say to you that I am one of the earliest merchants of San Francisco. At the time I landed on those shores, before the peace with Mexico, that city contained but about two hundred and fifty inhabitants. We now number one hundred and thirty thousand. I could go on and tell you of the wonders of our State, but I fear you would think the story extravagant. Our Western friends have a saying, "As easy as rolling off a log." If you think of trying to roll off one of our big logs, I recommend you to make the experiment first on a two-story house, and see how that seems. (Laughter.) We hope that in the course of time, aided by the wise efforts of the merchants of this part of the land to relieve our country from its present depression, we shall be able to reap the rewards of our enterprise in the past, and be stimulated to yet greater efforts in the future. I thank you, Mr. Mayor, for your courtesy and liberality.

Mr. James W. Taylor, of St. Paul, Minnesota, was then introduced, and spoke as follows: —

My friend from the Golden Gate, San Francisco, has portrayed eloquently the resources of that great empire State of the Pacific coast, but far to the Northwest there comes a new New England into the union of this Republic. (Applause.) The eloquent voice of a son of Massachusetts has vindicated to the world the sagacity of the purchase of Russian America, and I am here to-night to say that the march of the American Empire is from this hour henceforth Northwest, until it unites with the shores of Asia, and embraces the whole coast of the Pacific. (Applause.) Do you know, citizens of Boston, that the name of your city is familiar to every tribe upon the shores of Alaska? The untutored savage of Alaska has heard of Boston, has heard of that great struggle for freedom which was rocked in Faneuil Hall; and among the savage tribes of the Northwest coast of this continent, whenever they wish to speak of an American, they call him a Boston man. (Applause.) Aye, the traditions of this city, the Cradle of Liberty, which come echoing back here in the voices of these men of the West, are familiar tales upon the Pacific coast. (Applause.) Sir, I represent the distant State of Minnesota, and whenever I rise before an assembly of my fellow-citizens, I know that one-half, aye, a majority of the faces before me first saw their mother's face here in New England. (Applause.) I ask no prouder name for Minnesota than the "New

England of the West." ("Bravo.") There we stand, the outpost of the Northwest; and, my friends, Minnesota will lead in the annexation to the United States, not only of the distant Alaska, but of all the intervening territories, until the only boundary of this great Republic of the West shall be the North Pole. (Laughter and applause.)

Mr. Allen: Gentlemen, you will now listen to some remarks by Mr. E. D. Holton, of Milwaukie.

Mr. Holton: Mr. Mayor, when I was a boy, there used to be a man going through the country by the name of Daniel Lambert. You may have heard of him. He was a man of most extraordinary corporosity, and there was a small man who went round with him, and it used to be shrewdly said, that he had more brains than Daniel himself. Now, Mr. Chairman, you here in Boston may be encouraged, for if my friend Mr. Walbridge does represent Daniel Lambert, and if Boston is the little man, it is sometimes said that he has got as many brains as Daniel has. (Laughter.) We are similarly circumstanced out on Lake Michigan. There is a Daniel Lambert out there, (Chicago,) and a small man walking along by his side, (Milwaukie.) You may have heard of our good town of Milwaukie. It lies at about the forty-third parallel of latitude, on the west shore of Lake Michigan. You see that I am a very young man, but I have seen every brick in that "city of bricks" raised from the ground to the eaves. (Applause.) Our population is now eighty thousand. Milwaukie is a large manufacturer of certain commodities; she maintains a foreign and domestic commerce. One of her articles of manufacture is lager beer. (Laughter.) The largest exportation of which goes down to our friend Daniel, (Chicago,) and is thus distributed to all his neighbors below. We are not a wine-growing country, and consequently we have to use lager.

You had a plain, simple man standing here a few moments ago (Mr. Bryson,) who made us a beautiful speech. I am afraid of that man. He travels up and down the Mississippi river, and goes to Congress and tells them of the eighteen thousand miles of navigation of that river, and justly demands, in my view, that Congress shall stretch forth its strong arm, and make every inch of that river, from its mouth to its head, navigable for the best steamers that float upon any waters. Standing on the shore of Lake Michigan,—though laying no claim to be either a prophet or the son of a prophet,—I think I see the millions of bushels from the great grain-growing regions of the valley of the Mississippi, on their way to the mouth of that river. We in Milwaukie have thrown out a thousand miles of railroad, which is all managed in our own city. We have brought about twenty million bushels of wheat a year, on the average, for the last five years, to the City of Milwaukie. Much of that has come from across the river. I am here with my associates to ask,—to demand, as far as we may,—that you shall give us the power to withstand this sandy-headed man (Mr. BRYSON) who has stood here as the advocate of the mouth of the Mississippi, and to see to it that our fifteen hundred ships shall find wharves here in the City of Boston. (Applause.) We are going to make a league with another man here (Mr. BARNUM,) who will carry you on to the Pacific Ocean, and send you whirling along his railroad through the gorges of the great river that empties at Mr. ASTOR's former home. I am going to make a contract, I say, and enter into a league with him, and I will go in for his railroad, and he shall have it, provided he will give me a ship canal to the sea. And if you men of New York, and these men of Buffalo and other cities, will not come into the measure, I will tell you what we are going to do; we are going to join hands with Vermont, and make a contract with Massachusetts, and we are coming down through the Hoosac Tunnel with our products. (Applause.) Prepare, therefore, Mr. Mayor, the public sentiment of Massachusetts for that measure. The navigation of the Mississippi river, the track across to the mouth of the Columbia, the continuous navigation of the lakes, by which our vast commerce shall have free access hitherward,—these are the threefold instrumentalities and powers which shall bind our Union in indissoluble and indestructible bonds.

Mr. Mayor, I was deeply touched,—the tears sprang to my eyes,—when I heard the respected Governor of this State appeal to us as *New Englanders.* Ah, how my heart came back to New England, going out from New Hampshire as I did, when he said, "Yes, all these men have a touch of the old, honest, Yankee blood in their veins!" Sir, we hear out West sometimes "about leaving New England out in the cold!" I tell you, when that day comes, we will come swarming back here like bees to the hive. (Applause.) God defend us from that day! When New England, which has given laws to the land,—which has given to it the great powers of genius and enterprise,—shall be "left out in the cold," you will not have standing-ground to hold her sons who will come crowding back upon you. (Applause.)

Mr. BARNUM, of Oregon, was then introduced, and spoke as follows:

MR. MAYOR, GENTLEMEN OF THE CITY GOVERNMENT OF BOSTON, AND OF THE BOARD OF TRADE: Hailing, as I do, from the farthest West, it gives me pleasure to greet the representative men of the City of Boston, and it gives me still greater pleasure to be able to say a few words for the farthest State in the great galaxy of States. You have all heard of the States upon the Pacific coast, but whenever you take into your mind the idea of the Pacific States, California alone stands prominent. The silver State of Nevada is almost overwhelmed by the golden tide that pours out from the gates of that mistress of the West, San Francisco. You almost forget that there lies upon our northwest border a State smaller in population, but older in years, than any other territory upon the Pacific coast. Before California was added to the Union,—before Nevada had been pressed by the foot of a single white man,—there was a territory by the name of Oregon, of which you may once have heard a little, but of which you have heard less since California and the great West have loomed up with their golden treasures before you.

Before I proceed to say anything of that, however, I desire to say here, that whatever there may be in me that is worthy of commendation, or whatever there may be in me of ability, I owe to my New England ancestry. In the blood that courses in my veins, I am proud to say, is commingled the blood of the Bay and the Nutmeg States.

A great majority of the people of Oregon are the hardy sons of New England. We bear through all our domains names that remind us of New England. The capital of our State is *Salem;* the great commercial town of our State is *Portland;* and we have, too, a *Boston* in Oregon. It is not so large as the Boston that sits here upon Massachusetts Bay; indeed, I may state that at the present time it contains within its corporate limits but three houses; but it will grow. We are reminded every day of New England, of this city; for wherever an Indian treaty is made, the name of Boston sounds oftener than any other word. The first white men that went to that territory, were the voyageurs and trappers of the Hudson Bay Company from England, and they became known to thousands of Indians in that vast territory, as "King GEORGE's tillicums." When LEWIS and CLARKE penetrated to the wilds of the West,—when ships from Boston, from Salem, from Marblehead, from Newburyport and from Portland—coursed round the Horn and visited that northwest coast, all the men who were known to belong to this country were by the Indians denominated "Boston tillicums," and they are so termed to this day. It makes no difference where a white man comes from; if he is a citizen of the United States, he is a "Boston tillicum." In every Indian speech, whatever remark the Indian may make, when he points to a white man, he calls him a "Boston tillicum."

As I said before, very little is known, unfortunately, too little is known, in this country, of that far Western State. You, gentlemen, in common with every American citizen, are proud of the name of NOAH WEBSTER, one of the great lexicographers of the world, who has produced that dictionary of our language which goes to all parts of the world as a standard authority. But I desire to say here, and I desire gentlemen to mark it, that NOAH WEBSTER, or the men who compiled the latest edition of his great dictionary, have not yet heard that there is a *State* of Oregon. I will tell you why. And I want the reporters to put this remark down. I want it to go to the literary men of Harvard and of Yale, and to all who have had a hand in the production of the latest illustrated edition of "Webster's Dictionary of the English Language," that its editors do not know the seal of Oregon, nor its motto. Upon yonder gallery is the escutcheon of your noble State of Massachusetts. Suppose a representation of a prostrate Indian, and underneath, the words, "Hic jacet Narragansett big Indian," would you take that as a compliment? Would you consider that the lexicographers who compiled the latest edition of Webster's Dictionary knew much about your State? Turn to the last edition of Webster's Dictionary, and you will find there a picture purporting to represent the seal of Oregon, which bears no more relation to the actual seal of that State than the representation I have suggested bears to the seal of your own State. The motto of Oregon is there given as "*Alis Volat Propriis*,"—("He flies with his own wings.") It is no such thing. Those words are not upon the escutcheon of Oregon. There is but one word upon the seal of Oregon, and that word is the most glorious one in the English language—"Union." (Applause.) Oregon was admitted into the Union in 1858,—ten years ago,—and since that time she has borne that single word as the motto on her escutcheon; and yet the lexicographers of Harvard and Yale have not found it out! I will simply add, that while the men of Oregon are all for the Union, the ladies there are also for union. (Applause.)

MR. ALLEN: Gentlemen, the entertainment of the evening has but just commenced. We will now listen to a little music from "The Grand Duchess," by our friend GILMORE. After a happy selection from this opera had been played, the toastmaster introduced Mr. EDWIN BYNNER, as an agent of the Western lines of transportation in Boston.

Mr. BYNNER: Ladies and Gentlemen:—Mr. Mayor, I take the liberty of addressing first the ladies, because I have noticed, that among all the orators of the evening, only one gentleman,—and that was the gallant gentleman from St. Louis, who entertained us so eloquently,—has made the first allusion to the ladies. Sir, I do not know what the other speakers of the evening may have been thinking of, but it has always seemed to me, that if there ever was a mistake in the Divine economy, it was in the creation of man before woman. (Applause.) I do not know, sir, by what right, either in the primeval ages, or in the age in which we exist, man could claim precedence of woman. I confess, for one, that I do not see how man could exist without woman,—(laughter,)—and hence I contend that the gentlemen who have addressed you to-night should have addressed their remarks, in the first place, to the ladies.

You have taken the liberty, sir, to introduce me to-night to this assembly as the representative of the different transportation lines connecting the great West with the East. I could have hoped that some abler and more fitting representative of those interests should have been selected to speak for them. Among literary men, it is an adage that printing is the "art preservative of all arts." Perhaps I may claim, in this commercial assembly, that "the art preservative of all arts," commercially, is the transportation art. We are entitled here to a representation, because, supposing the West has products to sell to the East, if there were no transportation lines to move those products from one end of the continent to the other, their industry at the West would be useless, as our commerce at the East would be useless.

It has afforded me great pleasure to listen to-night to the accounts which have been given of the prosperity of the different sections of the West, and all I have to say, in behalf of the interests which I represent, is that the idea that there is any conflict between the interests of the West and East is in my judgment, and I believe in the judgment of the members of this Convention, a grand mistake. We are citizens of a common country; our interests are common; our destinies are common; and so, commending the deliberations of the Convention to the care of that Power which presides over all our deliberations, and thanking you for the compliment you have paid to the interests I feebly represent, I bid you good night.

Mr. ALLEN: Gentlemen, you have heard from Portland, Oregon. There is another City of Portland, nearer home. I give you

*Portland, Maine,—The Star of the East*—It sparkles with enterprise.

I call upon Mr. T. C. HERSEY, formerly President of the Board of Trade of that city to respond.

Mr. HERSEY: Mr. Mayor and Gentlemen, — It is entirely unexpected to me to be called upon to respond to a sentiment here; but I am proud to be a representative of the "Pine Tree State," and of the City of Portland, and I can do no less than to thank the City of Boston and the Boston Board of Trade,—and especially the Committee in attendance at the Parker House,—for their kind hospitality to my associates and myself.

Mr. Mayor, the enterprise of Portland has been alluded to. I would say, that perhaps we are entitled to no more credit than other cities, but a year ago last fourth of July, more than one-half of our city was laid in ashes; and yet through the enterprise and indomitable perseverance of our active business men, with the aid of the capitalists, (I allude to the capitalists, because, in our good city, the capitalists have always done their part in this matter,) our city to-day hardly shows a trace of that devouring element. When enterprise is alluded to, I would say that I think we have our share of it, and I would not give a farthing for the prosperity of any city that would not be ruined at least once in ten years. Once in ten years, any city needs to be ruined; not as our city was ruined, by fire, but as Philadelphia was ruined by her water works, as New York was ruined by her water works, as Boston was ruined by the Quincy Market, and again by her water works, and as Portland was ruined by her investments in the Grand Trunk Railway. Gentlemen, these things are what we require.

In times past, there has been some little quarrelling between Boston and Portland, but we are now ready to bury the hatchet, and to be received into her arms. I believe the business men of Boston have done as much, and I will add more (I have said it home, and I will repeat it here) than the same class of any other city, to aid in enterprises for the public benefit; and if Boston does not accomplish all she desires commercially, she is likely to accomplish all she wishes by annexation, and we hope that, if annexation is to go on, we may not be "left out in the cold." We will surrender at the sound of the first gun. (Applause.)

Mr. ALLEN: I now introduce to you Mr. S. G. FORT, of Oswego, a strong man, who will open his batteries in our behalf.

Mr. FORT: Mr. Mayor, — Nestled down upon the shores of the beautiful Ontario is the city of my home. It may not be known to the inhabitants of Boston that we have two forts in that city. One of them was built by Uncle Sam, and over it floats that flag which never yet has surrendered to any foe, (applause,) and the other is a sort of walking *fort*, and the last walking he did was to walk to Boston, and the first thing he did when he arrived here was to surrender. (Applause ) We came from our homes expecting to return at once; we came promising ourselves that not more than two days, at most, should find us in this city; we came to Boston, we have been entertained by her people; and to-night, I believe, the delegation from Oswego feel, almost unanimously, that we will "fight it out on this line if it takes all winter."

We stand upon the shores of Lake Ontario; we give our hands to the West, and we give our hands to the East. We feel that we have one common country, one common interest; and in behalf of that country, in behalf of that interest, we shall always labor. We find represented here in Boston every Board of Trade in the United States of America, unless, indeed, they have a Board of Trade in Alaska; and at the next meeting we shall expect to see delegates from that territory, and, if they are not all shaken to pieces by that time, from St. Thomas as well. (Laughter and applause )

The night is too far spent, and speeches have been too long in vogue for me to venture to take up your time this evening; and in behalf of the Oswego delegation, thanking the Boston Board of Trade and the good people of the City of Boston for their kindness, I bid you a hearty good night.

Mr. Allen: I have now the pleasure of introducing Mr. E. P. Dorr, of Buffalo.

Mr. Dorr: Mr. Mayor, and Gentlemen of the City of Boston and of the Board of Trade: My friend Mr. Marsh, the President of our Buffalo Board of Trade, has asked me to say a word of response to your kind notice of the Buffalo Board of Trade. It is with extreme diffidence and hesitation that I stand up before you, citizens of Boston, to do so. The City of Boston,—that had her Board of Trade, her long line of prominent and eminent merchants, and her fleet of ships traversing every sea,—the City of Boston that attempted, but did not succeed, to enact a prohibitory tea drinking law,—and all long before the City of Buffalo had a solitary white inhabitant, or even a name, except as given by the Indian that roamed unmolested over what are now her peopled streets,—the City of Boston, now complimenting and welcoming within her princely domain Buffalo's representatives,—her Board of Trade, and the Board of Trade of her sister cities of the North, and South, and

West. Mr. Mayor, the City of Buffalo and her contemporaries of the West, are the cities of yesterday; your City of Boston, so full of the great memories of the past in all that has tended to make our common country great and glorious, dates back among the earliest records of the settlement of this country; and it would seem illy fitting for so young a city as the City of Buffalo to attempt to put her young pamphlet page of history alongside the revered book-bound page of the City of Boston; and yet, settled as Buffalo is, in part and in common with all the cities of the country, by people emanating from this city and other parts of glorious old New England,—is it not fitting that the son should turn with a proud face and a beaming eye to the father, and say: See what we, your good children, have done? The lesson from parent to child, and child to parent, may not suffer in the comparison, and the result may not only be not lost on either, but may result in much good. In that view, and in that spirit, Mr. Mayor, may I be allowed, without egotism and without self-gratulation, to speak a word that may interest you, of our city, to which you have so very kindly just alluded. The City of Buffalo, standing as it does at the foot of Lake Erie, is, with her sister cities of Oswego and Ogdensburgh, the natural receiver by water carriage of a goodly share of the products of the great Northwest seeking their Eastern markets through the various outlets of the transporting routes of the country, commencing with the great and rapidly growing City of Chicago, the largest primary and the largest entrepot grain market of the world, with her network of railroads and canals, all pouring their inexhaustible supplies of products of wealth into the hands of the most energetic men that ever peopled and made a city, down to the City of Milwaukie, of which we cannot say much less in deserving spirit at least, and embracing Detroit, Toledo, Cleveland—all cities and peoples which we are proud to own as sisters, and proud to be bound together with them by a common tie of interest. All these cities, Mr. Mayor, bring to Buffalo in immense quantities, by water and by rail, the combined products of the great West, and these are thence distributed through the arteries of transportation all over the cities of the East.

Mr. Mayor, the Buffalo Board of Trade is a young institution,—an emanation of only a few years' growth. Buffalo, now a city of one hundred and thirty thousand people, was, thirty years ago, a city of twelve or fifteen thousand. The City of Buffalo was the first to invent, by one of her honored citizens, and to put in use for commercial purposes in the transfer of grain, that new, indispensable invention, the grain elevator. Without it to facilitate the handling of grain, the whole Northwest would at this day be many, many years behind its present commercial advancement. Many times, Mr. Mayor, within the past six or seven years, have vessels entered the port of Buffalo with two million bushels of grain, and been all unloaded and out of the harbor within twenty-four hours; and in one instance have three millions and one-half bushels of grain been unloaded, and the vessels out again, within thirty-six hours. Buffalo has capacity in elevators to unload and handle, and transfer to her canal boats, this vast amount of grain, besides capacity for other varied products. I spoke only of the lake cities that have added so largely to her commerce and prosperity. I would include in honorable mention the territory and cities beyond the lakes, and prominent among them the great cities of Cincinnati and St. Louis, either of them fitting, in all respects, to be called the great emporium in common with its peers of the great Northwest.

Mr. Mayor, a few words more, and I am done. There are two ways to move the products of the earth,—two motive powers requisite,—money to buy with, and a natural power to turn it homeward to its destination. Would you, as a father, accept from the son a word of advice as to its marketing? If you desire to participate in the prosperity of this stream of golden wealth from the West to the East, we would say to you: Take your money, father, and go West; only take a small part of it, to experiment with, at first; shake off a part of the prudent caution of benevolent old age; go Westward among your sons; you will be proud of them as soon as you know them. Mix the caution of the East with the prompt energy of the West. Give the West, so sparsely scant of capital, the helping hand of your overloaded money-hoarded coffers of the East. Stand on your feet in the great City of Chicago, to illustrate the point, money in hand, and say, I want to purchase one hundred thousand bushels of wheat to send to Boston, on Boston merchants' account, to tranship to Europe on the steamer *Ontario*, to encourage her noble-hearted projectors. Say to the agent of that network of transportation in Chicago, I will buy this grain if you will send it to Boston as cheap for me, and by the same routes, either Oswego, or Ogdensburgh, as I may select, as you do to New York; and it will be done, and your question of side issue is solved. Money is the lever, and you have enough of it to move even Niagara Falls, if you wish to do it. When you touch the yellow kernel of the cereal, you touch in it commercial advantages to manufactures and to commerce, a mine of wealth, compared with which the copper and mineral stocks sink into utter insignificance. Legislation to protect commerce, and an interchange of views of men engaged in kindred enterprises, are very useful; but we cannot at a saving make water run up hill by spending money, when, if let alone, it will run down hill of itself.

I would say to you, good fathers, come up and see your sons, and visit them on their farms in the West, and buy something to take home and send abroad to your ancestry across the water, on the other side. Don't sit still, expecting your sons to come to you to sell their products, when the younger cousins,—another branch of the family, and in many cases not to the manor born,—come up ahead of you, while you are staying at home "waiting for something to turn up," and take the lot all to themselves. Return this visit of your Western relations, bring your greenbacks with you, and settle this mooted question of an unequal distribution of Government funds (I am on the Currency Committee) to the New England States in a satisfactory manner to our Western friends, and in a short time you will have need of more *Ontarios* and *Eries*, and Mr. CUNARD will be sorry he ever left a port from whose citizens his line for many years had such a generous support.

Mr. Mayor and gentlemen, excuse me if I have tired your patience, or have wandered from my subject; and allow me to thank you in behalf of my worthy friend, its President, and my colleagues of the Board of Trade of Buffalo, for the kind reception and princely entertainment of the citizens of Boston and of your time-honored merchants, the Board of Trade of Boston.

Mr. ALLEN: In closing, I have no doubt every gentleman here, whether a resident of Boston or otherwise, will unite in a sentiment invoking—

*Prosperity to the Board of Trade of the City of Boston.*

I have the pleasure of introducing to you the President of the Boston Board of Trade.

Mr. NAZRO: Gentlemen, at this late hour I should not attempt to say a single word to you, had not His Excellency the Governor informed us that this was a family party; therefore I feel at liberty, in bidding you good night, to say a single word. I feel, as a representative of the Board of Trade of Boston, under great obligations to our municipal authorities for what they have done for our guests on this occasion; and in behalf of the Board I tender to them its thanks for what they have done for us; and preëminently would I thank them for the presence of the ladies who have graced our assemblage here to-night. Gentlemen of the Convention, I beg that you will take with you the friendly greetings of the merchants of Boston. They have welcomed you here with joy; they hope many times to meet you again: they delight to have you visit them, and they hope to visit you. They hope that these Conventions, which have been established now as an institution of the land, will continue, and that the merchants of the United States will meet and discuss the various questions in which they are interested, together.

But, gentlemen, called up here at this moment, I am very much in the position of the young lawyer who undertook to make an address at the opening of a new bridge. It was his first speech, and he had prepared himself to speak most eloquently. He began with, "The timbers with which this bridge was made, a short time ago, formed a part of the vast howling wilderness." Here his memory failed him, and he repeated the sentence a second, a third, and a fourth time. Then he made a desperate effort, and said, "Mr. Chairman, the timbers of which this bridge is made, a short time ago, formed a part of the vast, howling wilderness; and I wish to goodness they formed a part of it now." (Laughter and applause.) Now, gentlemen, I do not mean to say that I wish any of our friends formed a part of the "vast howling wilderness," but I do say that I mean to get out of the woods as quickly as possible. I thank you for the attention you have given me here. I hope you will remember Boston; remember our City Government; remember the merchants of Boston, and remember the Board of Trade. I bid you good night. (Cheers.)

Mr. Allen: Gentlemen, the entertainment of the evening will close with a grand concert from our friend Gilmore, at the other end of the hall.

The band accordingly played a *pot pourri* of national and popular airs, concluding with "Yankee Doodle," which was loudly applauded.

At the conclusion of the music, three cheers were given for the band; and, at a quarter before eleven o'clock, the company separated, with enthusiastic cheers for the Board of Trade, the City of Boston, and all concerned in the conception and management of the entertainment.

# VISIT TO THE LEGISLATURE.

---

THE Convention, having accepted an invitation to visit the Legislature of Massachusetts, was waited upon at two o'clock on Friday, the seventh of February, by the Joint Committee of the two Houses, and conducted to the State House.

On arriving in the hall of the House of Representatives, where the two branches of the Legislature, with the Governor and Executive Council, were assembled, the President of the Convention was assigned a seat on the Speaker's platform, at the right of the Governor. When all were seated, Mr. SCHOULER, of the Senate, Chairman of the Special Committee appointed to wait on the Convention, addressed the President of the Senate, who occupied the chair, as follows:

MR. PRESIDENT: As Chairman of the Joint Committee of the two branches of the Legislature to convey to the National Convention of business men assembled in this city, the invitation of the General Court of Massachusetts to appear here in the State House on this day, to be received by the Legislature and to be welcomed to this ancient Commonwealth by his Excellency the Governor, I have the honor at this time to present to you, the President of the Convention and the Convention itself, in acceptance of the invitation extended to them.

The President of the Senate, Mr. BRASTOW, then addressed the President of the Convention as follows:

Mr. PRESIDENT: The two branches of the Legislature are assembled in convention for the purpose of welcoming you and your associates to our State Capital. And in behalf of the Legislature, I have the pleasure of tendering to you, and to the distinguished gentlemen representing the Boards of Trade of so many of the commercial cities of our Union, a most hearty and a most cordial greeting. (Cheers.) But for the purpose of more fully and more emphatically expressing to you the deep interest felt by the Government, and by the whole people of our State, in the objects of your National Commercial Convention, permit me, sir, to present you to the Chief Executive of the Commonwealth of Massachusetts, His Excellency Governor BULLOCK.

The Governor welcomed the Convention in the following words:

MR. PRESIDENT, AND GENTLEMEN OF THE NATIONAL COMMERCIAL CONVENTION: By request of the Senate and the House of Representatives of Massachusetts, it is my profound pleasure to meet you here, and in the name of the Legislative and Executive Departments of the Government to welcome you to this Commonwealth, and to express the respect in which yourselves, and the cause you represent, are held by all our people.

I may properly say that the proceedings of your body are likely to form an epoch in the history of the industries of this country. The pursuits of agriculture, commerce, manufactures and the mechanic arts, of which the joint welfare has been the subject of your deliberations, constitute the base of the prosperity and social life of the people of all the States. Those interests are united in one common destiny. There is no such possibility as isolation or separation in the empire of modern labor. All these activities and employments make a charmed circle, from which no link can be spared without detriment and disaster to the whole. The country owes much to you for your efforts to harmonize and strengthen these mutualities and reciprocities of relationship.

The communities of men are also subject to the same law of unity. So long as there is a New York, an Ohio, a Missouri, Massachusetts cannot afford to be without them, and they cannot afford to be without her. There cannot be a complete or a satisfactory union of interests without a union of States. You therefore will undoubtedly concur with me, that for the most full development and adjustment of all the forces of American industry, it is of the first importance that there should be an early and an enduring reünion of all the States of this Confederacy in one common cause, and under one common flag. I cannot doubt that such assemblages as yours, so intelligent and so impressive, will aid in promoting the restoration of an undivided nationality for which all sections are anxiously looking.

Gentlemen, the hearts of the people of Massachusetts greet you with cordiality, and their hands will unite with yours in the objects which you have assembled to promote. (Loud applause.)

The President of the Convention, Mr. FOX, responded as follows:

YOUR EXCELLENCY, MR. PRESIDENT, MR. SPEAKER, SENATORS AND REPRESENTATIVES: As President of the National Commercial Convention, I am instructed by a special resolution to express to you the profound sensibility of the high honor conferred by the chosen representatives of the ancient Commonwealth of Massachusetts in inviting us to meet them in this hall.

To you, Governor, what can I say? Your greetings have been so cordial and warm that we are delighted to recognize in you a firm friend of the great industrial interests which we are here to-day to protect and advance. (Applause.)

I have the honor of presenting the members of the National Commercial Convention of the United States of America to the civil authorities of the Commonwealth of Massachusetts. (Loud and continued applause.)

At the close of these proceedings several of the delegates were introduced to the Governor, the President of the Senate, and the Speaker of the House, and the Convention then retired from the hall.

# INDEX.

PAGE.

www.ingramcontent.com/pod-product-compliance
Lightning Source LLC
LaVergne TN
LVHW010246110826
845151LV00004B/1402

* 9 7 8 1 4 2 5 5 2 3 3 4 3 *